STUDENTS OF ENGLISH

What does English mean to those who study and teach it? Why do students choose English? What do they think of the way English is taught? What do they feel they are gaining from their studies? How can literature be assessed? This book reveals what students and teachers think about the subject. Using material gained from questionnaires and interviews with over 800 students between the ages of 15 and 21 and their teachers, the author provides us with a broad assessment of attitudes and responses to English Literature as an academic subject.

He has asked basic questions about the expectations students have of their courses as well as those of teachers concerning their students. He examines the transition between school and university and the ways in which that transition is viewed from both sides. Syllabuses and university courses of study are scrutinised, as are exam-board decisions and the choices teachers make from the reading lists offered.

What is revealed is of major interest to teachers, examiners, and policy-makers in the field of English studies. There are illuminating revelations of attitudes on such urgent issues as the improvement of the examination system and the need for more continuity between 16+, A level, and degree courses. The author discovers considerable strength of feeling on matters such as the use of continuous assessment and the need to allow provision for a creative as well as a critical response to literature. Here we have a thoroughly clear, empirical study of current views and attitudes on the teaching, learning, and examining of English that also indicates how those involved think the study of literature might be strengthened in the future.

Robert Protherough is Senior Lecturer in the School of Education at Hull University with nearly 40 years' teaching experience in schools, colleges and university. Previous books include *Encouraging Writing*, (Methuen, 1983), *Teaching Literature for Examinations* (Open University Press, 1986), and with Judith Atkinson and John Fawcett, *The Effective Teaching of English* (Longman, 1988).

STUDENTS OF ENGLISH

ROBERT PROTHEROUGH

ROUTLEDGE
London and New York

First published in 1989 by
Routledge
11 New Fetter Lane, London EC4P 4EE

29 West 35th Street, New York NY 10001

© 1989 Robert Protherough

Typesetting by LaserScript Ltd, Mitcham, Surrey.
Printed in Great Britain by Billing & Sons Ltd, Worcester

British Library Cataloging in Publication Data

Protherough, Robert
Students of English.
1. Great Britain. Higher education
institutions. Curriculum subjects:
English literature
I. Title
820'.7'1141
ISBN 0-415-01637-1

Library of Congress Cataloging-in-Publication Data

ISBN 0-415-01637-1

Contents

Acknowledgements   viii

Introduction   1

1 English as a subject   5

Perceptions of English   5
The coming of subject-English   11
One subject or two?   21
Why choose to study English?   26
What is to be gained from English?   28
The relationship with other subjects   32

2 The students of English   36

The 16+ divide   36
The balance of the sexes   41
Their family background   44
Their academic record   46
Who go on to university?   48

3 Development and continuity   54

Student views of continuity   55
Views of teachers and lecturers   60
Development of personal response   66

4 Courses of study   78

Literary studies   80
The literary curriculum   82
Student views of literature and criticism   93
Views of literature courses at different stages   100
The perceived influence of English courses   113

5 Teaching and learning   117

Unanswered questions   117
Perceptions of teachers and learners   122
Proposals for change   128

6 The assessment process   136

  Doubts about examinations   136
  What is to be assessed?   142
  Students' views of assessment   144
  Staff views of assessment   148
  Examiners' views of assessment   153
  Examinations at 16   157
  Examinations at 18 and beyond   165

Conclusion   172

Notes   185

Index   198

For Hugh and Mark,
two of the many

Acknowledgements

I am grateful to the University of Hull for the research grant which made possible the investigation on which this book is based. Considerable help was given me by staff in the university's computer centre (particularly by Mr Allan Reese) and – as always – by the staff of the Brynmor Jones library.

I am indebted to the many students and teachers in schools and universities who gave up time to complete questionnaires, and to those who talked with me at a later stage about their views. The survey was only possible because of the willingness of heads of department and others to cooperate in its organisation.

It would be impossible to list the many who have helped to shape the book by their writings and conversation over many years of teaching in school and university. Some of the more conscious influences appear in the lists of references. More specifically, however, I gladly acknowledge the helpful suggestions made by Judith Atkinson and by my wife, Margaret, who read the manuscript in draft. A few brief sections have previously appeared in different form in *English in Education*, *The Use of English* and my earlier book *Teaching English for Examinations* (Open University Press, 1986).

Robert Protherough

Introduction

Uneasiness remains even today about the very notion of *studying* something called 'English'. Surely, the argument still runs, the necessary abilities of reading and self-expression should develop naturally in the pursuit of other subjects. Shortly after the last war Professor D.G. James characterised this view:

> To be well read in English is regarded as a most desirable thing, as essential even to a cultured person: but to *study* English, to give three years of academic labour to it (to say nothing of a life-time) is a doubtful business.[1]

More recently George Steiner posed the rhetorical question:

> Is a man who has spent his last years of school and his university career in the study of English literature to the exclusion of nearly every other language and tradition an educated man?[2]

There is a pervasive uncertainty about the nature of the discipline, about its objectives and about the values it achieves.

When people study something called 'English', what are they actually doing (and what do they think they are doing)? More specifically, what happens when studying 'English' is equated with studying literature (and what do we mean by 'English' literature)? What are considered appropriate ways of writing about literary works or of trying to create them? How can a student's progress and development in 'English' be legitimately assessed? On what grounds can changes in the methods of 'English' instruction be termed advances or retreats? Ultimately, why should there be people who are paid to teach 'English'? How do we justify our existence? Would the world be very different if we were all wiped out overnight?[3]

Plenty of questions like these exist - frequently suppressed - but they receive few answers. Indeed the questions themselves seem only rarely to be put, and replies are not often sought from those who are being passed through the system: the students themselves. This book is primarily concerned with such people and with their responses to the idea of studying 'English' (which is hereafter normally referred to without the quotation marks, but still with the sense of a dubious term that has not been adequately defined).

The relationship between a subject for study and those who study (or teach) it is a highly complex one. Perceptions of a subject and its worth are crucial to those who are deciding whether to commit time and effort to studying it and what its significance is for a future career. Equally, though, the importance of a subject is defined by the kinds of people who select it and by the level at which that study is carried on.

The short history of how English came to be a separate subject for study at university, and how it attracted an increasing number of specialists, has been extensively chronicled.[4] What has received relatively little attention is the parallel history of what it means to study or to teach that subject, and in particular, how students perceive the initiation process by which in successive stages they come to see themselves (and to be seen by others) as students of English. One recent study commented at the very beginning on this peculiar omission:

> Somewhere at the heart of the discipline is the figure of the student, subject of all these vast technologies that surround him or her yet never brought to the surface in analysis ... the student is the 'lost object' of the discipline, ever present but unacknowledged, untheorised.[5]

Where and when does the process we might call studying English begin? Up to the age of 16, virtually all secondary pupils will have lessons in something called 'English', part of the essential core of the curriculum, as a matter of course. When they talk about 'doing' or 'taking' English, though, only exceptional individuals in the pre-examination years will refer to it as studying the subject. There seems to be a transitional period, marked by making some choice of subjects, by external assessment and by an increased concern for future qualifications, during which students of English - and of other subjects - somehow emerge. The crucial stage of this transition comes immediately after the statutory leaving age, when courses are concerned to provide qualifications that will give entry to higher education or to some career.[6] In 1985, just under three-quarters of those taking A-level or equivalent examinations actually applied for places in higher education,[7] and it is with such students that this study is particularly concerned.

In the 1960s and 1970s, increasing attention was paid to this transition between school and higher education, much of it closely related to the principles and methods of selection for college or university,[8] Almost all of that work, however, was concerned to establish a general picture, without differentiating between the situation of different subjects, except in broad terms of arts or science. This study is more limited and subject-specific. It shares the concern of those earlier papers about 'problems involved in the transition from school to university' and about the significance of those values inhering in such a rite of passage. Like most of them it defines the transition as essentially 'extending from the fifth year of secondary schooling to the first year of university', though with obvious implications for the periods before and after.[9]

The Students of English research project, initiated in the School of Education at Hull University, was carried out in three stages. A pilot study of about two hundred O-level and one hundred A-level students took place in the Hull area, and some of the results of this have already been reported.[10] A more detailed regional study drew on just over 260 students at the end of the first year of their English A-level courses and some 200 English undergraduates at the end of their first year at university. The schools represented were drawn from different inner city, suburban and country areas and included some independent as well as local authority schools. The undergraduates came from a range of Oxbridge colleges, 'older' and 'newer' civic and post-war 'new' universities. In addition, just under a hundred of the teachers and lecturers working with these students completed questionnaires. In the third stage, interviews and group discussions were held with a number of those in school and university who had participated, some of whom had seen interim reports on the first two stages.

The undergraduates in the study were all taking 'single' or 'special' honours in English, and were thereby recognised as specialists in the subject. This does not imply any adverse judgment on those from joint degree courses, or studying English in colleges and polytechnics. Lecturers who have worked in both sectors of higher education know that some students on B.Ed. and similar courses are more capable and achieve better results than others reading English at university. However, the range of courses in which English is an element is at present so diverse that it would have been very difficult to create a wider sample that was in any sense representative.

Although this was not a scientifically balanced sample, as it depended on the willingness of schools and university departments to participate, and on the co-operation of those within the institutions, it does seem to have been representative. Comparable demographic details relate quite closely to those obtained in larger national investigations (notably the 1970 Schools Council and the 1987 OPCS surveys).[11] Accordingly, where it seems appropriate, the percentages falling into different categories of the analysis have been given. However, as the chief concern is with the views of students and those who teach them, representative written and spoken comments put most of the flesh on the statistical bones.

The first two chapters of this book provide the background for what follows. They attempt to define rather more precisely what meanings are attached to 'English' in the transitional years and who the students of the subject are. Previous studies are related to relevant information from the survey. The remainder of the book quotes more extensively from the comments of students. The third chapter concentrates on the theme of continuity and development during the successive changes through 16+ courses, to A-level and to undergraduate work in English. The final three chapters develop this theme with reference to particular topics: the nature of the courses that are offered, the methods of learning and teaching, and the forms of assessment that are practised. A brief conclusion considers some of the implications.

1

English as a subject

Perceptions of English

It is only in recent years that serious attention has been given to *perceptions* of academic subjects: the ways in which they appear to students (or, occasionally, to parents, employers or teachers). An important early article of 1974 ranked student attitudes to a range of school subjects on four scales - interest, difficulty, freedom and social benefit - and found, among other conclusions, that 'pupils in all sub-groups show considerable agreement as to which subjects are found both dull and difficult - mathematics, physics, French and Latin'.[1] Since that time there have been studies of the variant perceptions of different subjects, particularly at moments of curricular choice ('why choose French?').[2] Among the variant factors influencing selection, there has been sustained attention to perceptions of 'gender-appropriate' subjects (a 'sexual division of knowledge')[3] and to 'ability-appropriate' subjects. Woods found, for example, that by the third year of secondary school pupils had 'internalised teacher definitions of success and failure and their application to themselves with the usual labels'. More able students tended to define their subject likes and dislikes by referring to 'official', traditional educational reasons whereas the less able explained their preferences in terms of fun, being easy, freedom, or being with their friends.[4]

Because of growing concern about the supply of scientists, more attention has been paid to scientific subjects than to others, but a number of comparative studies have commented on different aspects of the particular way in which English is perceived. In the Duckworth and Entwistle article, referred to earlier, English was ranked in the middle of nine specified subjects for interest, but was seen by pupils as the *least* difficult subject, the one offering *most* freedom and, for boys, the one with *most* social benefit.[5] It contrasted markedly with the profile of subjects like languages and physics, which were generally perceived as difficult, lacking in freedom and not very interesting. In the *Young School Leavers* inquiry, 'English was universally valued by the 15-year-old leaver ... of great use ... of great importance' and (with mathematics) as the subject that pupils most wished they were better at. The same importance was attached to the subject by the sample of those aged 19-20 and by parents.[6]

In his analysis of secondary pupils' responses, Robert Witkin showed that whereas some subjects are valued because they are interesting or entertaining and allow them to work in their own way (notably art, drama and music) and others because they are important, helpful and clearly explained (like mathematics and geography) English was unique in being highly rated for both sets of reasons. English was given the most affirmative ratings in response to the two statements that in this subject 'I feel I have learned something important to me' and 'my lessons are fun and I really enjoy myself'.[7] Several sociological studies have concluded, in the words of Howard Gannaway, that students feel that in English 'both the subject matter and the teachers are interesting'. He goes on:

> It is almost as if one has to be a really *bad* teacher of English in order not to be rated highly by the pupils, and a number of reasons were given for liking English teachers. It would appear that English lessons and teachers represent a happy coincidence of agreeable features, so that many pupils find something good about the lessons.[8]

Paul Bench found that three-quarters of his sample of O-level candidates enjoyed English Literature as a school subject 'very much' or 'reasonably' (60% of boys, 86% of girls), and only 6% said they enjoyed it 'hardly at all'.[9]

There is some ambiguity in public perceptions of the relationships between the importance of English and its difficulty, compared with other subjects. There has been no serious questioning of the need to place English at the core of any national curriculum. Indeed, in a recent attitude survey, 87% of respondents placed reading and writing at the top of those curricular subjects perceived as essential for 15-year-olds.[10] However, precisely because everybody takes it at school the subject can be perceived as less 'serious' and demanding than those taken by an academically able minority. Although English has the greatest number of candidates for examination at 16+ (and English Literature the third greatest) and although for some years it has been second only to mathematics (inflated by double entries) at A-level, it is still an 'easy' option in some people's minds. There seem to be three main reasons for this. Some people feel that the 'softness' of English is indicated by the fact that it became established more rapidly in girls' schools than in boys', and that it was chiefly studied at university by women. Others believe that English teachers are more tolerant in their expectations and more sanguine about its benefits than other subjects. For a few, the weakness is somehow there in the subject itself, too obvious to need argument. Graham Hough said of English at university: 'It becomes the bolt-hole of those who can't do mathematics and are too lazy to learn a language properly'.[11] Significantly, when parents were asked in a recent survey whether they would find it 'easy' to help their children with school homework at O-level, 60% claimed that they could easily help with English, but only 15% felt capable of assisting with Mathematics or French.[12] The arguments used in the late nineteenth century to oppose the introduction of English to universities still live on: it is too pleasurable, it could be undertaken in leisure time, it is hard to assess rigorously (very much the arguments now being used to prevent separate status being given to media or cultural studies).

When students say that they do 'better' in English than in other subjects, or that they 'like it better/more', does this mean that standards in English are lower (as some would complain) or that the students are encouraged to perform at a higher level in that subject? The third follow-up stage of the National Child Development Study, examining the perceptions of the first group staying at school compulsorily to 16, found that they rated themselves more highly in ability in English than in other subjects. Nearly a quarter of the cohort thought themselves 'above average' in English (24% as compared with 16% for mathematics and 14% for science) and only 11% rated themselves 'below average' in English (compared with 27% for mathematics and 26% for science).[13]

It is striking that their teachers also rated pupils' English abilities more highly than other teachers did for their subjects. English teachers estimated that 16% of their 16-year-olds were capable of an A-level pass in the subject (whereas teachers of mathematics, science and modern languages thought this of only 11% of theirs).

They were also more sanguine about younger 'above average' pupils believed capable of an 0-level pass in English (26%, compared with between 17% and 21% in other subjects). At the other end of the ability range they said that only 11% had 'little if any ability in this subject' (17% in mathematics, 19% in science, 28% in modern languages).[14] Another study has shown that A-level English groups are twice as likely as mathematics groups to contain students who have failed at 0-level, but who are nevertheless being encouraged to continue with the subject.[15]

An analysis of school predictions of the chances of their university candidates obtaining a good honours degree again showed that opinions were most sanguine about English students. Schools rated 83% of them as likely to gain a good honours degree (compared with 78% for French or German, 75% for mathematics, 67% for geography or 53% for biology).[16] The same emphasis seemed to continue at the end of the first year at university. First year assessment placed more English students (42%) in the 'high' category and fewer (6%) in the 'fail' category than in any other subject. (For comparison, ratings of French or German students placed 34% in the 'high' category and 10% in the 'fail'; mathematics 28% 'high' and 18% 'fail').[17]

Such an attitude towards their students is just one indicator of the way in which English teachers perceive themselves and their work as distinct from those in other subjects. Although English is also unusual in the wide range of paradigms held by those who teach it,[18] and although it is notoriously 'the least subject-like of subjects, the least susceptible to definition',[19] those involved in the subject unite in attributing to it a unique and particularly important role. They see themselves as more widely concerned with students as developing individuals than with particular subject-matter. The emphasis in English is on personal experiences, on the affective inseparable from the cognitive, contributing to learning in all areas of the curriculum and of life. Whereas the acquisition of most subjects begins and ends with the teaching of that subject in school, children bring to English a wealth of existing language experience and the boundaries of what they do in it through English have no fixed limits.[20] The Schools Council survey demonstrated that English teachers had a different scale of objectives from those involved in other subjects, were much less concerned with facts, techniques or concepts, and much more concerned that pupils should be aware of aspects beyond the syllabus, should relate learning to their own lives and experiences and should be helped to counter the limitations of their environment.[21] More specific case studies have illustrated the kinds of tension that exist in some schools between English departments and the rest: 'This English department certainly saw itself as being very different from the rest of the school', 'The department took up a dissident stance towards the culture of the school', 'Their subject identity served to distinguish them ... from the teachers of other subjects'.[22]

The ambiguity in perceptions of English outside the profession has already been mentioned. Those subjects of which we expect most are also those which we criticise most if they fail to meet our expectations, and those expectations change as society changes. Mr Kenneth Baker has encouraged what he calls the 'consumers' to have a greater voice in education, but - unfortunately for English - politicians, parents, employers and professors of other subjects have conflicting views about what abilities should be developed and how, and they express these views with a confidence they would not dream of adopting when speaking of chemistry, say, or German.

Despite evidence that national standards of reading and writing are rising rather than falling [23] and that examination standards have, if anything, become more demanding,[24] a perception of English as somehow 'failing' has been sedulously cultivated by certain groups. Such a view is advanced by those who disapprove, on political or other grounds, of certain features of current English pedagogy. Their perception is that in some previous generation children read and wrote better than they do today and that this was because teachers in those days had different, preferable aims and methods.

There is a remarkable similarity between the strictures advanced in the late 1920s and early 1930s, those of the Black Papers and associated documents in the late sixties and early seventies, and those orchestrated around the responses to *English from 5 to 16*, of which Dr John Marenbon's pamphlet is perhaps the best known. In each of these periods the basic complaint has been that an obsession with freedom and creativity has led to the abandonment of formal grammar teaching, that children cannot use language well because they lack an understanding of its structure, and that many of the unattractive features of contemporary life can be attributed to this negligence of English teachers. So, in 1931, it was asserted that children cannot be 'trained' to use language without understanding its structure, and that 'one is tempted' to attribute to the abandonment of grammar the 'incoherency of the popular press'.[25]

In 1969, Professor Cyril Burt, writing before his research had been called into question, asserted that in the name of 'self-expression ... bad spelling, bad grammar, and the crudest vulgarisms are ... freely tolerated' by teachers. As a result, we 'wonder' whether this 'may not largely be responsible for much of the subsequent delinquency, violence and general unrest that characterize our permissive society'.[26] In 1987, the press release for Dr. Marenbon's pamphlet (headed 'The disastrous state of the teaching of English') similarly alleged that teachers were 'sweeping aside discipline in favour of creativity' and could 'render our children illiterate'. His case was that English should be seen as 'the subject in which pupils learn to write standard English correctly', and that for this they 'will need to learn' traditional classical categories.[27] A classical scholar himself, Marenbon believed that Latin should be taught 'widely' in schools, because 'it ensures a supply of English teachers whose grasp of Latin will make their command of English and its grammar firmer and more explicit'.[28]

In each of the three periods mentioned critics seem to have been stronger on rhetoric than on hard facts. Indeed Marenbon can only counter the evidence of the Inspectorate, of the Assessment of Performance Unit (APU) and others by seeing them as part of a gigantic conspiracy, and by launching an attack on the concept of expert opinion ('To look ... to experts for advice about the teaching of a subject such as English is unquestionably to invite confusion').[29] Would scholars so glibly discount expertise in any academic area apart from English? Because we can never be wholly satisfied with standards of literacy, the same complaints recur: there has never been any golden age. It was in the days of universal grammar teaching that one major work began 'The average English boy cannot write English' and that a leading authority said to the English Association:

> Whether boys leave school at 13 or 16 or 18, whether they are destined for business, for the army, or for the university and the learned professions, in all cases alike we hear that they are frequently unable to write their own language with any approach to clearness or accuracy.[30]

There were repeated bitter complaints that public school boys, with all the advantages of Dr. Marenbon's classical grammar, simply could not read, write or talk adequately. In 1914, for example, 'Few will deny, for it has been abundantly proved, that the average public schoolboy cannot write good English', and in the sixth form boys reading aloud 'continually stumble over and mispronounce the simplest words'. A pupil leaves at 18 or 19, 'able hardly to write a coherent sentence, with no knowledge of punctuation, no vocabulary, no power of expression, having read practically nothing...'[31] Simplistic diagnoses and remedies ignore such judgments from earlier periods.

These tensions between different perceptions of English arise partly because our expectations increase and partly because of the way in which English has come to be shaped as a discipline. Therefore, before going on to consider why students say they select the subject, what they believe is to be gained from it, and with what other subjects they believe it is best combined, there is a need to consider briefly how subject-English came to be.

The coming of subject-English

It is hard for us to imagine an educational system in this country where learning English was not important, and where English as a subject did not have a leading place. At present English is seen as central to our school curriculum; English examinations at 16+ attract more candidates than any other subject; something like a million young people every year in England and Wales seek external qualifications in English literature, and English is studied world-wide by many of the 300 million or so who speak it as their first language as well as by a similar number who learn it as a foreign language. However, this assured place has only recently been won. English did not even become established as a coherent curriculum subject until long after classics, mathematics or theology, and later than history or modern languages or science.

This is not, of course, to say that there was no instruction in learning to read and write, in spelling and grammar, or that children were never acquainted with literature in the vernacular. Professor Ian Michael's scholarly work *The Teaching of English from the Sixteenth Century to 1870*[32] devotes over two hundred pages to listing books that were intended to aid these processes. However, such guides were concerned with particular aspects of language ability seen in no clear relationship to one another. In an earlier article, Michael described some features of 'this apparently chaotic material', in which:

Some spelling books contain grammars and some grammars contain spelling. Skill in finding words is exercized in logics as well as in rhetorics and books on composition. The analysis of judgment of literary style may be part of anthologies, handbooks of elocution, composition or rhetoric.[33]

These disparate activities were not then seen as integrated parts of a single subject. They were taught to separate, discrete groups rather than to the entire school population, and they were not the responsibility of teachers who saw themselves as qualified and responsible in English. In a study of the ways in which teachers have been presented in imaginative literature, it is significant that although references to and descriptions of lessons in classics, in modern languages, in mathematics and eventually in science are common enough in the eighteenth and nineteenth centuries, there are virtually no descriptions of English lessons until well into the twentieth century. The concept of an English *teacher* is even later to appear.[34]

Histories of the curriculum make it plain that there is nothing divinely ordained about the way in which societies define particular areas of study as worthwhile, mark their boundaries, and decide who should participate in that learning and how. Whether subjects are supposed to represent 'disciplines' with their own characteristic forms of knowing and experience, or whether they are separated from each other more arbitrarily, they are all progressively shaped by a series of social and political interactions.[35] In the later part of the nineteenth century, certain professions increasingly assumed the right to select, organise and validate those forms of knowledge they perceived as valuable.[36] In particular the universities, both by defining such knowledge and by placing the responsibility for it within subject departments, took a significant part in framing the pattern in schools. There too the secondary curriculum is divided into subject 'territories' and teacher roles are largely defined by their subject specialisms, which are themselves dependent on university qualifications. The success of schools is judged by the acceptability of their courses and students as measured by the examination boards, which were originally (and to some degree remain) the creation of universities for their own purposes.[37] The debates over new school subjects (humanities, environmental studies, psychology or philosophy) are associated with changes in the power structure and values of the groups involved. Within such a pattern, the history of English as a subject only begins from around the turn of the century.

The first recorded use of the word 'English' meaning an academic subject for study is given in the Oxford English Dictionary as 1889, where it is defined as 'English language *or* literature as a school *or* university subject *or* examination'. The triple alternatives (and especially those between language *or* literature and subject *or* examination) are symbolic of the tensions within a new, emerging subject. A variety of studies makes the same basic point:

In 1880 English as an autonomous academic discipline did not exist.[38]

Before the turn of the century English did not exist as a separately identifiable school subject at either elementary or secondary level.[39]

English did not emerge as a major school subject until the 1890s [in the USA].[40]

For centuries the term English had simply signified nationality or the language itself. The ability to read and write the mother tongue has, of course, long been perceived as desirable, though the idea that this should be a universal accomplishment is very much more recent. Mastery of English in this sense of basic literacy was seen in Elizabethan England as the key to social advancement, necessary for commercial expansion and desirable for Christians who could then read the Bible for themselves. A vast range of books and techniques was available for those who wished to educate themselves, of which Edmund Coote's *The English Schoole-Master* (1596) is probably the best known.[41] Richard Mulcaster, appointed the first headmaster of Merchant Taylors' school in 1561, where he had Edmund Spenser and Lancelot Andrews among his pupils, was perhaps the earliest educationalist to argue in English in favour of educating children in the vernacular.

I honour the Latin tongue, but I worship the English ... our English is our own, and must be used by those to whom it belongs.[42]

He was aware, however, that there was 'reasonable doubt' about priorities in early education, 'whether English or Latin should first be learned'. Mulcaster believed that we should 'read first that which we speak first, to take most care over that which we use most' because studying English offered 'the best chance of good progress owing to the natural familiarity of our ordinary language'.[43] To us this sounds such common sense that we may overlook how startling the idea was in its time. Ascham may have written *The Scholemaster* (1570) in English, but the title page clearly expressed its purpose: 'a plain and perfect way of teaching children to understand, write and speak the Latin tongue'. From the middle ages onwards *Latinum* had come to mean language in general, and *grammar* meant exclusively Latin grammar. Cleland reported in 1607 that many parents in aristocratic families 'caused their sons to be brought up only in speaking of Latin with their tutor'.[44]

The depreciation of the vernacular as a subject for serious study meant that it was seen as appropriate only for artisans or others unfitted for the education of a gentleman or for the very earliest stages of learning. Charles Hoole, for example, dismissed it as an easy first step: 'For this learning to read English perfectly I allow two or three years' time, so that at seven or eight years of age a child may begin Latin'.[45] Because of the low educational value placed on the mother tongue, it was assumed that educated teachers would not be concerned with 'the elements'. Brinsley wrote that it was 'unbefitting to our profession'.[46] Edmund Coote believed that such instruction would be given by 'such men and women of trade, as Taylors, Weavers, Shoppe-keepers, Seamsters, and such others, as have undertaken the charge of teaching others'.[47] Even Mulcaster himself was forced to admit that 'good scholars will not abase themselves' to the teaching of reading.[48] Describing the work of the 'petty' schools, Lawson and Silver sum up that 'teaching the elements was regarded as menial work - work which only the poor were expected to take up'.[49]

This situation remained substantially unchanged for many years. Until well into the nineteenth century a two-tier system existed. Basic instruction in reading and writing was given in dame schools, charity schools, elementary schools and mechanics' institutes. At secondary and university level it was simply assumed that pupils should already have attained any necessary competence in the vernacular.

The ancient universities, public schools and grammar schools ignored English throughout the nineteenth century. This neglect was partly because of the confidence in the superior humanism of the classics, and partly because of the vernacular's association with working-class education.[50]

Nowhere was there any concept of English as an organic field of study. As late as 1900, the Board of Education's Schedules for each age group show Reading, Writing and English as separate subjects, possibly taught by different teachers, and 'English' exists simply in terms of formal grammatical knowledge.[51] In the school curriculum, the activities were 'further fragmented into "Recitation", "Spelling", "Handwriting" and so on', with separate periods for each.[52] Also in 1900, Alice Zimmern was publishing an article in *The Journal of Education*, putting forward what was clearly a revolutionary proposal that authorities should 'treat literature not as an isolated study, but as part of English'. Indeed, she went further, to propose that a single teacher should take on and unify half-a-dozen separate activities, to which she now gives the name English:

> Give all the English in a class to one teacher: let him add together the hours now given to reading, grammar, composition, recitation, and literature, and redistribute them at his own discretion according as need may arise.[53]

The complex series of changes which resulted in such an establishment of English as an academic subject gained impetus from increasing dissatisfaction with the results obtained from the study of classics. In the first thirty years of the nineteenth century, regular attacks in leading journals like the *Edinburgh Review*, *Westminster Journal* and *Quarterly Journal* argued that other essential elements were shouldered out of the curriculum by the exclusive concentration on the classics, which had degenerated into grammatical drill and memorising, with no real knowledge of literature or culture.[54]

In the late 1860s appeared two influential works, F.W. Farrar's volume *Essays on a Liberal Education* (following his 1867 lecture 'On some defects in public school education') and Matthew Arnold's *Culture and Anarchy* (1869). In the first of these books, Henry Sidgwick argued against the 'various unmeaning linguistic exercises' and in favour of a modern humanism. To ensure this, he wrote, 'Let us demand ... that all boys, whatever their special bent or distinction, be really taught literature', which meant that for most pupils the study of Greek should be replaced by *English* literature. Arnold, although writing from a slightly different stance, also proclaimed that if education was to have a truly humanising, liberal centre, ensuring the survival (or salvation) of English society 'besotted with business', then experience of the best that has been thought and said would, in large measure, have to be experienced through English literature.

The sub-text beneath these arguments has to be examined. The writers still assume both the superiority of the classics over English literature, and the fact that the most able pupils will continue as classical scholars. English is seen as supplying the want of classics for the less able and those further down the social scale. One recent study has concluded:

> Thus the 'new' English made most headway in low status areas of schooling - in the education of girls, the children of the working-classes in elementary schools, and the lower middle classes in the new state secondary schools.[55]

It was hardly surprising, then, that some prejudice against English continued in the public schools and the older universities. Thring's progressive regime at Uppingham in the 1880s offered a curriculum in which all boys studied classics and mathematics, history and geography, a modern language or science or drawing, and all 'learn singing who can' - but not English.[56] Margaret Mathieson has written of 'the reluctance of headmasters to include English literature in their curricula'.[57] Although the members of the Taunton Commission (1864-8) had suggested that English language and literature should be part of the curriculum in their proposed national system of secondary schools, they suspected that it would prove impossible to find staff who could teach such a subject adequately.[58]

In 1904, the *Code of Regulations* of the Board of Education establishing a four-year secondary course required all state schools to include English language and literature in the curriculum. In one sense this could be seen as the first significant acknowledgement of English as a subject. On the other hand, it has to be remembered that these Regulations were introduced because inspectors reported that English was commonly neglected, that many schools continued to teach other subjects under the guise of English, and that English was significantly divided into two separate subjects, frequently taught in isolation. The implications of this division will be discussed later. In 1906 the English Association was founded and strove from the beginning to unify those separate elements 'into a single, recognized school subject with its own specialist teaching force'.[59] Perhaps most important of all was the decision of the new Secondary Schools Examination Council, established in 1917, to include English among the approved subjects for Advanced study in the Higher School Certificate (and not, as was originally intended, only as a subsidiary subject). A similar process was going on in the United States where examination requirements for university entrance were a major force in establishing a sense that English could be 'the equal of any other studies in disciplinary or developing power'.[60] In his 1906 Presidential address to the MLA, Albert S. Cook of Yale said that 'English has been thrust forward with a rapidity almost alarming'.[61]

The confident tone of the Board of Education's 1910 Circular might suggest that the battle for English was over. Drawn up in consultation with the English Association, this publication asserted that it was not 'necessary to dwell upon the importance of the subject' because 'the claim of English to a definite place in the curriculum of every Secondary School is admitted'.[62] However, there was also evidence of the 'failure ... in many schools' to establish the subject properly or to give it 'fair treatment in the Timetable'. Most depressing of all was the comment on 'the very low standard of the teaching'.[63] The Circular was clear about the damaging effects of assuming that 'any master or mistress can teach English'.[64] The Newbolt Report was critical of the lack of qualifications of most teachers involved in English work. It was estimated in 1920 that 'certainly not more than one-third' of those leaving colleges with a certificate were 'qualified to take English with a class'.[65] Unfortunately the Bullock Report and the studies of Her Majesty's Inspectors indicate that the heresy persists and that at least a fifth of secondary English teaching is still undertaken by staff with no kind of qualification in the subject.[66] Repeated attempts to obtain acknowledgement that English is a shortage subject have been rejected by the Department of Education and Science.

The relationship between the existence of the subject and the qualifications of the teacher was even clearer in the public and grammar schools, where English was by no means established at the time of the 1914-18 war. S.P.B. Mais wrote from Sherborne School to say that in public schools 'it cannot be pretended that English is taught as a subject at all' and that the crying need was for

17

'specialist masters in English'.[67] At the time, those involved in teaching it were either non-graduates of low esteem (later versions of the 'writing master') or graduates of other subjects, not formally 'qualified' in a subject that had not previously existed at university level. These were mostly classicists who brought with them into the new subject the approaches developed in the study of the old. Writing in support of the new English tripos at Cambridge, A.C. Benson based his case on a supposed *future* (not present) need of qualified English teachers:

> I believe that English is very shortly going to become an integral part of every school curriculum ... and teachers for this purpose will have to be found and trained.[68]

Particularly in the public and grammar schools the impression remained for some time that English *should* be taught by specialists in other subjects. Lord James has recorded that when he went to Manchester Grammar School as late as 1945, only one of the masters in that large school was qualified in English.[69] This may in part explain the ambivalence of some of those who taught English when it came to recognising it as a subject in its own right. It may also help to explain the relatively late appearance of organisations related to the subject and to its pedagogy. The English Association did not come into being until thirty-five years after the foundation of the Mathematical Association and considerably later than the Modern Languages Association, the Geographical Association or the Classical Association. There were professional associations for teachers of domestic science in 1896, physical education in 1899 and the natural sciences in 1903. By contrast, the National Association for the Teaching of English (NATE) was not founded until 1962, lagging well behind similar groups for teachers of mathematics (1952) and drama (1959), and still further behind such minority subjects as Spanish and Portuguese (1947). NATE was also half a century behind its American equivalent, the NCTE, founded 1911. Awareness of the world-wide role of English resulted in the eventual formation of the International Federation for the Teaching of English - but not until 1983.

After such a late start, English has established itself with extraordinary speed as a central subject (perhaps *the* central subject) in the curriculum. At school level, the crucial event was the publication in 1921 of the Newbolt Report, *The Teaching of English in England*. Highly critical of 'inadequate' nineteenth century attitudes and methods, the authors put forward a passionate and idealistic case for English in every child's timetable and for the notion that all teachers are (or should be) teachers of English. In particular they stressed Arnold's argument for the power of literature to strengthen men and women in times of cultural crisis. People would lead 'starved existences' if they lacked 'that unifying influence, that purifying of the emotions which art and literature can alone bestow'.[70]

> We believe that in English literature we have a means of education not less valuable than the classics and decidedly more suited to the necessities of a general and national education.[71]

In other words, English was coming to be seen (in political and social terms as well as educational ones) as a unifying force. The Report criticised the differences in aims and curricula that separated the 'special treatment' of public schools from the severely practical emphasis in elementary schools, and which 'widened the mental distances between classes in England'.[72] The improved teaching of English in all schools was seen as an important way of bringing about desirable changes in individuals and in society. This emphasis on the wider responsibilities of the subject and of its teachers marked a significant difference from other subjects, and has remained an animating principle for many English teachers. Writing on the claims made for English in schools, Margaret Mathieson has remarked on the fact that this principle unites those who, in other respects, differ widely in their views.

> Elitists and radicals are, in a broad sense, all 'progressives'. They share a long-standing faith that good English teaching can achieve desirable changes in individual personality and the social structure... It is a faith which they have in common with the subject's earliest supporters. As soon as proposals moved beyond a concern about the skills of reading and writing they concentrated upon its power to affect the quality of children's lives.[73]

The Newbolt Report also offered a vision of a unified professional concern with the new subject, in which teachers in schools and in universities would jointly adopt a 'missionary' role. It suggested that the university professor of literature 'has obligations not merely to the students who come to him to read for a degree, but still more towards the teeming population outside the university walls'.[74] However, instead of establishing such closer links with schools, with national educational policy, with adult education or with wider issues of literacy, most university English departments seemed to turn inwards. One recent study of English in higher education sees this as a time of distancing from non-university concerns:

> The identity of English studies during the inter- war period was forged, not out of the discourses of the Newbolt Report, but rather in terms of the subject's consolidation as an autonomous academic discipline and learned profession.[75]

From 1921 onwards the centrality of English in the school curriculum was a recurrent theme. In *The Teaching of English in England* (and in George Sampson's influential book *English for the English* which shortly followed it) the subject was presented as 'the one indispensable preliminary and foundation of all the rest'.[76] The Spens Report of 1939, saying that of all subjects 'English is most capable of giving a meaning and a unity to the whole course' up to the age of 16, suggested (using italics for emphasis) that

> for the majority of pupils *we think that the school itself should adopt a unifying principle in its curriculum, and we recommend that it be found in the teaching of English*[77]

The Norwood Report of 1943 recorded similarly:

> the supreme importance of 'English' has been stressed ... an 'element' of education which is of vital importance to all subjects and should be the concern of all teachers.[78]

Terry Eagleton has summed up the cumulative effect of such heady assertions that English is 'the central and dominating subject': 'In the early 1920s it was desperately unclear why English was worth studying at all; by the early 1930s it had become a question of why it was worth wasting your time on anything else.' English at Cambridge had come to be seen as 'not just one discipline among many but the most central subject of all'.[79] When Denys Thompson wrote the first editorial of a new journal, *The Use of English*, in 1949, he proclaimed that 'English is more than a subject'. Much of its more recent history has been that of a colonising process in which the boundaries of what might be counted as English have expanded, taking in drama here and linguistics there, communications, media studies, semiotics and cultural studies, women's studies and a range of 'integrated' courses. English is becoming a site on which many new interests can find a home, and where existing concerns are remade:

> Traditional conceptions of literature, for example, are criticized, refused or re-evaluated in the light of theories which connect them to questions of material production, class relations and the ideological construction of subjectivity. Not only that but the boundaries of what is considered appropriate for study have shifted dramatically.[80]

One subject or two?

Has the early twentieth century unification of English ever been really complete? Is English one subject or two? The only word to signify the joint 'study of English language and literature' seems to be *Anglistics*: a late coinage (OED 1930) of continental origin that is largely unknown and unused here. The two-part division marked by the 1904 *Code of Regulations* simply reduced the even greater fragmentation of 'English' activities on those school timetables where they existed at all. The forward-looking Board of Education report of 1910 saw that 'literature' and 'language' were simply convenient terms for aspects of what should be a single concern.

> The instruction in English in a Secondary School aims at training the mind to appreciate English literature, and at cultivating the power of using the English language in speech and in writing. These objects are equally important, and each implies the other. Without training in the use of language, literature cannot be fully understood or properly appreciated. Without the study of literature there can be no mastery of language: it will not only be loose, incorrect, and awkward, but will also be insufficient for the demands of life.[81]

We have not really got much further than this in the last seventy years. However, it is significant that for reasons of convenience, the report then went on to consider *Literature* and *Composition* in separate sections. This division was later reinforced by the coming of formal examinations, where English language was accepted as a separate subject before English literature. The division has been maintained through the changes from School Certificate to O-level, and although GCSE introduces a unitary subject called English, with a literary element, it also retains a separate, additional subject called English Literature.

The most significant effect has been seen in the HSC or A-level, where *English* was taken to mean exclusively English *literature*. In a way this echoes the nineteenth century distinction between the study of the classics and the vernacular. As was suggested in the preceding historical sketch, the twin aspects of English were encouraged for different reasons and for different clienteles. English language was perceived as providing the basic literacy required by workers in an advanced industrial society; it was for the many. English literature, embodying the values that religion and the classics seemed increasingly unable to supply, was for the able few, the specialists; it was reserved for the secondary stage and the universities. A pattern of language skills for all and literature for a few was thus established and has tended to persist.

After twenty years of discussion, two boards have introduced a new subject at Advanced Level called English Language or English Language Studies. The London Board's original proposal was for two examinations in varieties of written and spoken English and a written project on a specific area of spoken language, based on transcripts and analysis. Significantly this was referred back for further consideration by the Secondary Examinations Council. The Joint Matriculation Board (JMB) also put forward a scheme involving two papers and a selection of course work. The JMB states the aims of its syllabus as 'to combine learning about the nature and function of language in human thought and communication with learning how to use English more effectively'. The study should be 'more systematic' and display 'more advanced expertise' than in O-level language.

It is significant, however, that both of these proposals are for language *alternatives* to literature, and that they originate largely from the influence of those who are specialists in language or linguistics at universities and colleges. They are an attempt to give language studies in school an equal status to literary ones. They are not really attempts to bridge the gap between the two. At present such a combination is only available in the slightly uneasy compromise of the AEB alternative syllabus, English Language and Literature. The proposals for new AS courses being submitted to the Secondary Examinations Council suggest that there is considerable uncertainty whether AS English should model itself on A-level English Literature or on GCSE unitary English. The Oxford Delegacy propose an AS syllabus in English literature 'as demanding in its standards as an Advanced Level syllabus' but with 'much reduced content'. The intended overlap with A-level is made clear by the statement that the two courses will be, in the Board's phrase, 'co-teachable'. On the other hand, the Joint Matriculation Board claim that their syllabus 'has been designed to enable centres to provide a combined studies course in English Language and English Literature at a level where the discipline of one area may reinforce those of the other to produce an integrated course'. Other boards propose to have it both ways by allowing a choice of modes. The AEB offer AS English (linked with A-level Language or Literature) as an alternative to AS English Literature (linked with the board's two English Literature syllabuses). An even more complex mix of options enables the Welsh Joint Education Committee to suggest that, 'Depending on the options taken, candidates' certificates could be titled *English*, *English Literature* or *English Language*'. Although such AS courses will not, by definition, be taken by those intending to specialise in English, they will inevitably influence views of the nature of English studies beyond the age of 16.

At the older universities, the tension between language and literature was intensified by the fact that philological and etymological studies were recognised as scholarly concerns well before literary ones. For nationalist and historic reasons it seemed plain that Old English should be the basis for new courses. The proponents of English literature needed the association with Anglo-Saxon and Middle English to give their subject academic respectability, but simultaneously they feared the emphasis and approach of those involved in language studies. Although an Honours School of English Language and Literature was founded at Oxford in 1893, in the teeth of strong opposition, there was no separate chair of literature until 1904.[82] When a Chair of English Literature was eventually founded at Cambridge University, specifying that the holder should treat the subject 'on literary and critical rather than on philological and linguistic lines', it was another six years before an English Tripos actually came into being, in 1917.[83]

The philological emphasis in language studies, which tradition had made dominant, was slow to adapt. Even after the 1939-45 war, working in the Honours School of Language and Literature at Oxford involved a heavy diet of Anglo-Saxon, Middle English and History of the Language. A student with a philological bent might take a language option which virtually eliminated any literature later than Chaucer in favour of such studies as Old Norse or Old High German and still emerge as a graduate in English Language and Literature. It was not possible, however, to select a literature option and to avoid the compulsory language studies. The university argument that 'Literature is a branch of language'[84] - to quote the title of an article in the *Universities Quarterly* in 1951 - lived on to become an acrimonious source of dispute in schools some years later. The growth of linguistics as a discipline, and particularly the publication of *Language in Use*[85] seemed to provoke either/or disagreements, symbolised in the title of one article: 'Is literature language? Or is language literature?'[86]

Despite his assertions that 'English should stand or fall as a single School of study' and that any division between Language and Literature is 'an utterly unjustified dichotomy', Professor D.G. James had to admit that 'there frequently exists a good deal of tension between "Literature" and "Language" in English Schools'.[87] Indeed this is still manifested in the titles of such schools. They may simply be known as *English*, there may be separate departments of *English Language* and *English Literature*, the two may both be included in the title, one may be omitted as in *English and Related Literature* (York), or a different orientation may be implied as in *English and American Studies* (East Anglia).

Because of the origins of university courses in language, few have questioned the assumption that the language to be studied should be exclusively that of the past and of literature; still fewer the notion that language studies have little or nothing to do with *using* language. Indeed, in England it still tends to be assumed today that university English departments have no direct responsibility for the written or spoken language use of their students. Undergraduates learn to write by writing essays about the books they read.

The situation in the USA, with its much wider intake of students, is very different. Traditionally the two aspects within English, literature and literacy, have been seen as mutually supportive, because American teachers 'knew early that they were helping to form rather than merely preserve a culture'.[88] A recent study has

24

described how, at the end of the last century, Harvard 'became the first great university to dramatize the split between scholarship and composition that would become so typical of English departments down to the present day'.[89] The ubiquitous 'Freshman composition' courses are seen as a necessary - though separate - preparation for literary studies. As in England, however, teachers of literature rarely have anything to do with the teaching of writing.

> The senior tenured faculty continued to teach and pursue research in literature while the graduate students taught composition - but studied literature. After graduation, they gratefully abandoned the teaching of composition (with its onerous hours of theme grading and its ill-prepared students) and turned to serious research and teaching in literature.[90]

The situation is gradually changing, because of pressures from two directions. From schools, there is increasing understanding that there is no clear division between what one does in teaching writing and what one does in teaching literature; that tests of literary abilities are largely tests of writing; that students learn to tell stories about stories. Teachers are becoming aware that 'writers are always reading ... and readers are always writing'.[91] From literary theory, particularly under the influence of deconstruction, a related view has become more common within universities and colleges:

> Reading is itself a kind of writing, or writing is a trope for the act of reading ... any artificial detachment of one from the other will be a disaster for both disciplines.[92]

> ... the desire to bring together composition and literature, writing and reading, and the teaching of them ... displacing the either/or thinking that has too long dominated the pedagogy, especially of English, in secondary and post-secondary education.[93]

> We have often been guilty of trying to teach writing or reading as if they were divorced from one another ... Reading is the way in which we evaluate or express (not develop or complete) writing skill; writing is the way in which we evaluate (not develop or extend) reading skill ... one learns to write to read to write.[94]

It is possible to change students' attitudes and approaches to texts in a course whose goal is to turn readers-as-consumers into readers-as-producers of their own readings of texts and of their own written texts.[95]

To what extent such views may bring about changes in the perception of English studies is still unclear. One lecturer said candidly in discussion:

> We don't know quite where we are within this department about creative writing/a curious mixture of anxiety to encourage/and fear of releasing unreal ambitions/and linking those to forms of academic assessment that we feel we cannot legitimately operate/but the fact that you don't know where you are/seems a very bad reason for not encouraging it/there are very real problems in fitting it into the larger programme of what we do now/and deciding how to assess/but writing in an English course/should be as significant as practice in art or music.

Why choose to study English?

From the sixties onwards a number of studies have examined the reasons students give for selecting their university subjects. Most of these compared responses between broad fields: arts and science, sometimes with separate categories for 'mixed' courses or engineering. The general results were reasonably consistent. One early study found that arts students were much more likely to see interest as their major motive for choosing a subject and were much less likely to mention vocational use than students as a whole.[96] Similarly, a 1982 investigation at Loughborough University found that Arts students were more likely to refer to interest in the course and personal satisfaction, and less likely to consider the implications of their course for specific careers or for financial rewards.[97] By contrast, a large-scale survey of science undergraduates and their motivation concluded that 'undoubtedly the most common single factor was ... better jobs and higher salaries'.[98]

These surveys and another concerned specifically with A-level choices[99] were used to identify the five most commonly cited reasons for selecting a particular subject. Both the A-level and the university students in our sample were asked to rate the relative importance of these five factors in their decision to study English and to add other significant reasons of their own if they wished.

Teachers and lecturers were asked to say how important they felt the same five factors were in affecting their students' choices. All four groups agreed in ranking 'liking for the subject' as far and away the most important element, and the students were even more emphatic than their teachers (81% A-level students and 90% undergraduates rated this 'very important' as compared with 73% of A-level teachers and 81% lecturers). All the groups agreed in placing next 'previous academic success in English', though this was perceived as 'very important' more frequently at university level (by half of the students and lecturers). After this there was some variation of opinion. Both the teachers and the lecturers thought that the next most significant factor would be 'influence of English teachers', but this was rated much lower by undergraduates and as the least important by A-level students (only 11% of whom thought teacher influence 'very important'). It is perhaps worth noting that another survey suggests that parents also rate teacher-advice very low in considering the choice of subjects for their children.[100] By contrast, both student groups suggested that their 'ideas of what the course would be like' were considerably more important. The final factor, 'future plans or choice of career', was seen as the least important by three of the four groups, described as 'very important' by only one in ten of the undergraduates and by none of their lecturers (one of whom wrote that a major motive in choosing English for some undergraduates was their 'resistance to vocational hard-sell').

Further confirmation of these results comes from the wider OPCS survey for the DES published in 1987. That study considered 'reasons for choosing A-level subjects' across the curricular range, though using a somewhat different list of factors. 'Liking' and 'previous success' were again overwhelmingly the reasons most frequently cited by those taking English. 'Found subject interesting and enjoyable', mentioned by 77% of English students (and a similar proportion for history or modern languages) was only cited by just over 50% of those offering mathematics, physics or chemistry. The possession of a good O-level or CSE pass (given as a reason by 44% of English students) was also more likely to be mentioned in relation to English or French than for science subjects. On the other hand 'instrumental' reasons (needing the subject for a course or job or to help with other subjects) were virtually three times more likely to be mentioned as reasons for choosing the science group than for English.[101]

In the free responses invited by the questionnaire, many other reasons were advanced by individuals or small numbers of respondents. The only one to be repeated a significant number of times was the idea of English as 'the least disliked third A-level', 'the lack of another alternative' or the subject that best fitted with other (preferred) options. More is said about this in a later section of this chapter, 'The relationship with other subjects'. Teachers were rather more likely than their pupils to see the forced choice as a significant motive. Some of the other reasons that were offered were sardonic: 'Why not?' from an A-level student, 'I didn't want to get a job and thought I liked English', or 'the high percentage of females' from undergraduates, 'ignorance of other subjects' or 'the illusion that English is easy' suggested by teachers and lecturers. However, the great majority seemed to share an idealistic belief in what the subject had to offer. At school this was described as 'a chance to develop interest in books', 'opportunities for self-expression', 'desire to improve my standard of English', or 'a chance to read widely'. At university, people talked of 'wanting more expansive knowledge and ways of thinking', 'following an enjoyable subject in breadth and depth', 'a sense of unfulfilled potential', 'a desire to be stretched', 'the notion that this subject of all the arts would have the greatest use for me personally', 'the subject's social relevance', 'desire to be creative', as well as more personal, narrower motives like 'a second chance through late entry' or 'urge to be a medievalist'.

For a few students the choice had always seemed inevitable. One young man remarked in a sixth form discussion group:

> I never considered anything else/having been told on various occasions that I'd got flair for it/and with my father being an English teacher/I enjoy it/and its my favourite subject by a long way.

What is to be gained from English?

Reasons for studying English are inevitably related to the ideas which individuals form of the advantages they might gain from work in that subject. The pilot study had suggested that there was a major difference in the ways that students on O-level courses and those, only a year older, on A-level courses described the benefits they felt were available. Their free responses were analysed into three major categories: those seen as literary and subject-specific (developing critical skills, increasing knowledge of texts, gaining information about books, learning to read more closely), those concerned with practical curricular or vocational advantages (help for other subjects, qualifying for further courses, preparing for a career), and those that pointed to personal affective benefits (pleasure and enjoyment, increased awareness or self-understanding, extending of experience, stimulus for ideas). Those sampled were free to mention more than one benefit, and the older students were more likely than the younger to respond with two or more which could be classified in different categories.

Percentage of students responding in each category

	literary	practical	personal
O-level	80	30	15
A-level	50	63	80

At 16+ about 3% said that English literature offered *no* benefits ('it's pointless'; 'the books are fictional so no information of value is gained'), but those who were more positive saw the advantages in very different terms from their teachers. Whereas English teachers rate personal, affective aims as overwhelmingly the most important, practical learning through books as next most significant and specifically literary objectives as the least important of all,[102] O-level students neatly reverse their teachers' order of priorities. Not only do few of them seem to find personal pleasure in their courses, a number suggest that the work is essentially done to please other people. One girl says that parents approve of the subject because 'they like to think their children are getting some culture' and another that 'having an O-level in English Literature proves to prospective employers that you have an understanding of written work'.

The shift of priorities by the A-level students, mirroring more closely the views of their teachers, could be explained by a number of hypotheses:

- that students develop as they continue their literary studies
- that they are progressively conditioned by those who teach them
- that A-level courses lay more emphasis on personal response and less on formal learning than O-level

- that those who have *not* experienced personal benefits tend to abandon the subject at later stages

In the main stage of the survey, respondents were asked to indicate the relative importance of seven supposed benefits that might be gained from a study of English. These seven were drawn from the pilot survey and from other similar research studies. Those responding were also asked to mention any other benefits that they found significant, though few did so. The results confirmed the impression of the pilot study that older students attach more significance to what English does for them as people and less to its practical and vocational advantages. The concept of 'pleasure and enjoyment' was ranked first by both groups of students, and classed as 'very important' by 63% of the A-level and 88% of the undergraduate samples. Those taking A-level tended to rank practical advantages like 'improving your own use of language' or 'gaining useful knowledge and information' rather more highly than the university students, who gave the highest ranking after 'pleasure and enjoyment' to the two other personal benefits: 'extending of experience' and 'increased awareness and self-understanding'. Both groups ranked vocational motives, 'becoming qualified for a future career' at the bottom of their list. It was the only item seen as of 'no importance' by a significant number of A-level students, and only 16% of undergraduates thought it 'very important'. In responses elsewhere, a number of students made comments such as 'careerwise I do not think it can help me'.

It is interesting to compare these views with those of the people engaged in teaching who were asked what they thought their students might gain from English. A-level teachers rated the benefits very much like the university students that once they had been. They put 'pleasure and enjoyment' followed by 'increased awareness and self understanding' at the top, attached less importance than their pupils did to 'improving their own language use' or 'acquiring useful knowledge and information', and placed 'becoming qualified for a future career' at the bottom. In this they were different from the university lecturers, the one group that did *not* see 'pleasure and enjoyment' as the chief benefit (it came fifth in their rank order). For the lecturers, 'development of critical ability' followed by 'improving their own language use' and 'extending their range of reading' were the most important benefits.

The development of critical ability was rated 'very important' by 90%.

If the impression given by this small study is accurate, then there is something ironic about the developing perception of what a literary education can achieve. Younger pupils believe, contrary to the aims of their teachers, that literary advantages rather than personal ones are significant. University students give overwhelming importance to the personal despite the fact that *their* teachers see literary advantages as most important.

Relatively few suggestions were made about other benefits to be gained. Some students in both groups mentioned an increase in confidence, social awareness and enhanced capacity for communicating with others. Their teachers tended to mention intellectual rather than social advantages: 'extending ability to think for themselves', 'improved aesthetic taste', 'discipline for independent learning', 'clarity of thought', 'historical awareness', 'understanding varied uses of language', 'becoming socially aware and critical'.

The lack of specific applications to particular careers can be seen as either a strength or a weakness of English studies. The degree of openness ('it prepares you for everything or nothing', as one student said) came out clearly in discussions with first year A-level students who were uncertain about their future destinations. A minority thought that their courses would be of direct benefit in what they hoped to do later. One who wanted to enter a library studies course at university said that, if she then got a library job, English 'would have helped me gain a knowledge of texts and authors which could be useful in that type of work'. Others said that it could be helpful 'if I get to drama college', or 'at university reading English or English and French (though it won't help for any future job)', or 'in the development of ability to criticise and justify, which will be useful in journalism'.

Much more common, however, were remarks which pointed to indirect benefits. One student who hoped to enter retail management said that the extension of critical observation through literature 'should help me in day to day situations'. Another, thinking of sports studies and recreational management, said that 'English will have been a help, but only in improving my ideas and thoughts about various aspects of life - the actual books studied will be of little use'. A future art student mentioned the value of 'help in essay writing'. Others, intending to apply for higher education

31

courses in history or law or politics, pointed to 'reading skills' or 'ability to analyse ideas' as advantages that English would have provided. One who was interested in film and television as a career saw English as keeping her options open: it was not directly relevant to her immediate plans, but might be important 'if I change my mind and do a totally different career - it is an academic A-level whereas Art is not particularly'.

Most frequent of all were the suggestions of personal benefits and pleasure that were gained independently of qualifications or vocational use. A potential history student expressed a belief that 'Literature will help me after the sixth form, not since it will help my studies but since I have developed a keen interest for literature, and I'm sure I shall not stop enjoying reading after I leave school'. Another who hoped to study nursing said that 'the work in literature has been no help in actually getting into a hospital, however it has been of general interest to me'. Two going on to art and design courses talked of 'broadening literary horizons' and 'having a wider range of books to read in spare time'. Another said that 'English has developed my ability to form my own ideas and given me an appreciation of literature which I'll be able to enjoy throughout life'.

The relationship with other subjects

English is no longer associated clearly with any specific subject group. The students in our A-level sample were offering it in combination with over thirty other subjects drawn from the whole range of the curriculum. History and general studies (the latter compulsory in some institutions) were the most popular with both sexes, but neither was being taken by even half of the students doing English (116 in each case). Economics was the next most popular subject (63). Rather under a quarter were taking geography (58) and under a fifth French (45). Other subjects being taken by a significant number of students were in order of frequency sociology, German, art, biology and mathematics.

Some subjects were more popular with one sex than the other. Proportionately more boys than girls had chosen mathematics, physics, geography and economics to accompany English; more girls than boys were studying a modern language other than French, biology and sociology.

The variety of courses comes out most clearly in examining the actual subject combinations which individuals offer. In the days of the traditional Arts Sixth, most students offered English with French and history,[103] or with history and geography, or with French and another language. Indeed, the popularity of the first of these groupings may have confirmed the gloomy suspicions of some respondents to the Secondary Schools Examinations Council. They said that if English was admitted as an Advanced course then it would frequently be combined with French and history, which 'would not provide a sufficiently strenuous curriculum'.[104] Such critics might be better pleased by the present situation. The extent to which once conventional groupings have broken down is indicated by the fact that the three cited combinations added together only account for 18% of those in the A-level sample. Of 261 students, only 12 were taking English, French and history; 14 English, French and another language; 21 English, geography and history.

Another way to consider subject combinations is to examine the patterns of O-level passes obtained by those going on to take A-level English. The categories of the Schools Council research study *The Examination Courses of First Year Sixth Formers*[105] which classified students as strong, weak or 'no' in arts and in science are interesting here, though they need to be treated with care because of the researchers' decision to limit 'strong' arts to those who are taking Latin in conjunction with other arts subjects. In our sample only one in five students had offered Latin. However, looking at our English students in the Schools Council terms of relative science/arts balance, more would be classified as strong in science than in arts (70 as opposed to 31). Although 90 would be considered as having offered 'no' science (with girls a disproportionate number of these) it is striking that 57 would be classified as offering 'no' arts at 16+. The largest group for both arts and science is 'weak'. This reinforces the impression that English is now perceived as a subject that can be almost universally combined with any others as well as being a key subject in its own right. If, as seems likely, English is unique among major subjects in this respect, it is to be anticipated that views of what the subject 'is' and 'is for' will be more varied in English A-level groups than in those for other subjects.

In theory, then, as the student comments at the end of the previous section suggested, English should be helpful for people with very different destinations in mind. However, it is still only exceptionally seen as an appropriate accompaniment for mathematics or a science at higher level. Despite the frequent plans for a broader sixth form curriculum, university entrance requirements (or departmental requirements) still militate against those who follow 'mixed' courses. The OPCS survey of 1987 found that nine out of ten boys and eight out of ten girls who continued into higher education with A-level English were taking either arts and social sciences or professional and vocational courses.[106] Much of the variety revealed in the responses of our A-level groups disappears when we look at the subject combinations of those students who were accepted to read English at university. There is still evidence of the range of subjects with which English *can* be combined: a few undergraduates have taken it at A-level with law, theatre studies, mathematics, chemistry and twenty other subjects. Nevertheless, the majority of those who applied and were selected for university had followed a more conventional arts subject grouping at school. The situation is not significantly different from that revealed in the 1973 NFER study, when over 60% of the sample entering university English departments had taken history and rather more French or German. No other subject had been taken by over a quarter of the entrants.[107] In the current enquiry the same two subjects dominate, though their relative positions have changed. Half of the English students had taken history and nearly 40% French. Other subjects were again markedly less popular: one in five offered general studies; about one in seven geography; and just over one in ten German or economics. Comparing the subject combinations of the wider A-level group with those of the undergraduates suggests that those going on to read English at university are markedly more likely than others to have taken French at A-level, somewhat more likely to have taken history, and distinctly *less* likely to have taken general studies, economics or geography. It would be interesting to investigate further how far students anxious to go to university select (or are advised to select) subjects that they think will appeal to selectors as being 'appropriate'.

Just under half of the undergraduates were studying English exclusively: the remainder were taking 'minor', 'ancillary' or 'subsidiary' courses in a wide range of other different subjects (about twenty of them in all), ranging for example through Icelandic, American studies, linguistics, psychology, South East Asian studies, women's studies and education. The most popular was drama (offered by 13% of the whole sample), followed by classical civilisation or ancient history and philosophy. Four different modern languages accounted for 6.6% between them. It does not appear that English predicts limited subject combinations or interests at university any more than at A-level. This may be taken as further evidence that English encourages healthy individualism, or alternatively that its boundaries are so permeable that it hardly exists as a discipline in its own right.

2

The students of English

The 16+ divide

The introduction posed a question: where and how does the initiation process go on by which a gradually diminishing cohort of young people comes to see itself (and to be seen by others) as students of English? Who are they, and what do we know of them?

As Douglas Barnes and others have remarked, the English curricula followed by different groups of students have for years diversified sharply near the end of the compulsory phase of schooling and even more thereafter.[1] Although virtually nine out of ten took some kind of assessed English course in the days of O-level, CSE and joint 16+, and this is likely to continue with the coming of GCSE, there has always been a division between those who were also assessed for English Literature and those who were not. Although GCSE involves literary studies as part of a unitary English course, the separate qualification in Literature will continue. Over a period of years, those passing in O-level Literature have numbered just over half of those gaining O-level Language. Between a third and a quarter of this number later go on to pass English (actually English Literature) at A-level, and about a tenth of these will continue with English studies as the sole or major part of their studies in higher education.

It is after 16+ examinations that major differences in courses, and in attitudes towards them become marked. The transitions from English to 16+ English Literature (involving perhaps half a million young people annually) to A-level English (about 130,000 each year), to English at university or college, are the major concern of this book. However, it is necessary to remember that a considerable and increasing number of young people continue after 16 as English students of a quite different kind. Apart from re-taking 16+ examinations they may enter English or overlapping 'Communications' courses for the CEE or the CPVE. Especially in tertiary and FE colleges, English staff may be involved in teaching a bewildering variety of options - B/TEC, YTS schemes, national diploma and day release options - alongside conventional academic courses.

What John Dixon wrote ten years ago remains broadly true:

> In 1978 there are conflicting definitions of the curriculum in the two main sectors of full-time education. Vocational FE departments have moved decisively to communications ... In schools (and thus in the academic departments of FE) the examination curriculum is generally defined in 1951 terms. Thus, beyond 16, drama and media studies tend to be seen as extensions of English.[2]

Although there is some slight evidence of inter-penetration between these two main clusters of 'English' courses,[3] the general impression is that they cater for distinct sets of clients. A national survey in 1987 found that of those working towards advanced post-16 qualifications 86% were taking solely A-level courses, 12% B/TEC courses and only 2% were taking both.[4] Indeed, some feel that recent political developments have intensified the division 'between learning how to write job applications and an uncritical reverence for something called the English literary heritage'.[5] The first chapter suggested how different groups of 'consumers' of education have distinct views about what is meant by English, and about what abilities courses should aim to develop. For some, English should provide those skills in functional literacy that are needed to obtain and to carry out certain kinds of employment. For others, English is concerned with developing personal and social qualities, and the process centres on the study of literature. These perceptions inevitably rub off on the groups of students who are exposed to them.

For example, compare with the reasons that A-level students gave for selecting English (discussed in the last chapter) the feelings of those in further education colleges.

In a survey of just under five hundred students in seven colleges it was found that although 79% thought that English should be a compulsory subject at college their reasons for the belief were overwhelmingly vocational and utilitarian. English was important because it provided the skills necessary for careers: competence in written English and the ability to speak 'properly'.[6] Very few saw any importance in the reading of literature and 'not one student suggested that English might help in living a happier, fuller life'.[7] An analysis of their reasons for wishing to continue with English studies revealed that the four mentioned by over 40% were, in order, to learn to spell, to learn correct grammar, to learn to 'speak properly' and to choose and use correct words.[8] Other reasons included: to lose accent, to write letters, to fill in forms and - more generally - to get a 'good job'. Students' free comments included references to such desired abilities as being able to 'fill up forms properly, write properly', 'write words down without having to think', 'pronounce words properly'. It is hardly surprising, then, that in describing those activities that they favoured in English classes at college, the students concentrated on talk and discussion (with a repeated emphasis on 'eradicating accent' or speaking 'correctly') and on the formal aspects of writing ('spelling', 'filling in forms'). Whereas such topics were mentioned by between 60% and 90% of those responding, only 5% or 6% mentioned plays, reading or writing poetry.

The utilitarian impression conveyed by those who wished to continue with English is strengthened by the opinions of those who did *not* wish to remain students of English. Overwhelmingly the most common reasons given were that English had nothing to do with their other college courses (87%), that it would not be needed in their chosen job (83%) or that it had already been 'done' at school (76%). 'All had disliked English at school and were against the inclusion in their college courses of what they saw as another subject of the school curriculum'. They made such comments as, 'It's a waste of time and doesn't help a mechanic', 'We should have learned enough of it by now', or 'I hate English, can't stand it never could'.[9]

In a small-scale but more detailed study of staff and students' responses to different kinds of 16+ courses in English and communications, Nicola Burston found that the range of satisfaction varied very widely (from 27% to 100%) when students were asked whether they had found their particular course interesting or enjoyable.[10] The large measure of satisfaction expressed by her A-level English students depended on their enjoyment of the activities, especially their encounters with particular texts, and their broad view of the subject as concerned to develop their self-understanding and awareness of life.[11] Asked about specific gains, individuals claimed that the work had 'developed my thinking', 'I can communicate better', more 'able to read and understand'.

By comparison, those on Certificate of Pre-Vocational Education (CPVE)/Foundation, Youth Training Scheme (YTS) or vocational courses expressed their sense of the subject's importance and their complaints about it in pragmatic terms of preparation for a career. English is 'essential for secretarial work' or is 'not really that useful for nursing'; it 'helps with dealing with customers' or teaches 'how to complete forms'. It follows that courses 'should be specifically geared towards relevant work', 'appropriate to the actual work', there should be 'more vocational work', 'more in line with retail work'. If courses seem to have no such application then they are described as 'no use whatsoever', 'no use at all'. For some, examination grades were the chief end of the exercise: teachers should 'spend more time ... getting folders done so we can get decent grades. Instead of doing 'useless time-wasting projects', they should help the students with 'getting through'.[12]

An earlier study had obtained very similar results from the free responses of students and staff in FE colleges. Their views were found largely to be echoing those of the employers, who were also the subject of this enquiry. The chief complaints made about young employees concerned their errors of spelling or grammar and their failings in oral (especially telephonic) communication. Asked what particular capabilities they were seeking, employers answered, for example:

> The ability to express oneself in a clear and concise manner, and to understand business terms.

> Ability to spell, ability to compose straightforward business letters and memoranda in concise and grammatical English.

> Reasonable spelling, writing and comprehension in order to be effective in their job.[13]

Such instrumental views select as important only a few of the many abilities that an English teacher might normally hope to be developing. It is hardly surprising then that members of staff gave very varied answers to the question 'How great a role should the study of literature play?' in their courses, ranging from those who wished it to have a more significant part to those who thought it 'secondary', 'optional' or unsuitable as 'a basis on which to teach'.

One significant reply suggested that 'If the students are academic, then the class should study literature', but otherwise not.[14]

To sum up, then, the evidence suggests that although students on courses other than A-level are still taking something called English, they did not think of themselves as English students: that term seems reserved for those taking a specific kind of academic course in literature. Governmental pressures and the attempt to eliminate the CEE have resulted in a stiffening rather than eroding of the distinction between vocational, work-oriented courses in English skills and those essentially traditional literary courses from which will come eventually most of those who will return to the education system as teachers of English. However, this may not remain unchanging in a time when curricula, modes of assessment and the organisation of 16+ education are all under debate.

One significant influence on student perceptions of what 'English' is and does will be the increasing popularity of tertiary colleges, in many of which the co-existence of very different kinds of 16+ course is gradually replacing the hard division between school A-level literature and FE communications. This flexibility itself may produce problems, of course. One tutor described to me his college in which 'English' staff were involved in A-level courses in English literature, in English language, communications, and media studies, as well as in 16+ and vocational courses. The blurring of what English can offer at 18+ is accompanied by such practical problems as the extent to which staff need to specialise in particular areas, how far the work crosses departmental boundaries, and questions about how far students can be encouraged to combine courses within the wider 'English' area. Literature, language and communications can all be seen as a helpful preparation for further work in higher education, but would taking two (or even three) to the exclusion of other subjects strengthen or weaken a candidate's application? How far are admission tutors conscious of the kinds of course (and the kinds of learning experience) that underlie the titles of these A-level qualifications?

What follows concentrates on the emergence of that group of young people who are coming to think of themselves as English students, first in conjunction with other subjects and then exclusively. Is there anything distinctive about them as a group? In what ways do their views change as they move from school to higher education? Are there tensions between the perceptions of students and of those who teach them, or between teachers in school and in university? Is it true, as John Dixon suggested, that 'the 18+

tail wags the dog', and that by implication what happens at 18 is dictated by what happens at 21?[15] We rarely ask such questions because we are so used to the hierarchical process that ends stage by stage with individuals being certified as somehow proficient in English that our energies are absorbed by keeping the process running as efficiently as possible.

First then, what sort of people elect to study English when it becomes a matter of choice after compulsory schooling? If you knew that you were to meet an anonymous A-level student, you could gamble with the odds in your favour that it would be a girl (odds of 3 to 1), from a middle-class family background (6 to 4), with a good academic record (6 to 1 that she has five or more O-levels and 3 to 1 that they include grade A or B in English Language). If it was a first year English undergraduate that you were to meet, then the odds would be even more in your favour. The chances that it would be woman remain at about 3 to 1, but it would then be 3 to 1 on the middle-class background, and 9 to 1 that she had three or four passes at A-level including an A or B in English. These three aspects of English students as a group are considered more fully in the following sections.

The balance of the sexes

It was suggested in the first chapter that English was seen from the beginning as a subject likely to be popular with girls and one at which they would do well. Even before they were admitted as undergraduates at Oxford, women outnumbered men in English classes and were generally felt to be more enthusiastic. English was more quickly established in girls' schools than in boys' and standards there were believed to be better. The 1922 Consultative Committee recorded a 'general conclusion' that 'in this subject the average achievement of girls was distinctly superior to that of boys'.[16] To that degree English has always been 'a girls' subject', although eventually it began to gain rapidly in popularity among boys.

Over the last quarter of a century there has been a significant shift in the proportions of the two sexes studying English. At O-level in the early sixties rather more boys gained passes in English language than girls (51.7% in 1960), but the proportion had fallen to 42.63% in 1980. Although the proportion of boys passing in English Literature remained remarkably constant between 1960

(40.36%) and 1985 (39.25%), those going on with the subject to pass in Literature at A-level fell steadily as a proportion throughout that period from nearly 42% to 29%.

Proportion of passes gained by boys in A-level summer examination[17]

1960	41.73%
1965	39.01%
1970	36.35%
1975	33.31%
1980	30.68%
1985	29.37%

This did not reflect a decrease in the number of boys taking the subject, but a marked increase of girls remaining at school beyond the leaving age. At the time of the 1967 Schools Council enquiry boys still outnumbered girls in the sixth form by over six to four, and less than a third of either sex were in mixed schools.[18] It was almost wholly the increase in girls taking A-level English that caused the significant rise in popularity of English as an A-level subject (from being fourth after mathematics, physics and chemistry and only slightly ahead of history, biology and French in 1960, to being a dominant subject well ahead of all others except mathematics in the second half of the seventies). At present nationally the ratio is about 7:3 in favour of girls: 71% to 29% both in numbers taking A-level English courses and in numbers passing.[19]

There is some reason to believe that the imbalance may be greater in mixed schools (balancing the disproportionate popularity of mathematics and science among boys there). Nationally in 1985 over 40% of boys were taking exclusively maths and science courses at A-level compared with only 17% of girls.[20] In our A-level sample girls accounted for 78% of the total. This was thought to exaggerate the difference because two girls' schools were included and the two balancing boys' schools that were invited felt unable to participate. However, the rather larger sample of 662 pupils in an HMI survey carried out at the same time similarly found that 79% of those studying English A-level in twenty mixed schools were girls and only 21% boys. The report added that these were 'proportions observed to be broadly similar in the individual schools'.[21]

As anticipated, there is evidence of a balancing decline in the proportion of men going on to study English at university. Nationally in 1965 just under 46% of those on English degree courses were men, but this proportion fell to 32.5% in the 1985 entry. In part this reflects the increasing participation of women in higher education. Whereas in 1961 they only accounted for a quarter of full-time university undergraduates, by 1980 their share had risen to 40%.[22] As early as the sixties it had been noted that irrespective of class women were twice as likely to read arts subjects as men.[23] Again our sample, which depended on voluntary completion of questionnaires, somewhat exaggerates this difference, men accounting for only 26.4% of all respondents.

Fears are sometimes expressed that this gender imbalance in student groups may be part of a spiral: that the teaching of secondary English may be increasingly seen as women's work, thus intensifying the view of English as a girls' subject. It is true that in the long term there has been a shift since the late fifties and early sixties, when just over 40% of the graduates successfully completing professional training were men. However, there seems no evidence at present to suggest that the situation has altered recently. Although women teachers of English outnumber men by about two to one, there has been no significant change for twenty years in the proportions of the sexes training to become graduate English teachers. (There is a marked difference from initial teacher training courses leading to B.Ed. degrees and concerned largely with preparation for primary schools, where nationally at present women outnumber men by more than six to one).[24] In 1969, men accounted for 33.3% of those entering PGCE English courses at university (and 31.65% of those accepted for such courses in all institutes of higher education). In the 1986 English entries, 32.74% of those on university courses were men (and 32.66% of those on all PGCE courses).[25]

There has, of course, been a recent general decline in the annual number of those graduates accepted to train for secondary English because of government-imposed cuts. Between 1980 and 1986 the number fell by 40%, from 1241 to 753.[26] The future picture is unclear, but there may be some cause for concern in that the percentage of male English graduates leaving university for teacher training fell from 12.8% in 1980-1 to 6.32% in 1985-6.[27] Prediction is particularly difficult because of those currently in higher education 27% say that they are unsure whether or not they will take a PGCE course, as opposed to only 3% who certainly will and 70% who will not.[28]

Their family background

The students in our sample demonstrate the cumulative social imbalance that results from an educational system in which fewer than two out of ten remain at school until the age of eighteen (as compared with more than eight out of ten in countries like Japan, Sweden and the United States), and in which the participation rate in higher education falls well below that in countries like Australia, Belgium, Spain and Italy.

The crucial discriminator seems to be the decision to remain at school beyond the statutory leaving age. It has been calculated that those born into the two upper social groups are six times more likely to stay on than the rest. A survey of 1977 found that whereas only 23% of fifth formers had parents in the Registrar General's classes 1 and 2, 60% of sixth formers did so.[29] The present study of English students echoes that finding.

Although the significance of social class background is manifested at the age of 16, it has its roots in the earliest stages of children's lives. A wealth of previous research has analysed the inter-connection between social class, parental attitudes to children remaining at school, examination attainment, parents' own education and the intentions of children.[30]

The OPCS survey is the most recent of a number concluding that 'analysing by social class yielded very similar results to analysing by parental qualification'.[31] Whereas 85% of children in social class I had at least one parent with a degree or other higher qualification, 'this proportion declined markedly across the next three social classes'.[32]

In our A-level English sample, about six per cent had fathers who were unemployed or retired, but those parental occupations that could be classified with some accuracy showed that just over half of the students come from the two upper social groups and very few from the two lower groups.[33] In the sample of English undergraduates, nearly 10% had fathers who were retired or unemployed, but of the remainder, three quarters came from homes in the top two social groups and under 6% were drawn from the partly-skilled and unskilled groups. This reflects the general finding that those from the upper groups not only predominate in applying for university but are also more successful in gaining places. One recent study has calculated that 55% of those applicants from social class I and 41% of those from class V are accepted. It has also been demonstrated that the proportion gaining scores of 13-15 on their three best A-levels drops according to class from 24% in class I to 10% in class V.[34] The Robbins report of 1963 found that the chances of a professional worker's child following a degree level course were eight times as great as those for a manual worker's child and that the proportion of university students from working-class homes (about 23%) had not changed significantly throughout the period from 1928.[35] One more recent verdict on the post-Robbins years has been that 'the expansion of higher education was a policy that was essentially a response to middle-class social pressures and that provided for mostly middle-class students'.[36]

The following table compares the social background of English students in the survey with two other national surveys and with the national census. As will be seen, there is no evidence that students of English - at A-level or at university - differ markedly in family background from students as a whole, except that the undergraduates are somewhat more likely than the average to come from the upper two classes. It is perhaps worth noting that the OPCS survey of A-level students, which divided boys from girls, reported that English was one of a group of subjects that 'seem to attract proportionately more boys from Social Classes I and II'.[37]

Percentage of -

		men in 1981 census	A-level English sample	OPCS sample B	OPCS sample G	Under-graduate English sample	All students accepted for university 1982
I	professional	4.6	15.2	16	14	24.7	23.9
II	intermediate	18.7	45.5	47	48	51.8	49.0
III	skilled	49.6	31.8	28	29	17.7	21.3
IV	partly skilled	17.2	7.6	9	8	5.9	4.9
V	unskilled	7.5	0			0	0.9
	(unclassified)	2.4					

English students came to university from a wide range of educational backgrounds: 36.8% from comprehensive schools,

27.4% from independent schools, 16.9% from tertiary or from further education colleges, 15% from grammar schools and 3.7% from other institutions or private tuition. Since over 90% of children are now educated in comprehensive schools, a disproportionately small number seem to have become English students by such a route. However the 1987 national survey also remarked on the fact that boys at independent schools were distinctly more likely to take English at A-level than boys in maintained schools (25% as opposed to 16%). There was no significant difference between girls from the two sectors.[38]

Their academic record

In terms of previous academic performance, those who choose (or are selected) to study English tend to have done well. Of those on A-level courses in our sample, only 14% gained fewer than five O-level passes at grade C or better (compared with 35% of all those taking O-level English nationally), 28% had eight passes and 18% had nine. Boys were rather more successful than girls in gaining seven or more passes (73% compared with 56%).

Most of those in the first year of their university studies had successfully taken three or four subjects at A-level (accounting for 65.4% and 28% of the sample respectively). This mirrors the national figures which show that 93% of those entering English degree courses had passed in three or more subjects at A-level. Just under 5% had taken only one or two A-level subjects and fewer still had offered five. The average A-level scores of those accepted for English at university have steadily risen during the 1980s,[39] and most of those responding to the questionnaire were well qualified in terms of their 'points' score. (It is possible that the more academically successful students were over-represented in our sample). Certainly their A-level scores seemed above the national average. It would be dangerous to attach too much significance to such a small sample, but most of the Oxbridge students had scores of 14 or 15, and the average points score of those from the newer civic and the post-war universities was about 12.5.

What was the level of their performance in English itself? In general it can be said, as in the HMI survey, 'that students had taken both English language and English literature at O-level and had achieved good grades in those examinations'.[40] There were, however, some differences in performance between the two subjects. Whereas nationally there is a tendency for a higher proportion to gain grades A - C in literature than in language (64.3% as opposed to 52% in 1985) - partly because literature attracts a smaller and presumably more selective entry - this does not seem to be true of this sample of those who continued with English to A-level. Of those who had taken both subjects (about nine per cent had not offered literature) virtually identical proportions had gained grades A - C: 96% in language and 95% in literature. However considerably more students had done well in language than in literature. A third gained A and almost 40% B in language, compared with 20% A and 36% B of those who were entered for literature. These results are again roughly in line with the HMI survey, which found that about 70% had A or B in language compared with 60% in literature.[41] As the A-level course is essentially literary, it seems puzzling that those following it have not been more successful in O-level literature. Discussions with students suggest that they see their performance in English as essentially global, rather than as artifically divided, as one said, 'into separate bits labelled Lang and Lit'. Teachers seem relatively unperturbed by low grades in literature because they see that examination as a poor predictor of future success in the subject, offering little reward for critical sense, depth of response or breadth of reading. It will be interesting to monitor GCSE results over a decade to see whether any shift in performance is revealed.

Although the HMI generalisation ('There was no evidence ... that girls were better qualified')[43] seems true overall, there are signs of differential performance in the two 16+ examinations. In this sample, boys scored more grade As and more Bs than girls, and fewer Cs in language. The situation was very different, however, in literature, where approximately 23% of the girls who entered were awarded grade A, as compared with 10% of boys (and 50% of boys had only grade C compared with 36% of girls). This may, perhaps, be one of the contributing reasons for the preponderance of girls in English A-level groups.

As might be anticipated, almost all of those on English degree courses had been awarded grade A or B at A-level (65% A; 31% B). Their results in supporting subjects were also generally good: two-thirds of them were at grade A or B (30% A; 36.5% B; 18.5% C and a few lower grades).

Who go on to university?

The notion that there should be academic requirements for university entry beyond matriculation at 16 is a relatively recent one. Unlike many other countries, Britain did not establish a national policy for university entry and the present situation has evolved during this century. The right of grammar schools and, more recently, comprehensive schools and sixth form colleges to be responsible for the advanced stages of secondary education has been conceded. However, this right has depended on offering special subject courses closely tied to the requirements of universities who have indirectly validated what the schools were providing for pupils of 16-19. The clearest indication of the tensions resulting from the lack of any specific national policy has been the recurring debate since 1944 over the sixth form curriculum. Repeated attempts to widen the curriculum and to avoid the early abandonment of 'core' subjects have foundered because of the competition for university places which depend on obtaining high grades in certain subjects and consequently neglecting others. (An A-level pass in English is of virtually no significance to selectors for physics or chemistry, and English selectors pay almost as little attention to those science subjects.)[43] At the time of writing, this is one of the problems exercising the Higginson committee in its consideration of the A-level system.

Although only about a tenth of those taking English at A-level go on to specialise in the subject in higher education, they form an important group for several reasons. It is their success that is seen as validating their school's academic reputation. They are the people from whom most future English teachers and lecturers will be drawn. Their perceptions are likely to be influential in forming more general ideas of what English is and what its values should be.

Becoming an undergraduate studying English at university is the result of a two-stage process: the decision of the student to apply for that subject and the decision of the university to accept. The questionnaire attempted to find out something about each of these stages.

From the student viewpoint, entry to an English degree course was rightly perceived as highly restricted. According to the 1972 Schools Council survey, English required the highest average standard offers of all the major academic subjects considered.[44] The demand for grades of BBC or better remains the norm,[45] and the universities involved in this survey all expected points scores of between 11 and 15. It may have some implications for academic planning that considerably more A-level students wished to continue with their English studies than thought they had a realistic chance of doing so.

Asked whether they hoped to continue studying English after A-level at university or college, 12.7% of our sample said 'yes', 34.2% 'possibly' and 53.1% 'no'. Girls were slightly more likely to answer affirmatively than boys, and slightly less inclined to answer 'possibly'. Those with parents in the upper two social classes were markedly more likely to respond 'yes'.

Asked whether they ever regretted taking English at A-level, about a fifth of the sample said that they did, boys being more likely than girls to respond in this way (29% as opposed to 19%).

However, there was no automatic correlation between the answers to these two questions. Over a third of those who said they regretted taking A-level English still said that they definitely or possibly intended to continue studying the subject at a higher level. Similarly, a third of the 'regretful' group said that they *would* advise a friend to take the course on which they themselves were engaged.

This apparent paradox was resolved by the explanations which students gave. Some said simply 'I don't enjoy it' or 'it is not what I expected', but a third of them grounded their reasons for dissatisfaction in what they perceived as their own weakness. They made such remarks as, 'I sometimes do not believe I have enough ability', 'when receiving a low graded essay I feel demoralised and ask myself "Why am I doing this?"' 'I sometimes think I'm no good at it ... also I'm too lazy' or 'Sometimes I feel that I am not up to the standard of others in my group'. About half of them blamed the teaching or the nature of the course, saying 'Teachers not very good', 'the teachers are not prepared to help you', 'teaching methods are tedious', 'one teacher is not as interesting as the other'. One said she particularly regretted her decision 'when the teacher is doing most of the talking and not giving us enough chance to contribute ideas'. Others said, 'I dislike some of the books being studied, and the course hasn't been very well organised', 'the texts are not to our liking', 'the course has very often proved uninteresting and tedious', or 'sometimes I find the work we do trivial or pointless'. The implication of the comments is that the subject *itself* is not viewed as uninteresting, but the particular syllabus or teaching style in which it is manifested. Some students clearly felt that at university things would be better, and that the

A-level course was a necessary preliminary stage to be got through.

Those in the undergraduate sample, representing a more selective group, were less likely to express regret at having embarked on English at university, but even there about one in ten confessed to some reservations ('it has made me wonder what the point of it is'). Some were honest enough to add, 'but I'm not sure whether I'd be any happier doing something else'. They were less likely than the younger students to attribute weakness to themselves or their teachers, and more likely to explain their regrets by dissatisfaction with the courses offered and their value ('I'd rather be doing something more practical').

Teachers have to decide which students are to be encouraged to aim at university entry, and lecturers to determine who will be admitted. It would be helpful, therefore, if they employed the same criteria, but the survey suggests that this is not wholly the case. In two related questions, teachers were asked what chief qualities they would look for in deciding whether to advise an A-level student to apply to read English in higher education, and lecturers were asked what qualities they would look for in selecting a student for their own undergraduate courses. Overwhelmingly the most frequently mentioned quality was enthusiasm for literature, the desire to read widely (cited by 81% of the lecturers and by nearly 90% of the teachers). After this, however, there was less agreement.

It would be dangerous to build much on minor differences in a small sample, but there seems some indication that teachers in school are more likely to attach importance to subject-specific criteria, especially the ways in which students respond to texts, and are less likely to look for more general intellectual and academic qualities. They used phrases like: 'ability to respond to texts personally and articulately', 'perceptive individual response to reading', 'ability to argue a perceptive, individual response', 'perception in response'. *Enthusiasm*, *interest* and *enjoyment* were the other most frequently used terms, together with words like *willingness* or *open-mindedness*. Although intellectual abilities are sometimes mentioned (usually in combination with one or more of the terms quoted above) the overall emphasis seems to be on attitudes towards reading.

After love of reading, lecturers were most likely to look for intellectual curiosity and a liking for ideas (mentioned by about 40%), ability for clear, logical self-expression, general intelligence and academic ability. Compared with the teachers, they made much more use of terms like 'intelligence', 'talent', or 'general academic ability' (or began a longer reply with such terms). They may look for 'A-level grades', or 'a run of good O-levels'. Compared with teachers, most of whom seem to think alike, the lecturers offer a wide (sometimes bewildering) range of other criteria. According to some, the chief qualities to be sought include 'good library use', 'interest in history', 'knowledge of Latin and Greek', 'ability to do the work logically and rigorously'. According to others, what matters is 'potential for development', 'independence', 'emotional openness', 'psycho-social curiosity', 'sense of humour', 'desire to transform the self and change the world', 'co-operative personality', or 'independent interest in the arts'. A good deal would seem to depend on who is going to examine the application or to interview the candidate!

In one discussion with a group of lecturers it was suggested that these differences simply reflected the fact that school teachers were concerned with the *general* suitability of their students, lecturers with the *particular* requirements of their department and of their own courses. Because of the competitive situation they could 'take for granted' the qualities of responsiveness and perception that teachers thought so important. However, in view of the general complaints about the ability of students from school (discussed in more detail in the chapter *Development and Continuity*) there has to be some doubt whether the selection process works wholly effectively.

English universities are characterised as institutions by their freedom to control entry (compared with other countries), by the extent to which this control is in the hands of subject departments, and by some reluctance to discuss or make public the assumptions on which that control is based. 'Questions about the criteria by which qualification is to be recognized, and its relationship to the goals of the institution, are seldom posed'.[46]

The lack of any agreed policy over criteria for entry makes it difficult for both sides. Teachers in school said that they were preparing candidates for university entry without necessarily knowing where students were applying, where if anywhere they would be interviewed, or what qualities particular tutors would be seeking. There was rarely any chance of matching candidate to course. For their part, lecturers remarked that there was 'little sense of homogeneity in standards or in priorities from school to school'. It was extremely difficult to compare students from very different educational backgrounds with any fairness. As one said, there is a need 'to make sure we are not excluding people who actually might be very interesting to have because they happen to have been taught in what is from our point of view a somewhat eccentric department'.

Ian Robinson is one of very few English lecturers to have written openly about the shortcomings of the system.[47] He has described plaintively the task of selecting students to read English at Swansea, and the lack of help afforded tutors by the UCCA forms, especially about whether a candidate 'is sensitive enough to make a good English student'. The basic irony is that the very fact of competing for places must militate against the development of that sensitivity in those wishing to read English. He says that his decisions are not over-important, that 'the result is only admission to or exclusion from University College, Swansea, not Heaven', but the whole pressure of society on the student and on the school is to exaggerate the importance of that decision. The 'genuine interest' in literature which Robinson says is vital can be driven out by an anxious desire to provide what examiners and interviewers seem to want. As soon as teachers who read his article become aware that one element in the selection process is setting tests which demand 'Who wrote the following?' 'Give approximate dates for the composition of -' or 'Name three characters from each of *six* of the following', some of them will inevitably begin drilling their unfortunate students in such items of information at the expense of time actually spent reading and responding to the books themselves.

Discussions suggest that both schools and universities are locked into a system where they have to make assumptions that individuals - when pressed - admit are unsatisfactory. University selectors have to assume the validity as criteria of O- and A-level grades and the reports of head teachers, supported in some cases by interviews and by the consideration of written work (which one lecturer said was 'the most reliable single predictor of final performance'). However, different research studies have described the correlation between A-level grades and degree class as 'very low' or 'always weak', particularly in arts subjects. Indeed, 'for men studying English ... A-level predicts hardly at all'.[48] An investigation at Keele University suggested that there was virtually no difference in mean degree marks even between those with an A-level pass in English and those without.[49] Similarly at the Open University 'it is difficult, on the basis of their performance in Open University literature courses, to distinguish between students who *have* the formal qualifications demanded on an UCCA form and those who don't'.[50]

For their part, schools assume the validity of the decisions made by English selectors, and therefore organise students' choice of subjects, A-level work and interview technique in such a way as to satisfy what appear to be university criteria. This accommodation to the perceived wishes of the universities relieves the latter of any need to reconsider their practice. Reid's conclusion was that 'selection policies are almost universally characterized by extreme conservatism which manifests itself in a mistrust of the unfamiliar'.[51] When interviews take place, 'selectors are looking for confirmation of their impressions rather than seeking to disprove their hypotheses'.[52] There seem to be virtually no attempts to standardise the interviews of different lecturers or to agree on criteria, even within a single department.

There are reasons to believe that the effects of these two interlocked sets of assumptions are harmful. Schools complain that the pressure on candidates not just to succeed but to get the high grades required by universities has a damaging effect on courses and on styles of teaching and learning.[53] The needs of a few can dominate a whole group; wider reading can be sacrificed to more detailed study of a few texts. Lecturers also complain that students with three As can arrive over-taught and passive; the results reflected the work of teachers rather than the ability of the learner. The students themselves can have been damaged, as Peter Marris wrote, so that they arrive at university with 'the wrong mental set'.

> They have been studying so long to qualify for admission that they have lost sight of any further aim... They have lost the initiative in their education. The cleverer pupils, they were drilled for examination successes, while duller streams may have enjoyed a more creative scheme of learning, and when they arrive at university their attitude is receptive but passive ... treating it as yet another examination to pass before at last they grasp the ever-receding reward.[54]

The next chapter considers in more detail the views of students and their teachers as they move progressively through the different stages of education in English.

3

Development and continuity

Forty years ago, a group of articles by separate hands combined in asserting that a 'central educational problem' was the 'intellectual continuity' of studies from the examination years in school to the conclusion of degree courses.[1] In the words of one of the authors, Lucy Sutherland, 'the years between entry to the sixth form at the age of 16 and graduation from the university at the age of 21 or 22 are, or at any rate ought to be, a single, continuous and indivisible stage'.[2] The introductory note said that all the contributors assumed that achieving this *continuity* (a word which, like *indivisible* and *co-operation* is sprinkled through the pages) is a task that must be 'shared between the universities and the schools', taking it 'for granted that schools and universities must work on the same principles' and that 'they have each something to contribute'.[3]

The same articles, however, make clear a gulf between these aims and the reality. The author quoted above indicates the difference between her *are* and *ought to be* when she writes that 'in actual practice, there is clearly a good deal of dissatisfaction, both in the universities and in the schools'. She adds that 'university teachers are not satisfied with the preparation of many of the students who come up to them from the schools'[4] while, according to the author of the introduction, 'schoolmasters clearly think that the colleges and universities are not doing enough or trying enough'.[5] In a later issue of the same journal, in a series devoted specifically to 'English studies in the universities', the introduction complained magisterially that:

A great many students come to the university inadequately prepared for their work. A good deal of the basic reading that ought to have been done between twelve and eighteen has simply not been done; and the consequence is that students have to spend time acquiring a background, whereas they ought to be relating their reading at the university to a background already possessed and known.[6]

How much has the situation altered during the sweeping changes since 1950 (which has a symbolic significance for me as the year in which I began to teach English)? To what extent has *continuity* been achieved, and how far do those teaching English in schools and universities see themselves as involved in an *indivisible* process?

Student views of continuity

Students seem to gain little impression of continuity from the successive courses which they follow. In fact this survey confirms the impression described elsewhere of 'a broken-backed curriculum'.[7] The majority of those entering 16+ courses, A-level courses and degree courses in English complain of major differences from the work done at earlier stages and assert that they feel inadequately prepared for the new demands.

At 16+, only one student in the O-level sample said that she felt there was no significant difference between the work that she was doing and that which she had done earlier in the school. In that sample, 40% felt that they were being expected to read more complex and demanding texts, and 75% believed that their study methods had changed, that reading had to be 'deeper' and 'more analytic', looking 'between the lines' and 'learning to criticise'. Preparation for an examination meant that instead of a single reading for enjoyment they were now 'studying over and over'.

- Previous reading in school was fairly relaxed whereas with the books being studied for O-level you have to be careful not to miss any details.
- The books have hidden meanings which you have to find.
- We are thinking what information is between the lines.

A number of comments suggested that this change of gear could have been avoided if work earlier in the school had been adapted to make the transition more gradual. Girls said, for example, 'I didn't feel prepared to study these books' and 'Looking deeper into books was something I feel we should have been better prepared for in previous years'.

One sad effect of entering this new stage was that for many their enjoyment of reading actually diminished. The results of the survey reinforced the findings of the Assessment of Performance Unit that fewer than half of fifteen-year-olds felt that studying books in school helped them to increase their enjoyment.[8] Some (about 9%) did say that they were reading more or that their pleasure in books had increased. On the other hand, however, 20% said that they were reading less, and another 8% claimed that their enjoyment had diminished, or that they had been 'put off' authors.

A more recent sampling of GCSE groups suggests that, although dissatisfaction is less marked, there is still a sense of unanticipated demands:

> In the 3rd year we used to have lessons where you could choose books and read them for whole lessons, which was great because I love reading when it's a good book and I have chosen to read it. But at home I don't have much time for reading and now it has to be at home and it's a book that I haven't chosen completely by myself.[9]

It is the new pressure of formal assessment, of course, that accounts for much of the change in curriculum and method. O-level students were quite clear that different motives underlay the selection of texts:

> Earlier books were chosen because we would like reading them. Now they are chosen as part of a course, not necessarily likeable, and to increase our understanding of word-play etc.

Equally they were aware of a different rationale for the ways in which books were to be read and studied:

> It seems as though we are reading the books only to answer the exam questions, not for ourselves.

Although the continuous assessment for GCSE may remove the examination pressure, it substitutes others:

> You have to worry about doing good work for the whole year, instead of just doing an exam.

The approaches may be nearer to those practised earlier in the school, and there is some element of personal choice, but a new sense of urgency still remains:

After lower school, English for GCSE seems much more serious.

English in the 3rd form was more kind of relaxing. The lessons were more leisurely.

The transition to the sixth form has traditionally been marked by changes in staff-pupil relationships and in the implied position of students in the school, as well as in work. In an earlier survey, only one in ten pupils felt that there were no differences between life in the sixth and in the lower school.[10] Although the changes are generally perceived as beneficial, 55% of the English A-level cohort felt that there were ways in which their 16+ courses had failed to prepare them adequately for what one called the 'stark gap between O-level and A-level, widened by the very different ways of thinking and work'. This had caused them difficulty in adjustment. They were left free to express the perceived shortcomings in their own words, but almost all referred to three major points (a few mentioning more than one). Being unprepared for the range of the curriculum, the amount of reading required, was mentioned by about a quarter of those who were dissatisfied (24.7%). Previously they had 'spent the majority of the two-year course concentrating on just the three set books'; they were 'not encouraged to read other books outside the syllabus'. Whereas previously a detailed knowledge of a few texts had been adequate, now there was a sense in which their reading could never be 'complete'; 'there are always *other* novels by Jane Austen or plays by Shakespeare'.

Just over a third of the A-level candidates (34.25%) believed that they were unprepared for independence, the need to make up their own minds, to take responsibility for their own work. Students said, for example, that at 16+ 'we were told exactly what to think, not encouraged to make personal responses'; 'too much taken from text books and the teacher dictating'; 'the JMB course consisted of notes from the teacher which were learnt and personal response wasn't accepted as valid'; at O-level you 'copied and regurgitated in the exam what the teacher said'; 'now we are expected to think more for ourselves, whereas before we just gave back what we had memorised from the teacher's notes'. Previously 'we got told what we needed to know' whereas at A-level there is 'a change to being free to use your own mind'. The major perception of difference, mentioned by over half (56.6%) in slightly different formulations, was in the 'depth' of study, manifested in the level of understanding of texts, of critical discussion and of the written work required. Students remarked that they were 'not prepared for the actual depth of criticism', that previously 'we didn't do enough critical work'. 'At 16+ you are not taught how to criticise books, you are just expected to like and enjoy them'.

In subsequent discussion, groups generally seemed to feel that their O-level courses had not been designed as a satisfactory preparation for literary studies at a more advanced level; they were 'a preparation for communication skills rather than for the actual specifics of A-level literature'. Indeed, several students felt that they had gained more from their work in history than in English. One said, 'I thought that my O-level History prepared me more for English by way of studying sources and what you had to do with the material, learning to back up your ideas, knowing what to put in and what to leave out'.

They felt that it was 'a shame that we didn't study books in this sort of detail earlier in the school', and pointed out that critical approaches could well have been used with children's novels. The lack of detailed discussion was felt to be most obvious in poetry. A boy said:

> One thing we were not taught in the fourth and fifth years was how to look seriously at poetry/I didn't feel prepared to look at structure and style and imagery/and to say what we thought about the poems/we weren't taught about that/we had to learn that in the lower sixth.

Others agreed that poetry in the lower school was chosen to be 'immediately enjoyable', with an emphasis on humorous poems that would not require analysis or discussion. This 'wasn't enough to prepare us for what we have to do now'. One said that her immediate reaction was 'What the hell is critical appreciation?' when she was first faced with such a task, and another added that 'the literary terms you're expected to use are suddenly sprung upon you'.

One step further on, looking back from their degree courses, undergraduates were even more critical of their previous courses as a preparation for university. Nearly three-quarters of them (72.6%) believed that there were ways in which their A-level work had failed to equip them for the new demands. One said brutally that 'A-level was a waste of time, boring and excruciating'. The feeling is not universal, of course. Another undergraduate wrote that 'the level and depth of study of English literature at school was far more taxing, interesting and exciting. At University nobody is interested in your ideas anyway'.

When they express their sense of this supposed inadequacy of A-level, however, it is striking that the differences from students two years younger are only in degree, not in kind. In fact they make precisely the same criticisms of their A-level courses that students of 17 or so made of their O-level work. Virtually half of them (49%) felt unprepared for the greater range of reading on a degree course, and particularly for breaking away from the concept of 'set texts'. They said, for example, that 'A-level work was getting buried in individual texts without putting them in some kind of context'; we were 'taught that everything has to be in the analysis of set texts' with 'no sense of literary movements'; 'at university the emphasis is on an author rather than a text'.

Although, as described earlier, a third of A-level students felt that they had been forced to think for themselves and to be independent, as compared with the spoon-feeding of O-level, a similar proportion (35%) of undergraduates associated independence with university and rote-learning with A-level. They said that in the sixth, you 'were not encouraged to think for yourself', it was 'committing quotes to memory', whereas university 'requires a more self-reliant attitude which is not encouraged enough at school'; school 'doesn't prepare you for working on your own, a necessary university discipline'; 'I was unprepared for the amount of unsupervised work expected'; 'we were not taught how to make our own notes from texts or critical works but relied on the teacher'.

Similarly, the third perception of change - a more advanced critical level - was the same as that put forward by the A-level group, though it was less frequently mentioned by undergraduates. About a quarter of them (25.9%) remarked, for example, that at school 'there was no emphasis on critical theory: an emotional rather than intellectual approach was encouraged', 'no sense was impressed on us of literary criticism as a separate body of discourse', we were unprepared for 'different schools of criticism'.

The major similarity in the opinions of the two older groups prompts questions about whether there is, in fact, a break in continuity beween the two stages, or whether what has been recorded is simply the dissatisfaction of more mature students with what was offered to them when they were younger. How far are the transitions from one form of assessment to another simply seen as convenient frames for comparison rather than as phases in an unbroken development?

Dissatisfaction with previous stages of education, and a tendency to blame children's shortcomings on what has gone before, are familiar patterns. Teachers of juniors are often critical of what was achieved in the infant school; secondary teachers point to shortcomings in the 'feeder' junior schools. The same seems to be true of those working with older and more highly selected students.

Views of teachers and lecturers

It was suggested in the last section that over half of the A-level students and nearly three quarters of the undergraduates believed that their previous courses had 'failed to prepare' them for the work they were at present doing. The views of those who teach them are even more critical. About four out of five teachers (79%) said that their students were 'badly prepared to study English at A-level after the 16+ courses' (which one called 'a quantum jump') and almost all lecturers (95%) made the same criticism of A-level courses.

In explaining their reasons the teachers were most likely to refer to the restricted range of the O-level syllabus and the pressure of the examination to confine reading to set texts. Over half of those who felt their students ill-prepared (53%) put forward some version of this argument in their own words. They referred to 'lack of reading beyond set texts', 'little time to develop wider reading essential at A-level', 'not widely enough read' or the 'literary indigestion produced by studying for O-level exams'. One highly qualified and very experienced teacher suggested that the narrowness of the choice led to teachers selecting late nineteenth or twentieth century texts (apart from Shakespeare), which was an 'inadequate preparation for pre-19th century reading at A-level'. Another complained that the result of the course was that 'students see "literature" as being a Shakespeare play, a handful of odd poems and a novel'.

The next most frequently mentioned point concerned the perceived effect of O-level study in making students passive and dependent on the teacher for 'right' answers or views of texts. Over a third of the teachers (36%) felt that students became, if anything, *less* independent and self-confident in expressing their own responses during the O-level course. Typical comments included: 'students often lack the self-confidence to give their own ideas on the texts', 'they have not been sufficiently encouraged to think for themselves', 'they seem unable to work by themselves', 'some students arrive without the confidence to participate fully in the course at A-level'. One wrote that O-level 'encourages a passive response to teaching'; another that students 'become too reliant on ... the teacher giving information'; a third that the course results in 'over- reliance on teacher as transmitter of knowledge'.

The other feature mentioned by a significant number (about 18%) was a lack of adequate knowledge of one kind or another. This criticism - which could be less directly attributed to the impact of the O-level course itself - was variously focused. Comments referred to students' 'inadequate understanding of history', 'lack of cultural background', 'poor general knowledge', 'inadequate knowledge of Bible', 'inadequate knowledge of people as they really are', and lack of 'knowledge of critical terminology'.

It is clear that the points most frequently mentioned by teachers and lecturers coincide neatly with two of the three points stressed by their students. The teacher who wrote that O-level was 'far too limiting' because it 'tests memory not critical appreciation or personal response' was making a judgment echoed by a number of her own students. One or two believed that the adverse effects of 16+ were so strong that it was preferable to avoid literature examinations at that level. 'I prefer them to be "unprepared" ', wrote one, and another said that the lack of a separate literature course at 16 'does not mean that they are in any way badly prepared'.

Several of the teachers felt that the shortcomings they described were at least partially remedied during time spent in the sixth. One said, for example, that although many entered the course lacking in confidence, 'most overcome this at least by the end of the first year'. Another claimed that the lack of reading 'is soon remedied', and a third that in the sixth form students learn to prepare work in advance of lessons and 'develop their own critical ability'. Consequently, although they were so critical of O-level and CSE courses, teachers were much more optimistic about what was being achieved for students at A-level. Three-quarters of them believed that A-level courses were well designed as a preparation for higher education, and some went on to say that this fact was an example of the universities' 'stranglehold' on the curriculum. The needs of the majority were being sacrificed to the requirements of an influential minority. Although lecturers were not specifically asked about this dual responsibility of A-level teachers, a few showed awareness of the problems involved. One said, for example,

> I would like to think that we were taking seriously/and that schools were confident that we were taking seriously/the knowledge that most of the people who are doing A-level English/are not going to go on and read English at universities/and therefore that they ought to be doing things which matter/and are useful and productive for them/without this specialised destination in mind/and this is really in all our interests/of all English teachers in the 15-21 age group.

Those with such awareness, however, felt that the great majority of lecturers saw schools solely as the source of raw material. They referred to 'a strong tendency to see sixth forms as providers of suitably schooled intakes for university courses', and said that such colleagues 'like to get a nice finished product coming up from the schools that they can work on'.

For their part, the school-teachers were not only less confident about the course's relevance for those who would give up the formal study of English after A-level (58% felt that it was satisfactory), but also less certain about what it might achieve for such students. One exclaimed in some exasperation, 'How on earth do we know what their needs are?' The minority who felt the course unsatisfactory were asked to indicate in what respect this was the case. Six out of ten teachers in this category said in different ways that the syllabus was too narrow, that the choice of books was poor or that the emphasis was on disconnected works out of context:

- The course needs to be broader. Due to in-depth study of texts there is insufficient time to give students a broad-based introduction to English literature.
- NUMJMB A-level Literature is rather restrictive, concentrating on just seven texts. I would like to see a wider course, more scope for course assessment.
- The syllabus we use strikes me as more likely to put students off literature than anything else; studying six texts which have no connection (in the student's eyes) for which the students have had very little preparation prior to embarking

on the course. It suggests that literature is (i) inaccessible to the average sixteen-year-old; (ii) something 'great' in some mysterious way which no-one has explained.

One variant of this point of view said that an exclusively literary course was particularly unsatisfactory for those who would give up further study of English:

> Some continuation of O-level English language type writing skills would be useful, and a closer examination of different varieties of English other than literary texts. The new JMB English language A-level seems a viable *alternative* to the course we follow but a *compromise* course would be useful.

Nearly four out of ten said that there was too much emphasis on studying for the examination and not enough on enjoyment and personal response:

- First we teach them English literature (what writers have to say about people). Then we teach them Examinese (how to answer the questions without being quoted as a laugh in the Examiners' Report). They then go out of this 'Looking Glass' world and find it was the knowledge of literature and people they needed after all.
- It does not offer sufficient encouragement to see literature as enjoyable - to see it as a leisure pursuit. Too much stress is placed on study, which is only useful to those who continue to study.

The confidence of most A-level teachers that their courses were 'well designed to meet the needs of those going on to study English in higher education' was not shared by the lecturers who received the students. All but two of them felt that there were ways in which students had been 'badly prepared' for university study. (It may be of interest that the two are among the older and most experienced men in the sample).

In the opinion of lecturers, the chief weaknesses manifested by students from A-level courses (in order of frequency of mention) were:

- 1 a lack of adequate reading (mentioned by 54% of respondents)

- 2   passivity, lack of independence 26%
- 3   naive critical approaches to texts 23%
- 4   inability to express ideas clearly 18%
- 5   weakness in the mechanics of language 18%

Many other points were mentioned - ranging from lack of knowledge of foreign literature or historical sense to a lack of experience of creative work - but those listed above were the ones repeated from different universities. The *tone* of the comments is of some importance. Here is an illustrative collage for each of the major points.

1   'They do not have the "reading habit" '; 'they simply haven't read enough'; 'range of texts too small'; '*very* narrow range of reading'; 'ability to read rapidly and widely has not been encouraged'; 'few read any poetry'; 'concentration on the recent and crudely "relevant" '.
2   'They invariably arrive coerced into subservience by the demands of the A-level'; 'they are often timid and unadventurous and seem to require spoon-feeding'; 'too much coaching'; 'not enough independent thinking and reading'; 'receptive rather than active role preference'; 'insufficient enterprise and independence'.
3   'Their notions of practical criticism are naive'; 'lack of critical terminology'; 'criticism seen as truth rather than opinion'; 'not enough emphasis on discussion of texts, developing of a critical ability'; 'practical criticism is poor'.
4   'They have little sense of how to organise their ideas into an overall argument in an essay'; 'limited skill and experience in oral communication'; 'many don't think very clearly or write at all well'.
5   'Increasingly poor formal skills'; 'often dreadful ignorance of the basics of the language'; 'they know little about the mechanics of writing: grammar, punctuation, spelling, metre'; 'poor knowledge of grammar'; 'appalling deficiencies in spelling, punctuation, grammar, and ability to organise material'.

Assembled like this, the picture seems a grim one. Several points demand to be discussed. First, since almost all lecturers seem to feel that there are numerous ways in which students are 'badly prepared ... after their A-level courses', how is it that only a third of them said that the influence of the A-level examination is 'not helpful for undergraduate work in English'? It is particularly interesting that a number of lecturers specifically criticised the effects of the A-level curriculum and system of assessment but still recorded a belief that the A-level examination was somehow 'helpful'.

Second, how far are school teachers to be seen as responsible for the shortcomings mentioned? Only one lecturer said explicitly that an aspect of student unpreparedness was 'poor teaching (in some cases) of the subject at A-level', but many of the phrases quoted above imply weaknesses in teaching. This returns us to the major issue of dissatisfaction with previous stages of education. Since A-level teachers make essentially the same criticisms of students *they* receive at 16 as lecturers do of them at 18, where does the responsibility lie? Is it a case of successive courses failing to eradicate continuing student weaknesses, manifested at different ages? Or, since students make largely the same criticisms as teachers of courses they have passed through (as was discussed in the previous section), are there flaws in the nature of literary education, revealed at all levels? The only significant difference between the strictures of school-teachers and lecturers is that the former seem less inclined to point to weaknesses in students' language (though some do say, for example, 'Basic skills of grammar and punctuation, style and syntax are often lacking') and tend more to mention lack of background knowledge (though a number of lecturers also make this point). How far should those who teach (whether the students are 16-17 or 19-20) expect weaknesses to be eliminated at a previous stage, and how far should they see it as an inevitable part of their own task? (From the student viewpoint, it is noticeable that undergraduates are more critical of their courses and of the teaching they receive than A-level students are).

Third, the most emotional language used by lecturers seems to be reserved for students' shortcomings in language. 'Dreadful ignorance', 'appalling deficiencies' and so on make these sound morally reprehensible. This is perhaps the strongest marker of the feeling that remedying such weaknesses should be the task of someone else, that universities should at least be provided with students who can spell and punctuate. Without becoming involved in the rights and wrongs of such a belief, it is surely ironic that A-level English - like the bulk of undergraduate courses - is exclusively literary. The disappearance of the *Use of English* examination and the resistance (not least from university English departments) to the inclusion of a language element in A-level has led to a feeling that concern with candidates' language somehow stops at 16. It was lecturers with experience of universities outside Britain, or who had taught outside the university sector, who were most likely to say in discussion that English departments themselves had a responsibility to develop students' language abilities. One senior academic made the point that such development was, in any case, a life-long process, not one that could be accomplished by 18.

Fourth, universities are in a privileged position at the 'top' of an educational hierarchy. Unlike other teachers, lecturers can criticise the preparation of students who come to them, but are largely freed from any balancing need to account to others for *their* work. Those who accept graduates for research, professional training or employment may have individual criticisms, but no overall judgments of students are made. There is, for example, a widely held view that students entering post-graduate courses in teacher education have not been particularly well-equipped with the kinds of knowledge, skills and attitudes that will be most beneficial for English teachers. Such a view, however, has not been given any formal articulation. The only way of quantifying what a department has done over three years is to look at the spread of degree results.

From the practical point of view, it appeared in a discussion with a group of lecturers that although all had 'expectations' about the capabilities that students should display, what those expectations were varied widely from individual to individual. Unless departments can agree upon (and publish) some indication of what they expect, it is perhaps unreasonable to complain that students are 'not coming up to expectations'.

Development of personal response

In the papers originating from the Dartmouth Conference, Frank Whitehead suggested that in dealing with literature we all 'instinctively' proceed 'on the assumption that there exists in our students a developmental sequence'. Indeed, overlapping metaphorical epithets like *maturing*, *deepening*, *refining* alongside equally metaphorical terms like *sequence*, *steps* and *stages* recur as descriptions for children's increasingly *refined*, or *sophisticated*, or *critical* responses in the work of many major educational writers.[11] Until recently there have been few attempts to ground such generalisations in any description of *how* such a developmental sequence is manifested in children. Any attempt to investigate the ways in which taste, judgment, or critical response 'improve' with age are notoriously dependent on our criteria for distinguishing between 'better' and 'worse' readings or judgments and on the particular diagnostic measures that are to be used. Nevertheless there have been some tentative experiments to consider empirically how children progressively define the reading process, how they articulate their judgments of what is read, and how they come to interpret what they read.[12] This work has essentially been concerned with the response of children up to the age of 15. It has not yet been carried forward into the examination years.

There are several obvious reasons for this. Developmental 'markers' beyond the top of the 15-year-old range are harder to establish and more subjective. Examination courses and assessment can be held to 'contaminate' instinctive responses. The balance between teaching and learning shifts. Students become more self-conscious about formulating their responses.

More generally, however, there seems a disinclination to enquire too closely into development in the examination years except as it is manifested in the writing of essays and in examinations. Even many reader-response critics seem unwilling to move beyond the abstractions of the reader, the implied reader or the ideal reader to demonstrate what knowledge and abilities real readers actually deploy in practice and to show how these abilities develop - or not - in the educational contexts where learning is supposed to go on. Such a detailed investigation was beyond the scope of this enquiry, but some of the questions and discussions focused on students' *perceptions* of development.

At all levels there was a tendency to subsume any views of personal development in reading and response into the wider awareness of changing courses and assessment. In other words, students assumed that they were 'progressing' because they were doing work that seemed (or was presented to them as) more advanced than what had previously been undertaken. For example, asked whether they felt they had developed as readers, whether the reading in which they were at present engaged was 'more advanced' than that which they had done previously, nearly all echoed the points which they had previously made about the new demands of their courses (described in the earlier section of this chapter: 'Student views of continuity').

Almost all predictably believed that they had 'advanced' (approximately 95% of the O-level group; 91% of A-level students and 84% of undergraduates). Just as they attributed this to their ability to cope with what seemed more difficult studies, so the few who did not share this belief externalised their reactions into the failure of those studies to help them. For example, some undergraduates said, 'I don't feel that I've been stretched beyond the A-level standard of difficulty' or 'The first year is so slow and plodding that there seems little advancement'.

There is a significant difference in the ways that perceived progress is defined by the groups of students, although the same four or five points are repeated in a variety of ways. Of the basic metaphors, A-level students overwhelmingly preferred the notion that they were now capable of 'deeper' reading, of a more detailed, analytic kind, with more consciousness of technique. Over 70% made this point in one way or another. They said, for example: 'The course involves not just looking at the surface content of the text but going deeper into what the author is saying'; 'we have to "understand" in much greater depth'; 'earlier in the school reading was concerned with understanding the plot ... now the concern is with style and literary devices'; 'now you go deeper into the book and the author's ideas'; 'you are required to show perception and deeper understanding'.

Response to this increased 'depth' varied from the rueful ('I don't understand it now, and I always used to') to the confident ('As you become older, you grow in intelligence and maturity, and demand or look for more in the book you are reading. You are able to experiment with ideas that you were not able to perceive when you were younger').

About 30% of the undergraduate sample also used versions of the 'deeper' metaphor, but twice as many mentioned the ability to cope with a 'wider' range of reading, undertaken in the context of critical thinking and of some understanding of the social and cultural background.

How far do students perceive their examination courses as affecting their general reading? In the first questionnaire stage this was presented as an open question. The replies suggested that about a quarter of the O-level candidates thought that their literature studies had produced no real effect on their reading for pleasure out of school. Half of them felt that there had been perceptible advantages; they read more ('I have read nearly twice as much as when I didn't do literature'), or in a more thoughtful and understanding way, or they were able to cope with a wider range of reading and with more difficult books, though their formulation of this sometimes suggests a narrow view of what is involved ('I now tend to pick a book to pieces rather than just read it'; 'I have learned how to decipher Shakespeare... It turned *Romeo and Juliet* into something English'). On the other hand, nearly 30% made negative or critical comments. Some of them had apparently never greatly enjoyed reading, and had not changed their opinions: 'I don't read out of school, and I don't get much pleasure out of reading'; 'The only books I read are concerned with science and facts, and not novels, poems or plays'. Several felt that the imposed syllabus had destroyed enjoyment: 'Being forced to read books that I didn't enjoy puts me off'; 'The course has put me off reading at home because I am so busy reading and learning books I don't like'. Perhaps the most telling remark came from one girl who was reading less, and who expressed her dilemma in these terms: 'The books I enjoy are all below me now and I feel guilty about reading them. The sort of books I should be reading I don't enjoy'. It is hard to feel easy about examination courses that create this sort of split in an adolescent's mind between what she feels she *ought* to read and what she really *wants* to.

The effects of the A-level course on out-of-school reading were generally perceived as being beneficial. Nine students thought there had been no real change, but the other 87 respondents made 86 positive comments between them and only 27 negative ones. The most common of the latter were simply concerned with the lack of time available, but there were again a few sad suggestions that interest in books had been destroyed: 'It takes the pleasure out of reading for pleasure', one girl commented, and another wrote, 'You feel guilty if you read anything other than a classic'. The commonest positive responses were that tastes had been widened, that new authors and styles had been introduced and that reading with greater understanding and appreciation had strengthened the response to books in general, and 15 simply said that they now read more.

On the basis of these replies, A-level and university students were asked about the relative importance of the most commonly cited effects, and were able to specify others that they thought important. The responses of the two groups were very similar. Most important were the deepening of appreciation and the extension of range by introducing new authors and genres. Both groups ranked an increase in discrimination next, though this was less important for the A-level students. The least significant effect for both groups was 'increasing the amount you read'. Indeed, in their free responses a few students said that the result had been to *de*crease the amount they read for pleasure. They commented 'Don't have any time left', 'Do not read for pleasure outside course - many books to read for exams' or 'Amount of work has left me less time for reading outside the course'. One commented that the deepening of appreciation of literature 'has not affected the rubbish I read for sheer escapism, i.e. wet romances'.

The students were also asked the open question 'At present, which authors or kinds of books are your real favourites?' Predictably, literary authors, titles and genres were overwhelmingly most mentioned, sometimes with the addition of approving comments. A 16-year-old girl answered, 'Jane Austen - I like the sense of propriety; Thomas Hardy - his vivid descriptiveness especially in "Madding Crowd" '. Earnest preferences were stated for works 'in which ideas, moral values and opinions are discussed and discussed'.

Many were aware of the tug between different kinds of attraction. One 17-year-old wrote, 'Graham Greene is now my favourite author although before the course Catherine Cookson was my favourite ... I prefer quick-paced crime stories or books centred on oppression and the cruelty of mankind'. While some said obediently 'I'm enjoying my set books', others struck a more defiant liking for: 'mindless books to relax with when not having set books pressed on me', or 'For relaxation and sheer mindlessness combined with my love of clichés - Mills and Boon!' (However, the same student added a long list of other reading, including Tennessee Williams, Philip Larkin, Doris Lessing, Wilfred Owen and Colette). Two other responses read: 'Jackie Collins, Virginia Andrews, autobiographies of the rich and famous', and 'Harold Robbins, Jackie Collins, scandal and romance, astrology ... books about murderers (fact) occult'.

University students demonstrated healthily catholic tastes: between Marlowe, Beaumont and Fletcher, T.S. Eliot and E.M. Forster one sandwiched 'Sci-fi books esp. Asimov, Heinlein, John Varley, Ellisson'; another added to a list including Donne, Virginia Woolf and Scott Fitzgerald, 'but I also have an interest in superstition, mystical and predictions, hence books on such subjects and mystic novels e.g. Stephen Donaldson'. Undergraduates were more likely than school students to name categories marked by some particular quality or stance of the author: 'feminist authors', 'books by women writers', 'Christian books'. A few indicated the grounds for establishing their preference, like the 20-year-old who said that her favourites were 'Books in which I can identify with characters: Thomas Hardy, *Wuthering Heights*, D.H. Lawrence, Rupert Brooke and best of all *Hamlet*'. Some suggested that following a course in literature had actually 'reduced the number of people I count as favourites - now enjoy them all fairly equally'.

Fiction seems to be the dominant interest. The Whitehead survey of younger readers found that their preferences (whether assessed by records of recent reading or by their indication of favourite authors or titles) were 'overwhelmingly' for narrative fiction.[13] Following a course in literature does seem to increase the chances of other modes being mentioned, but over 80% of those responding in A-level and university groups mentioned fiction authors or titles in describing their 'real favourites'. The A-level results seem to confirm the familiar allegations about the low regard in which poetry is held in school: under 16% mentioned poems or poets (compared with nearly a quarter mentioning plays or dramatists). It is interesting, however, that A-level boys were rather more likely to mention poets and less likely to mention novelists than were the girls. The undergraduates were more likely to include poetry among their favourites, more than a third of them doing so (compared with a quarter mentioning dramatic works).

Since independence of critical thought is recurrently presented as one of the markers of development in literary studies, particular interest attaches to answers given to the question 'How far have you felt encouraged to make your own personal response to the books studied, rather than adopting ideas or judgments that you do not really feel?' The notion of *encouragement* was left deliberately vague, so that students could see it in terms of deliberate staff intervention, or of the pressures exerted by the group or the course, or of their own state of mind.

In the pilot study, rather over a third of the O-level students felt that they had been so encouraged, although there were considerable differences in the proportion between particular schools. Even within individual schools, however, students had formed very different perceptions. One group contained a boy who wrote that 'the teacher has at all times tried to encourage personal response' and another who said 'I have not been encouraged at all to make my own response to the books'. About 12% felt strongly that they had been *discouraged* from formulating their own response, that they had been 'brainwashed', subjected to 'force-feeding' or required to 'parrot' their teacher's views. Some felt, in the words of one, that

'I've never really been taught to give my own personal views on the texts', and others believed that their own opinions could not be developed because 'we have the teacher's viewpoint engraved on our minds':

- We are led to believe that the teacher's way of thinking is *RIGHT*.

- Sometimes ideas/judgments may be forced upon us.

- I think that the teacher does too much of the talking and all that one can do is to regurgitate their ideas.

In all schools there were students who felt that, although they were being encouraged to respond personally, there were unspoken constraints imposed by their view of the teacher as expert and by that expert's knowledge of what an examiner would require. Something like four out of ten O-level students expressed this belief that insincerity was forced upon them if they were to be successful.

- Although students may have ideas of their own, I think they feel they have to adopt the views of the staff if they want to pass the exam. Students feel they must accept the teacher's explanation as gospel.

- You are encouraged to put forward your own personal viewpoint but anything that is not conventional gets discouraged - everything gets modified. I write essays and don't believe a word that I say but get better marks than if I hadn't adopted other (i.e. teacher's) ideas.

- Personal response is encouraged to a certain extent, but ... I feel that we are pushed to feel what we are supposed to feel, not intentionally by the teacher, but because you believe what he says must be right.

- I have been encouraged to make a personal response to the books but I still would never dare to say in an essay that I detested or loathed a book.

The prevalence of such assumptions that there are 'accepted' views of texts and that one should provide 'what the examiner wants to read' was further tested in the main questionnaire stage, where the same question was put to A-level and university students.

This also provided an opportunity to test the hypotheses that there is a gender difference (particularly at school) in willingness to respond personally, that there is a relationship between use of published criticism and expression of personal responses, and that university students will feel more free to formulate their own views than younger students on A-level courses.

Before outlining the results, it can be said that none of the three hypotheses was sustained. The classification of male and female answers showed them to be virtually identical; there was no significant relationship between replies to this question and to another showing the amount of use made of printed criticism; and there was only a slight difference between the responses of A-level and of university students.

In brief, rather over half of each sample said that they were encouraged 'very much' or 'to some extent' to make their own responses (54.7% undergraduates; 54.8% A-level). Under a quarter had some reservations or felt that they were 'not much' encouraged (23.7% undergraduates; 18.7% A-level). A very small proportion replied 'not at all' (3.8% undergraduates; 4.2% A-level). More of the university students (14.2%) than of those taking A-level said that it varied according to the situation or the teacher, presumably because they were more likely to come into contact with a range of different lecturers.

The question was seen in black-and-white terms by many of the A-level students. Some of those who did feel encouraged answered in a single word or phrase: 'totally', 'very much', 'a great deal'. Others felt it necessary to back up such a comment with a qualification about the need for 'evidence', willingness to hear the views of others, or a sense of development, as can be seen from these examples:

- I have been very much encouraged to make my own response, but also to listen to others and appreciate their ideas.
- We have been greatly encouraged (too much - and I talk rubbish).
- If you have a firm enough point with backing evidence to uphold it then nothing or nobody can dissuade you from it even if a teacher is trying to brainwash you with his ideas alone.
- Am learning to form my own opinions, becoming more confident as I realise this is what examiners are looking for.
- Yes, the teachers encourage us (but not enough).

- I feel at liberty to say whatever I like as long as I am able to back up my argument.

Those at the other end of the spectrum complained that 'there is very little encouragement', 'many teachers do not regard personal response as important', 'you are made to feel you must say what the examiner wants to hear'. One remarked that 'you tend to accept teachers' views as law as after all they took a degree in English!'

- A lot of the time we have to say what is expected of us and not what we actually think.
- Teachers tell you what they think, you don't get the chance to air your views.
- Whenever I do make comments out of my own head, the teacher disagrees.
- We are suppressed into taking on outside judgments I don't feel for much of the time, as if there is no alternative.
- I find that most English teachers will only accept the traditional viewpoints and this allows little scope for individualism.
- Very little encouraged - teachers say that they will not give us judgments and ideas but then they always do and often say we are wrong when we have our own ideas, even if we can support them.
- I have written many essays where I have made personal responses and got terrible grades and others where I responded unnaturally and got good grades.

One particularly interesting example suggests a self-isolated student who feels under pressure from the group as well as from the teacher.

I have not been encouraged to make my own personal response. A general middle-of-the-road stance on all literature is taken. Controversial discussions usually end with the teacher deciding that that line of discussion should not be taken further, or will be returned to. Because my response is impulsive it tends to be controversial and is invariably squashed by the combined efforts of staff and students. Very often after consideration I tend to modify my view, though I don't admit it... All too often it appears that we will be giving the examiners what they want to hear - the same accepted ideas.

This student, who elsewhere stresses his wish to 'go it alone', said in a later discussion that he found his views threatened by others 'times too numerous to mention'.

The constraints hinted at in such comments suggest that the examination exerts the same kind of pressure at A-level as at 16+: the teacher is perceived as an authority who can give guidance about what an examiner expects or requires (even if the teacher denies this). There is a consequent pressure to feel what 'ought' to be felt. One student wrote, 'Teachers give us ideas which I would not really have thought were true but I am willing to try and understand them' (a literary leap of faith!) Others begin with a confident affirmation which has to be qualified:

> I always write my own opinions, no-one has ever affected my judgment, except the teacher who points certain things out and makes me come to my own decisions.

Just what is being suggested here? Why does she have to be *made* to come to her own decisions? The implication seems to be that the teacher 'pointing things out' is somehow not to be seen as 'affecting' her 'judgment'. Another student, asserting that personal response is vital and (like the last) that she 'always' speaks her mind, goes straight on to say 'but certain books do not allow this'. How do *books* prevent this? Does she mean that judgments about classic texts are too 'fixed' to be questioned?

Willingness to please is a recurrent note. 'I have not really adopted any sort of response', writes one, 'having agreed with most points made'.

- Mostly we are expected to follow traditional judgments then add any personal responses cautiously - to please the examiner not yourself.
- You feel confident in your own judgments if the teacher agrees but if not you don't believe in them enough to write them down in the A-level exam.

As in the pilot study, therefore, the most interesting responses to the question were those that in effect answered 'Yes, but...' The number of these suggests that although over half of the students claimed that they *were* encouraged to make their own responses, the actuality may be rather different.

- We are encouraged to give our own views but sometimes criticised about them and told they are wrong.
- We are all encouraged to make personal responses, but mostly the teacher's view is translated as being right.
- Quite far - but we are still expected ultimately to adopt some, if not all, of the teacher's responses.
- Quite well, but in class discussions our teacher often presents such a forceful argument that it is very hard to keep to my own opinion, even though I was convinced it was right.
- I have felt encouraged to a certain extent, but we are still expected to take note of other people's judgments and criticism.
- Master encourages to a certain extent, but always puts down our suggestions and then tells us to make our own observations when we do not know what to do or know if they are right.
- I have been encouraged to make my own personal response but often our teachers express their view as being correct, when there is no correct answer.
- We are encouraged, but it is often difficult to voice your views as the teacher says quite a lot.
- This is encouraged, but the teachers will still in the end favour their own interpretation.

The same tension between personal conviction and what proves acceptable to lecturer or examiner survives into university life. 'Encouraged to respond, but ...' remains the dominant mode. Undergraduates comment, for example:

- They say 'say what you feel' - but if you come out with a set academic response you get higher marks.
- I have always had my own ideas but whether I would ever argue against the department's view in an exam I don't know!
- Personal response is encouraged in tutorials, although higher essay marks are often gained by echoing the tutor's own opinion.
- The course appeared to require individual thought, but the exam did not!
- I always try to make my own judgments, but I feel that tutors have their own fixed ideas from which they will not budge and therefore you feel obliged to agree with them.

- I try to make personal responses but I still feel that it's best in exams not to deviate too far from the orthodox view.

One student who had recently completed her English degree course said in discussion:

I can distinctly remember/having one of my first essays at university handed back to me/with all the/I think/and/in my opinion/ ringed in red/and a comment along the lines of/I do not want to hear your personal response/that is not academic/I want to know your understanding of what the critics have to say.

There seem few signs, then, that the formulation of personal response becomes much stronger or more confident as students move through the system. The pressure of assessment is dominant. At all levels there seems to be a ladder of risk which only the very confident student will climb to the top. Least risky of all is simply to adopt the views of teacher or tutor, and to avoid formulating any of your own. There is slight risk in exposing your ideas in class or tutorial, and rather more risk if they conflict with the known opinions of the teacher. It is distinctly more risky to express such opinions in written form, in an essay or other project. Most hazardous of all is to put forward these ideas in an examination.

4

Courses of study

What do students think they are learning by studying English? What counts as 'knowledge' in this field? More specifically, how do students respond to their courses and which are the topics they find most interesting or helpful? What influence do they believe their studies have had on their lives? These are some of the topics that will be considered later in the chapter. First, however, it has to be said that courses are as they are because they are shaped in the particular contexts of their political and institutional frameworks, methodology, validation and assessment. In order to exist as a subject at university or in schools, English had to be defined according to pre-existing academic regulations. It had to be recognised as a subject that could be taught and examined in 'appropriate' ways. The swift rise of subject-English, sketched in chapter 1, has not been associated with any sense that its curriculum or criteria of assessment have been finally agreed, as was made plain by the very mixed *Responses* to *English from 5 to 16*.[1]

It is beyond the scope of this study to consider what impressions of 'English knowledge' are conveyed before the examination years, and this topic has been effectively discussed elsewhere.[2] At examination level in school, however, a number of institutional constraints have traditionally been clear: that English divides neatly into two (Lang. and Lit.), that courses are of one or two years duration, that literature is to be defined in terms of isolated set books, that students' success is to be measured by a final examination, and so on. Similar assumptions shaped university English, where for years 'language' meant Anglo-Saxon, 'literature' stopped in the 1830s, and literary studies were exclusively historical and critical. The reading process was defined in terms of the individual reader with a particular text (unlike much school practice), the figure of the critic was idealised and imaginative writing by students was seen as an irrelevance.

The extraordinary neglect of the subject of production in modern academic literary thought and in conventional literary thought is attributable to the notion of literature as an object and as existing in the past. Interest in the active process of making is suppressed in favour of the more negotiable activity of responding to an object.[3]

The interlocking of assumptions about the literary curriculum, its teaching and its assessment has been parodied in one view of the power structure within English:

A lecturer stands in front of a hundred students. He talks to them about 'Prometheus Unbound' and says how wonderful it is. He refers to other lecturers who have written down what they think in critical books. Most of them think it's wonderful too, but for different reasons. The students listen and take notes. They go away and read 'Prometheus', they read their notes, they read the critics.

They write about 'Prometheus' for the lecturer. Most say it's wonderful. The lecturer reads what they write. He recognizes what is said and is gratified: 'They've understood' he says. Or, he recognizes what is said and is displeased: 'They're just regurgitating the lectures', he says. Or, he doesn't recognize what is said and is displeased: 'They didn't understand what I was getting at', he says. Or, he doesn't recognize what is said and is at a loss: 'They're right to ignore the authorities, including me, but this stuff is absurd - "Margaret Thatcher is Jupiter, the Universities are Prometheus, and the Green Party is the Earth" - I ask you! And this - "I never could get beyond Act 1, however hard I tried. As far as I'm concerned the poem is the rock I'm bound to" - how am I expected to mark that?' It all gets sorted out in the end. Everyone gets graded, there's the vac., October comes, a lecturer stands in front of a hundred students. He talks to them about ...[4]

Radical critics suggest that such assumptions are no longer valid - if they ever were - and that English studies now provide 'a superb instrument' to educate a specific kind of literate, white, middle-class society that 'no longer exists'.[5]

Within this wider context, what of the courses that are offered? The coming of 'unitary' English in the GCSE does something to postpone the separation of language and literature, and it is now possible to take an A-level English course with elements of both (AEB syllabus 623, or London syllabuses 175 or 176). For most students, however, their teachers will select a purely literary course, or, just possibly, a language one (JMB English Language or AEB English Language Studies), foreshadowing the choice of language or literature options at some universities like Sheffield or Newcastle.

The majority of A-level students seems to have accepted unquestioningly (some with relief) the fact that their course will be exclusively literary. However, a few are surprised and displeased. Two boys in one discussion said:

- I regret taking English because it's all literature/I preferred language.
- It wasn't really stressed/on the syllabus/that there'd be absolutely no language work at all.

In particular, the confining of writing to critical modes produces complaints. Two girls comment that 'it would be better if we could do more imaginative writing' and 'more emphasis should be placed on creative writing'. It is perhaps worth noting in this respect that the 1970 Schools Council survey showed that *written* English (not literature) was well up among the subjects that pupils would have liked to take in the sixth form if the opportunity had been available and that four out of five of these would have liked to take such a subject at A-level.[6] However, the concern of this study is essentially with the nature of literary studies and with what seems at different stages to comprise the literary curriculum, and these topics are discussed in the next sections.

Literary studies

What is involved in the term 'literary studies'? For centuries the word *litterae* simply meant a knowledge of reading and writing, both literature and literacy. In the Middle Ages, the trivium (grammar, logic and rhetoric) continued to relate the two activities. Later, 'humane' or 'polite' letters involved the critical study of authors as a model for one's own language use. Increasingly, however, the attention shifted from the acts of composing and elocution, from generating ideas, to the analysis of rhetorical devices and the study of form and style, to critical activities. 'A similar shift in interest from the creative act to the interpretive act took place in other disciplines - in music and the visual arts.'[7] The works that were studied covered the whole range of writing, including history, biography, expository and didactic work. Not all theorists agree with the commonly expressed view that our current sense of literature - specifically imaginative writing of accepted worth - is essentially a nineteenth century creation,[8] and that increasing interest in English, or French, or German literature was linked to the rise of nationalism. Rene Wellek is one notable scholar who believes that some eighteenth century uses of the term have the current meaning.[9] However, the notion of *studying* such literature exclusively was certainly late to appear. Professor Colin McCabe has described as a three hundred year historical process the 'construction of a national literature as an object of study'.[10] When Sir Arthur Quiller Couch lectured at Cambridge 'On a School of English' in 1917, he criticised the statement of his professional duties which included promoting 'the study in the University of the subject of English Literature'. Repeating the word *subject*, he exclaimed, 'Surely - for a start - there is no such thing'. Although in what follows there seems some ambiguity in his use of the word (sometimes treated as *topic*) there is no doubt of his scepticism about what he calls a *convention*:

> the convention that English Literature could be separated somehow from its content and treated as a subject all by itself, for teaching purposes: and, for purposes of examination, could be yoked up with another subject called English Language, as other Universities had yoked it.[11]

The first chapter gave a brief sketch of the coming of English as an academic subject, which has to be accompanied here by an equally brief introduction to the literary curriculum.

As it has become practised, the study of literature is distinct in a number of ways from most other academic disciplines. By separating off the making and performance of literature, English distinguishes itself from other 'aesthetic' subjects, like music or drama. It provides no neat correlation between the courses offered and the future career. Politicians, and employers in a utilitarian age need little convincing of the value of studying science, engineering or medicine; the courses exist to produce scientists, engineers and doctors. The study of literature, however, cannot be given such direct practical justification. It may produce teachers and writers, but the purpose of the study is not primarily vocational.

Even more than other subjects, English merges imperceptibly into other disciplines. It is impossible to study literature of any period seriously without also being drawn into the study of history, of philosophy, of other literatures, of art and music and - of course- of the language in which the works are written. Can we study plays without becoming involved in theatre studies, or narratology without being concerned with films and television? Indeed, it will be argued that one of the major problems in literary studies is that so much needs to be known (in order to understand the discipline) that cannot be taught within it, but must simply be assumed.

The crucial difference lies in the particular way in which cognitive and affective approaches are inseparable: the reader's response to the text is an essential element in what is being studied. Criticism is not a purely intellectual activity; it involves feelings and attitudes (to 'life' as well as to 'literature'). Books are distinct from other objects of academic study by being, in Poulet's term, 'interior' or 'subjectified' objects.[12] Instead of moving towards some agreed 'truth', students of literature are involved in unique reading experiences, which exist to produce new perceptions of the world.

Ultimately the point of studying literature is 'not itself, in the end, a literary one'.[13] Terry Eagleton agrees in this with F.R. Leavis: 'Literary judgments are never merely literary', they are inseparable from those values which should determine 'the important choices of actual life'.[14]

The literary curriculum

Early in the 1980s, Raymond Williams could look back to a time, 'about half a century, in which courses in English Literature had an apparent and at times effective coherence. The central disciplines were literary criticism, literary history, literary scholarship, with some variation of order'.[15] He was clear, though, that 'the old unity' was now broken. In the same group of articles Iain Gilchrist attributed the crisis in English to its special nature as a subject for study:

... being studied in an intellectual context designed to shield it from the rest of experience, it has come to be viewed as devoid of relation to life, emptied of meaning, self-referential.[16]

Whatever one's views about the definition of literature and the extent to which it is a 'privileged' or special form of discourse, it is clear that the application of such a term to any group of texts is governed by a series of human activities. The survival of any work depends not only on retaining some degree of critical attention, but also on the available communication modes or technologies, and on the priorities and methods of the education system which mediate the text to successive generations.

At the student level, perceptions of what literature is are largely defined by a number of authors or texts nominated by other people as of particular value for being studied, taught and examined. This is one significant element in the progressive narrowing of meaning attached to the word *literature* itself. What counts as knowledge in this field comes to be identified with the contents of courses, lists of suggested reading and examination syllabuses. I have analysed in some detail elsewhere[17] a few of the impressions that might be gained from a close study of 16+ and A-level syllabuses over a period of years including these:

- that virtually all English drama was written either between 1590 and 1623 or between 1945 and the present day,
- that although stage plays are now seen as worthy of study, plays written for television are not,
- that for most students the English novel begins with Jane Austen and ends with Dickens and Hardy,
- that Chaucer and Milton are the only poets worthy of universal study,
- that the modern poets most appropriate for 16-year-olds are R.S. Thomas, John Betjeman and Ted Hughes.

Although some writers appear consistently (Shakespeare, Chaucer, Dickens and others) there are also many signs that examiners respond to shifting values on the literary stock exchange. Thirty years ago William Hazlitt was the most consistently prescribed prose author, twenty years ago there was a vogue for modern 'provincial realists', for some time Golding's *Lord of the Flies* was the most set text at 16+, but the popularity of all of these has waned.

Shaw has faded and Tom Stoppard currently has more plays on A-level syllabuses than any dramatist except Shakespeare. Dryden's *Absalom and Achitophel* was very popular thirty years ago but virtually disappeared from syllabuses in the eighties.

For many years examiners seemed to interpret English Literature as meaning texts written in English in England (or, occasionally, Britain); then it widened to include major examples drawn from the rapidly extending corpus of American writing; then again to admit writers from Australia or South Africa; and again to include the English works of authors like Achebe, Soyinka and Naipaul. At Cambridge the English Tripos extended the conventional range with subjects like 'Tragedy' (including French and German as well as Greek dramas) and 'The Moralists' (St Paul, Marx, Freud). Largely under the influence of the seminal *Literature in English* syllabus (Cambridge and the East African Examinations Syndicate), school examinations boards began to set Ibsen, Chekov or Brecht alongside Shakespeare and Arthur Miller. A living literature, to which new works are added year by year, cannot be defined (like Latin) in terms of an agreed canon.

The significance of policy decisions by the subject committees of examination boards is intensified by the choices made by teachers from the lists which they are offered. There are enormous variations in the numbers of schools opting for particular texts, showing in general a preference for plays and novels (rather than poems), for twentieth century works and for works that seem to be stylistically or culturally 'accessible' (Hardy rather than Henry James). According to one study of A-level choices, nineteen candidates opted to answer on *Tess of the D'Urbervilles* for every one choosing *Four Quartets*.[18] Teachers are not only concerned with selecting books that will be appropriate for their pupils. In a time of economic stringency there are strong reasons for choosing texts that are already in the stock cupboard and for ignoring an interesting new book that may only occur on the syllabus for two years. At A-level some teachers prefer texts that they themselves studied in some depth at university, and others say that they like 'books about which there's a good deal of published criticism'. In such cases they will be unlikely to select recent novels and plays or work by Caribbean, African (or even, perhaps, American) writers.[19]

This double selection has traditionally rested on a no-nonsense assumption that examiners and teachers make their nominations from an accepted canon of texts embodying particular values. Even today it is possible for an academic at Cambridge University to write with splendid circularity of these 'acknowledged literary masterpieces' that they can be defined as those texts 'which have come to be considered as literature, and whatever other texts resemble them in the respects which those who are familiar with literary texts recognise'.[20] Increasingly, however, there have been voices to complain that the 'established' canon excludes much writing by women, by those from other cultures writing in English, by many contemporary authors and by those working in other media than book-production. Texts do not simply 'come to be considered as literature' by some neutral chronological process: they are selected and re-selected by readers with their own values and for their own purposes. So it has been that a particular definition of a national 'heritage' of English literature became inter-connected with a particular construction of 'Englishness' itself. This model, still implicit in some syllabuses, has increasingly come under attack. George Steiner has argued that the 'linguistic centre of English has shifted' and that serious readers of literature will be 'less and less drawn to home ground'. He urged 'the obligation, the opportunity to make our sense of the history of the English language and of its literatures more comprehensive, more responsive to the great tributaries from outside'.[21]

More profoundly, Professor Colin MacCabe has questioned to what extent we can accept the values of the traditional literary heritage. What was 'constructed' over centuries, he writes,

> was indeed the literature of an imperial and Protestant nation inscribed with the assumption of the innate superiority of the English nation and people, the natural subordination of women to men and the unquestioned superiority of a particular class-based form of English.
>
> As we in the latter part of the twentieth century attempt to teach this tradition what can our attitude be to this cultural heritage? I assume that it is agreed that it cannot be one of unquestioning affirmation.[22]

Any definition of the curriculum in terms of set texts carries with it assumptions not only about the nature of literature but about society and about pedagogy. Raymond Williams described the effect of studying texts in relation to their 'background', as in the Cambridge English School and in some A-level syllabuses. In practice, 'the background' is supposed to be a general backing of facts against which this foreground we call literature is undertaken. The background is regarded - with all the implications of the metaphor - as a fixed unchanging scene, and against this the more significant activities of the making of literature are engaged in.[23]

Against this background works are given significance not only by the fact of their nomination but by the particular way in which it is implied that they should be read - though teachers and lecturers may practise and advocate quite different readings of the same texts. Tony Bennett has remarked:

Even when there is broad agreement about precisely which texts are to be regarded as 'literary', these may be held to be 'literary' in quite different ways and may, accordingly, be approached and studied from quite different perspectives with often radically different aims in view.[24]

At university, the literary curriculum is defined not in terms of set texts but by the courses on offer: the assumption that a reasonably balanced coverage of periods of literature, with some genre or thematic studies will somehow enable the student to become 'qualified'. Gerald Graff has written convincingly of what he calls 'the field-coverage principle', by which departments appoint specialists to cover what seem to be major periods or subjects within English Literature. The great advantage of this system, he writes,

was to make the department and the curriculum virtually self-regulating ... instructors could be left on their own to get on with teaching and research, with little need for elaborate supervision and management ...
Innovation even of a threatening kind could be welcomed by simply *adding* another unit to the aggregate of fields to be covered.[25]

Such a theory conveniently explains how departments and their curricula have remained largely unaffected by recent violent clashes of ideology. The myth of shared values could be maintained by allowing all lecturers to determine the methods and ideology they thought appropriate for their own courses. The system 'relieved them of the need to confer about matters of fundamental concern with colleagues'. Controversy was 'curiously screened from students and outsiders'.

> The presence of an array of fully staffed fields made it unnecessary for anybody to have a theoretical idea of the department's goals in order for it to get on with its work. The grid of literary periods, genres, and themes in the catalog was a sufficiently clear expression of what the department was about.[26]

In these days of the 'knowledge explosion', however, it is clear that no neatly agreed view exists of what an English graduate 'ought' to know. This is partly demonstrated by the range of courses and choices available at different universities (briefly discussed later in this chapter), dependent on the staff currently available. In addition, what is offered under such apparently identical headings as Augustan or Victorian literature can actually vary widely from department to department both in the selection of texts and in approaches to them. Not only is the field of literature uncontainable and expanding, but also the variety of *readings* of texts continually increases. It is not simply the obvious fact that each new critical position - Marxist, feminist, structuralist - points to different features of the same texts and evaluates them differently. Attention also needs to be paid to the fact that notions of *teaching* a text are equally changeable. The links between critical theory, concepts of reading and pedagogy can be illustrated by a brief examination of three key works on reading from the short history of English studies.

The earliest is the volume of lectures given at Cambridge University by the first Professor of English Literature there, Sir Arthur Quiller Couch, in the years 1916-1918. Published in 1920 under the title *On the Art of Reading*, these lectures revealed Q's awareness that 'the real battle for English lies in our Elementary Schools, and in the training of our elementary teachers'.[27]

From the teacher's point of view the Art of Reading means essentially the skilful performing of text to make it available, as Q himself did throughout the lectures, many of which are a tissue of extended quotations. His advice for school teachers is to take a poem like *L'Allegro* and read it to a 'class of 30 or 40' without interruptions: 'Go on: just read it to them ... Do not pause and explain ... Go on reading ... don't stop to explain ... don't discourse

... don't insist ... just go on reading, as well you can'.[28] When he describes his own methods of working with undergraduates, the picture is very similar. A student comes to him for a tutorial on Keats, they turn to 'Ode to a Grecian Urn' and then 'We read it together, perhaps twice; at the second attempt getting the emphasis right' and then 'From this we proceed to examine the ode in detail, line by line'.[29]

What is the justification for the methodology? Quite simply, that the Art of Reading for the student is to be passive, to let the author work directly on him. When Q imagines a questioner asking if it is really as simple as that, he retorts:

> Yes, even so simple as that, and (I claim) even so wise, seeing that it just lets the author - Chaucer or Shakespeare or Milton or Coleridge - have his own way with the young plant - just lets them drop 'like the gentle rain from heaven', and soak in.[30]

In another place he describes the desired stance as 'passive ... as a photographic plate which finds stars that no telescope can discover, simply by waiting with its face turned upward ...'.[31]

A crucial passage in the collection of lectures reads:

> ... the true subject of literary study is the author's meaning; and the true method a surrender of the mind to that meaning, with what Wordsworth calls 'a wise passiveness'.[32]

This *surrender* of the mind (the term is graphic) is to the *author's* meaning, which Q assumes will automatically imprint itself on the reader. This makes the teacher's role almost redundant. Information is not only irrelevant but dangerous, for it 'obscures what Chaucer or Shakespeare mean'. In these terms, therefore, Q can write that 'To be Hamlet - to feel yourself Hamlet - is more important than ... even knowing all there is to be known about a text ... Shakespeare means us to feel-to *be*-Hamlet. That is all: and from the play it is the best we can get.'[33] The happy certainty that he knows - and that his audience will agree - just what Shakespeare *means* us to feel, extends of course to the other authors quoted and discussed. By reading the Grecian Urn ode we get 'a working idea of the Ode and what Keats *meant* it to be'.[34] Elsewhere he can be confident that 'there is no mistaking what Browning *means*'.[35]

Q was perhaps the last major spokesman for the romantic and post-romantic tradition of criticism that took its cue from

Wordsworth's statement that the poet was 'a man speaking to men'. The reader is envisaged as being in direct contact with the writer, virtually as in face to face conversation. The poem is a transcription of the poet's voice, passing on significant experiences, ideas and feelings so that we can share them. Because critics in this tradition tended to ask questions like 'What does Dickens mean here?' or 'What is Keats saying to us?' knowledge of the lives and personalities of the writers seemed an essential area of study in recovering their full meaning: the contents of the author's mind.

The second text, only a dozen years later, is markedly different. In *How to Teach Reading: a Primer for Ezra Pound*, 1932, F.R. Leavis began his 'positive suggestions' with the brisk statement that

> literature is made of words, and that everything worth saying in criticism of verse and prose can be related to judgments concerning particular arrangements of words on the page.[36]

There will be no more passive exposure to the voice of the author; literary education is defined as a 'training of sensibility' through 'constant analytic practice' directed upon specific texts. So trained, the student -

> will be able to learn, and to teach, how to discuss profitably the differences between particular poems, to explain in detail and with precision why *this* is to be judged sentimental, *that* genuinely poignant; how the unrealized imagery of *this* betrays that it was "faked" while the concreteness and associative subtlety of *that* come from below and could not have been excogitated; and so on.[37]

The passage acts out the methodology: the repeated *this* and *that* imply the jabbing finger pointing at particular words and phrases on the open page. The purpose of the activity is essentially evaluative: the trained sensibility is the one that can discriminate - as Leavis suggests in the following pages - between Donne and Campion, Marvell and Morris. Leavis rejects the notion of 'a course of reading', in Ezra Pound's sense, in favour of limited close reading to realize principles that can later be applied to wider reading by those (a minority) who can benefit from such training. Again, the military images are significant: we are told of the '*equipment* and *training* that enable the student to *look after* himself'. '*Armed* in the ways suggested with a *technique* of reading, a *trained* sense for the *significant*, and types and analogues for dealing with further experience, the student may be left to educate himself (otherwise he is ineducable).'[38]

Although in Leavis's criticism the attention is always directed to those specific words on the page, demanding 'This is so, isn't it?' there is also continual awareness that those words depend on certain kinds of reading. In those few pages of the primer that awareness keeps breaking through. There are those asides like 'Otherwise he is ineducable' or the remark that those who cannot learn from *Seven Types of Ambiguity* 'were not intended by Nature for an advanced "education in letters",'[39] which have provided material for the accusations of elitism. There are the attacks on those whose readings are perceived as inadequate (the editors of the Arden *Macbeth*, the 'bad work' of Lamb and Swinburne the 'vested interests' in the old tradition), and the assumptions about what is and what is not worth reading. It will be unnecessary 'to read with any intensive scrutiny any large proportion of Victorian verse' or 'to spend much time weighing the intellectual pretensions of Meredith'.[40] As far as criticism is concerned, the student 'will have no use at all for Hazlitt or Lamb'.[41]

Redefining the object of literary enquiry and the style of reading meant redefining the nature of literary education. The attention shifted from the author to the work, the 'words on the page'. In the thirties and forties texts were described as 'well-wrought urns' or 'verbal icons': autonomous artefacts; the poet was seen as a maker, not a communicator. Author-centred questions like 'What is the writer's intention?' or 'Is he sincere?' were denounced as fallacies. Meaning was not what the author 'meant', but simply what was there in print; not a verbal imitation of something pre-existing but an object that comes to be in the act of making.

Because the meaning is apparently objectively 'there', accessible to those who can read properly, I.A. Richards could analyse the reasons for the 'wrong' interpretations and judgments which his Cambridge undergraduates offered when faced by unseen texts.[42] Others followed, like E.L. Black considering why college students could apparently not understand what they read.[43] All was apparently simple. Richards wrote later: 'In good interpretations the right parallels are at work; in bad interpretations wrong ones are'.[44] Good/bad; right/wrong; it was left for James Wilson, D.W. Harding and others to discover just how hard it was to apply those confident terms in practice.

Louise Rosenblatt in *The Reader, the Text, the Poem*, 1978, sees those words on the page, the text, only as a 'potential' or 'virtual' object: 'simply paper and ink until a reader evokes from it a literary work'.[45] Individual readers bring to the printed page their existing knowledge (of the world, of language and of texts) in order to make a poem for themselves: 'The reader's creation of a poem out of a text must be an active, self-ordering and self-corrective process'.[46] In the 'transaction' between reader and text, she argued that much more concern than the New Critics allowed had to be accorded to response:

> Whatever the reader may later add to that original creative activity is also rooted in his own responses during the reading event. His primary subject matter is the web of feelings, sensations, images, ideas, that he weaves between himself and the text.[47]

Rosenblatt's view of the nature of reading involves a rejection of the position that would mark off either certain texts (as Q did) or certain readers (as Leavis did) in a privileged position. Saying that the work of critics and scholars has represented only a narrow spectrum of response, she argues:

> Readers may bring to the text experiences, awarenesses, and needs that have been ignored in traditional criticism. Women, for example, are finding their own voices as writers and critics, as are the ethnic minorities and special cultural groups ... The aim should be to widen the range of critical voices.[48]

Poulet, Iser, Rosenblatt and - from a rather different stance - Norman Holland argue that 'meaning' is to be seen as a series of events in the reader's consciousness, constrained but not wholly defined by the text. Literary works cannot pre-empt how they are to be read at all periods, in all cultures, by all readers. Not only is the language itself forever shifting, so are the backgrounds, assumptions, knowledge and interests of the readers. In Culler's phrase, 'Each reader constructs a different text', becomes no longer a *consumer* but a *producer* of texts.[49] Between the 1914-18 war and the seventies, critics from different positions (illustrated rather over-neatly by these three examples) have chosen to emphasise different elements in the relationship between author, text and reader. By doing so they have implied (or directly stated) what the chief aims of a literary education should be and, by extension, what the major role for the teacher is. Teachers who followed Quiller-Couch encouraged their students to ask 'What does the author say?' and assisted them by speaking *for* the writer: performing the text and drawing out the 'intended' meaning. Those influenced by F.R. Leavis would ideally teach by example and by guidance how to point to the text, interpret it and evaluate it. Reader-response teachers, asking 'What does this text do?' rather than 'What does it mean?' see themselves primarily as facilitators, encouraging the framing and sharing of personal responses. The three emphases, of course, have never been mutually exclusive, but this simplified outline serves to illustrate some of the major shifts over sixty years. This continual re-drawing of the literary map is emphasised by changes in the way that students are certified as being at different levels 'proficient' in literary studies. Modes of assessment are considered in a separate chapter, but here it is enough to note that quite different views of reading and of teaching underlie the asking of such questions as:

- Give the chief facts in the life of Shakespeare until 1603.
- Give the substance of the Archbishop of Canterbury's speech about the honeybees. What lessons does he intend to teach by this speech?
- This play leaves us with mingled emotions of hope and sadness. With close reference to the play, show how far you agree with this statement.
- Would *The Old Curiosity Shop* be improved by being abridged? What would you cut out and why?
- How do you think Lady Macbeth is feeling, at the end of the banqueting scene, about her position, her husband, her relationship with him and herself? (You may, if you wish, write as if you are Lady Macbeth.)

This shifting of emphasis and approach may help to explain why A-level English teachers were so different from those of other subjects in the Schools Council Survey. On the one hand they were less likely than most others to complain that the approach demanded by the syllabus was out of date, that it was too wide or too demanding. (They were also more likely than others to believe that the syllabus encourages critical thinking and that it allowed ample time for pursuing fruitful ideas outside it.) On the other hand, they were the most likely of all subject teachers to say that they felt unable to keep up with recent developments in their subject.[50] Many of the teachers in our survey were uneasily aware that critical approaches and terminology had changed since their own university days ('Just what *is* structuralism?' asked one). Their own 'sense of academic security' seemed threatened, they were conscious of the overlapping questions, to which few felt able to give a definite answer:

- To what extent should English teachers themselves be aware of current critical theory?
- How far should it influence their ways of approaching texts with students?
- What instruction - if any - should be given to A-level students in critical theory in general?

University lecturers were equally divided in the answers that they would give to such questions. In a single department, two quite opposed views were propounded. One lecturer, saying that new ideas were 'in the atmosphere everywhere', felt that A-level students should be introduced to these concepts and acquainted with different ways of approaching texts. It was better that people should come to university with informed views rather than with what they had picked up from television programmes and colour supplements. Another, who wished that theory courses could be confined to graduate studies, would like to be able to say to schools 'forget it all', 'don't even try to take it on'.

Student views of literature and criticism

Concealed among the more specific questions put to A-level and university students was one which asked ingenuously: 'In a sentence, what does the word *literature* mean to you?' Fewer than might have been expected rejected this invitation, remarking stiffly, 'That is impossible in a sentence' (undergraduate) or, more vigorously, 'Come off it - what kind of a question is that?' (A-level). One or two understandably suggested that the word had no definable meaning: 'a vague generic term of no real substance', 'a totally artificial construct', 'an abstract, and trying to tie it down to a meaning gets you nowhere'. However, almost all of the group made an attempt - more or less serious - to grapple with an issue that has troubled scholars and baffled the standard reference books.

93

What was particularly interesting about the responses was that they seemed to illustrate the full range of critical positions: cultural heritage, reader-response, linguistic, deconstructive. Some seemed to have been more directly influenced by teachers or lecturers than others, but the overall impression is of a lack of consensus about the field of literary studies today. There were seven main clusters of repeated ideas, and examples of these follow.

One large group chose the all-embracing identification of literature with writing or print. According to some, literature is simply 'books', 'anything written', 'any form of writing', 'everything ever written'. This is the kind of usage encouraged by contemporary references to 'political campaign literature', 'discussion of the research literature' or 'our double-glazing literature'. Indeed, a number deliberately denied any qualitative implication:

- Prose and poetry, not all of which is particularly good.
- Any idea conveyed in writing, whether it be a political pamphlet or epic poem.
- Any piece of writing, whether of any quality or not.
- Even this questionnaire could be seen as literature.

A second large group saw literature as language marked by a particular imaginative quality, in the post-Romantic tradition. One undergraduate offered the basic materialist definition - 'black marks on white paper' - but added the qualification 'with the odd spark of magic'. These students differed from the first group in attempting to restrict literature to writing which is 'creative' or 'expressive', producing artefacts which belong to the world of 'art' or 'culture'. In these terms, literature is seen as 'the accumulation of written art', 'written beauty', or, more fully:

- The study of man's attempt to express himself through the written word.
- The assembled written culture of the world.
- The written record of personality and culture, recorded as prose or poetry for an audience of readers.
- The full range of creative expression (including television drama).
- Writing which uses language creatively.

Some within this group concentrated specifically on the linguistic markers defining the particular quality of literature in terms of a special language use. One cited it as 'organised violence committed on ordinary speech', and others wrote that works of literature were:

- Intelligible thoughts expressed in some distinct style.
- Works written using a particular code of language, where formal aspects of language are foregrounded.

A third group favoured what W.W. Robson called the 'honorific kind of definition' in the tradition of Matthew Arnold.[51] Literature is language of a particular richness and merit. A number of students seemed to imply that this is self-evident; literature is 'a recognisably good piece of work', 'high quality reading', 'any type of writing which is worth reading', or - more subtly - 'any form of writing which gains on re-reading'. The more developed formulations in this group included:

- Writing that is original humane and deep.
- Writing which offers some original thought, different perspectives, contains some beauty of form or style, or is just interesting or thought-provoking.
- Written or spoken language heightened and charged with as many deeper significances as possible.
- A written work of art that is aesthetically pleasing and usually fictional.
- Writing which is spiritually uplifting, morally valuable, stylistically exciting.
- Writing that has depth and social significance.

Some made the evaluative point by an implied or stated comparison with other written forms like the sixteenth century distinction between literature and blotterature. Literature, for them, is 'a better class of book', or is defined by what it is *not*:

- Anything above or outside the general media or pulp fiction.
- Books which are not trash.
- Literature explores human behaviour and ethics; anything else is merely entertainment.
- Books, poems or plays that are worth reading as opposed to trash.
- Novels, plays, poetry of a more meaningful nature than the paperbacks sold in newsagents.

A fourth, related group of definitions suggested that this particular quality of literature was shown by its ability to last, to enter the canon, to become part of 'the great tradition'. In these terms, literature is to be seen as 'writing which will be remembered for ever', 'writing which is of lasting value', or 'books and written matter that have a lasting quality and remain relevant through passing time'. This 'classical heritage' view of literature was presented in such terms as:

- All poetry, plays and novels that are commonly known to fall into the canon of 'English Literature'.
- The whole historical canon of fictional writing of whatever genre in whatever language.
- That which is judged by the society of the time to be of particular imaginative or intellectual merit.
- Our inheritance of written work over the centuries, excluding rubbish ...

The 'canon', the 'inheritance', is defined by the accumulated judgments of generations, 'hundreds of years of written thought'. At its simplest, in the words of A-level students, this meant 'the classic books', ' the classical literary masterpieces', or 'books written by the great masters'. The notion of 'classic' was generally seen as being conferred by other people, the 'experts': 'books fully acclaimed by critics', 'writing by people who are recognised', 'writing which "the experts" consider to be significant'. At its worst, classic equalled historic and possibly unattractive. Literature can be seen as 'books by people who are long dead', 'old novels of a past age', 'old books by Shakespeare, D.H. Lawrence etc. - having not enough interest to make you want to read in your spare time', 'boring, stuffy and out-of-date'.

The fifth and sixth groups balanced each other. They sought to define literature in terms of either the author's purpose and activity or the reading process and the reader's response. On the one hand, literature was seen as the writer's self-expression, the channel through which 'he' spoke: 'anything written where the author wants to convey a message'. Such students followed in the line of Sir Arthur Quiller-Couch's *On the Art of Reading*. The notion of intention underlies many of these formulations:

- Any type of writing that seeks to express the author's feelings and experiences and to communicate those feelings to an audience.

- Writings to give instruction and pleasure and insight.
- The communication of thoughts, ideas and sentiments in an acceptable medium to author and reader.
- Writing with more than a purely utilitarian purpose.
- Use of the written word as an individual expression of vision.

On the other hand, those who concentrated on what happens within the reader, after the fashion of Wolfgang Iser or Louise Rosenblatt, defined literature as 'writing which evokes some kind of response from the reader', which might include 'enjoyment' or 'pleasure', 'understanding', 'insight' or 'knowledge'. Broadly, literature is:

- Any form of written work that can generate a personal response from the reader.
- Any novel, play or poem which moves the reader.

In terms of more specific results, it is the source of 'knowledge and pleasure I gain from reading', 'writing which extends knowledge for the reader and inspires emotions':

- A medium through which we may learn to understand others and ourselves, but most importantly something to be enjoyed.
- Literature is like painting and music: it's pleasurable: it gives you the chance to eavesdrop on other people's lives, culture and society: it has no practical value, which is one of its major good points.
- Literature is a piece of writing through reading of which I gain greater understanding of myself or other people.
- Literature is the means by which we can get an insight into other times and people.
- A work that leaves with the person who experiences it a deeper understanding...

Lastly, for a considerable number of A-level students (but for very few undergraduates) the word *literature* had strong associations with *work*. At its most basic this was expressed in such terms as 'Literature means the study of books, authors, etc.' or in even more utilitarian terms, 'books for an exam', or 'all the books I would otherwise not have read'. Others said that literature was:

- A collection of words put together in an educational way.
- A study of any text to increase understanding.

- The studying of a text to find out the meaning and why it was written.
- The study of English at all levels of its history.
- The study of texts in order to discover what the author is trying to do.

The emphasis is shifted from what literature *is* to how it is being used; from being a source of pleasure or enlightenment to existing as a kind of puzzle in which students must 'discover' or 'find out' answers that will satisfy examiners.

There was little sense of an 'agreed' view coming from any school or university department. If teachers had firm views of their own, they had clearly not imposed them on their students, as four or more classes of definition were offered from all but the smallest groups. Indeed, it might prove an interesting introductory activity for a new group to use these examples as a basis for discussion and to see whether - as a result - they move closer to consensus.

How did the students perceive their reading of writing *about* literature? Asked about the use they made of published literary criticism, thirty-four of the A-level students failed to respond. Of the remainder, about three out of ten said they made little or no use of it, about one in ten claimed in different terms to use it a good deal, and some 56% said that they made 'some' use of it. Rather more than half of the sample gave some indication of the *kind* of use to which they put criticism. One student (ask a silly question?) retorted simply 'I read it'. Another, clearly defining *criticism* broadly, admitted 'I find York Notes useful'. One defined criticism as 'codswallop', another claimed to make 'considerable' use of it - 'I am a mindless plagiarist'. Some explained why they reject criticism:

> The people who write literary criticism have their own views and I don't like being influenced with biased views. I like to make my own decisions.

(It is interesting that she assumes that critics will be 'biased' but that apparently her own decisions will not be.)

The three most frequent replies accounted for almost three-quarters of all the responses, and examples can be given of each.

1 To give specific help for an essay or examination (mentioned by 30.4%):

- Very useful for essays and references.
- Introductions to books play a considerable part in my essays.
- I use it to help me make notes on the book I'm studying.
- I use it to gain extra information when preparing essays.
- A cramming tool at exam time.
- If I haven't an opinion about part of a book, I read what the critics say and shove that in my essay.
- I read it and put bits in my essays which it is very good for. Useful for revision and essay writing.

2   To encounter different viewpoints or interpretations and to prevent narrowness (22.3%):

- Guide to opposite viewpoints.
- It helps you to read other people's points of view and also makes you understand things that might never have occurred to you.
- They lead you away from being too opinionated or narrow-minded.
- Comparing critics to find out how they interpret the text.

3   To relate specifically to one's own views, to compare and perhaps to question ideas (19%):

- Using the criticism to spark off your own ideas.
- You can compare your criticisms with other people.
- I have looked at some criticism, using it to compare it to my own point of view and noting the differences.
- They help to build a wider variety of opinions in my own mind.
- Interesting to read other points of view to widen our opinion.
- I find it beneficial to criticise the critic or agree and then try to say *why* in my own mind.

Even when reading English at university, one in five of the students claimed to make little or no use of the critics. One said haughtily, 'I treat them with contempt'. Another, claiming to use criticism 'as little as possible' finds it 'usually ridiculously arcane and irrelevant and confusing. I dislike the scholarly élite that they formed.'

The kinds of use to which criticism was put were not significantly different from those expressed by the younger students. The most frequently mentioned (38%) was again specific guidance or material for an essay or other project, and a further 14.5% mentioned it as a starting-point (or even a substitute) for their own ideas. A quarter of those responding said that they used criticism to relate to their own views ('it should not be a replacement for a good knowledge of a text however') and another 13% found it helpful to encounter other viewpoints and interpretations.

Views of literature courses at different stages

The final question for students asked what advice they would give to a friend, a year younger than themselves, who was wondering whether to take the same English course that they themselves were following. The results were classified as strongly negative (Don't; forget it) or with a negative emphasis (Don't unless...); strongly positive (Certainly, don't miss it) or with a positive emphasis (Do if ...); or neutral (depending on the individual, explaining factors to consider, without any clear positive or negative emphasis).

About one in eight of the A-level respondents offered advice that would seem designed to dissuade friends from studying English. Boys were proportionately twice as likely as girls to offer negative comments, but only three expressed this in strong, unqualified terms:

- Forget it!
- It's boring - avoid it at all costs.
- Can you think of a better way of spending the time? If so, do it.

More frequently the note was one of warning: only take the course if ..., be prepared for ..., are you sure ...? Some typical replies were:

- Only do the course if you are genuinely interested in English literature.
- You must be totally sure that you can work for a whole two years even if you don't agree with the teaching methods and the examination and be sure that you have a real interest in English.
- Don't take it unless you're prepared to swallow other people's 'accepted' opinions, regurgitate them on paper and work hard to no real point.
- Warn them how much work is involved and how much it depends on you how much you do. Also, how much all the books and theatre trips cost.

- Only take the course if you are prepared to put in a lot of work at home and in class ... a keen interest in literature is also essential.

Positive advice was much more frequent, offered by over half the boys and nearly sixty per cent of the girls. Among those classified as strongly positive were the following:

- Do it! It's enjoyable, helpful and you become more artistically aware because of it. *Go for it.*
- I would say take English ... whether you pass at A-level or not doesn't matter, you learn so much during the course.
- Stay on definitely because even if you fail you will have a widened scope on life.
- I'd tell them to do the English A-level if they wanted to enjoy the subject as much as I am doing, because it's exciting, interesting and very enjoyable.
- I would advise them to do so. It's now my favourite subject and I have learnt a lot.

More qualified advice, but with a positive emphasis, was offered like this:

- You must be dedicated to do the A-level, but the course is certainly worth it!
- It's not a soft option and you have to enjoy dissecting and working on a line of a poem or paragraph of a book for half an hour to realise its full potential. Takes a lot more thinking about than a science, but do it.
- If you are interested in people, debating subjects and discussing people's attitudes etc. then take A-level English.

The 'neutral' category, accounting for about a third of all replies, offered practical advice to help in decision-making.

- Think very carefully about it before making the final decision. Go in with an open mind, if you do.
- I would tell her how much I enjoyed the course and warn her of the time that must be dedicated to it. Then I would leave the decision to her.
- I would suggest that they try hardest at the beginning of the course and get into the books that they are reading, and go to the teachers as soon as they need help.

- Find out what the course is like, because it is very different from O-level, although parts of it are very enjoyable.
- Discuss with the teacher, find out about syllabus, standard and time spent on work required.

Predictably, those who had previously indicated that they regretted taking English at A-level were more likely to give negative advice than those who had no regrets, but there was no precise correspondence. Over a quarter of those who regretted taking A-level English gave positive encouragement to their friends to do the subject and conversely 9% of those who expressed no regrets made remarks tending to dissuade friends from taking English. Those whose own satisfaction with A-level English was limited were particularly likely to give neutral advice (42% of them doing so, as compared with 27% of the others), which may indicate their awareness of how personal people's reactions were, manifested in the wide range of responses within many of the schools represented.

As would have been anticipated, in the more selective group of university English students there were few that offered negative advice (7.5%) and none in the strongly negative category. Friends were more gently dissuaded in terms of the need to think very carefully before committing themselves:

- Consider whether their interest in English Literature would be ruined by another three years of post A-level dissection.
- Only apply for an English degree if they can get complete satisfaction from studying the texts and critics. Warn them of the lackadaisical manner in which a student's interest is fostered by university tutors.
- I'd say think about it; it's a lot of work; you won't be top of the class here; they don't *tell* you anything; it's just as much a race to pass an exam as A-level was ...
- You have to really like English to put up with the fact that it is so unrelated directly to many jobs.
- As far as the course is concerned I would advise them not to apply here, but the teaching, although very variable, can be excellent.
- Only do it if you can't do anything else and are prepared to have all your preconceptions shattered. I'm sure it's good for you anyway.

More 'neutral' responses (nearly 40% of the total) acknowledged not only that individuals differ but also that university English departments are *chosen* and have different strengths and weaknesses. Many said that, to quote one, 'My advice would be tailored to the individual characteristics of that particular person'. It 'depends upon your area of interest', 'it's a matter of personal preference'. Individuals need to weigh up the relative importance of 'career considerations', 'personal benefits', 'work and attitudes required', 'enjoyment of the subject', 'the range of courses offered', 'methods of examination', 'quality of teaching', 'what the place is like to live and study in'. Consequently they were advised, for example, to 'read the prospectus thoroughly', 'look at the institution as well as just the courses', 'visit and interview', 'ask lots of questions', 'meet some tutors before you decide'. The overall emphasis of this practical advice could be very varied. Students might urge their hypothetical friends to question seriously whether English has anything to offer 'in preference to a more vocational subject', because 'literature is of little practical use'. Others say, 'Don't choose a course specifically with a career in mind - study what interests you most, despite any outside pressure to be practical'.

Over half the sample were prepared to recommend the courses they were taking with varying degrees of warmth. Many simply wrote, 'I would strongly recommend it'. One put, 'At least try it, if not you could regret it for ever'. When attempts to justify the recommendation were made, they offered some insight into the students' own priorities:

- I have not yet met a tutor who is not enthusiastic and willing to help.
- The Department is relaxed without being unprofessional.
- Professor ---'s Victorian lectures are brill.
- The course is varied and interesting and gives you freedom of choice.
- The place is cheap to live and quiet enough to be able to read in peace.
- It's a great place to study, quite excellent resources. It's worth coming here for the people one is likely to meet.
- The facilities are pretty well unparalleled ... this is a wonderful place at which to study.
- The course provides far greater scope for following interests than, I believe, equivalent courses do at other universities.

- English is the best course to take if you want to meet a lot of girls. Girls: try Engineering!

Words of warning were frequently combined with an enthusiastic endorsement of the course:

- Don't take either the Eng. Lang. compulsory first year course or the pretentious members of this Dept. at all seriously, do come - just enjoy yourself.
- Some elements of the course are quite boring, but *go for it*!
- I would say, yes, go for it ... whatever the difficulties of studying and socialising I believe it is a valuable, indispensable experience for anyone with enough brain cells.
- Size of department (huge) makes it impersonal but excellent choice of options, good standard of teaching.
- Go ahead! It is a stimulating and thought-provoking course ... but the work-load is heavy and demanding.

This general, if not unqualified, approval is not uncritical, as responses to another question indicate. The majority of students at all levels said that they had some complaints about the courses which they were following. Apart from those criticisms which referred to teaching (and are considered in a separate chapter) the commonest references at all ages were to syllabuses and to pressures of work.

Students taking O-level were twice as likely to mention the weaknesses of their courses as the strengths. The unsatisfactory selection of texts and the lack of choice ('we do not have a say in which books we do') were picked out by 41% as reasons for complaint. One said that as a result -

I think that I have been put off books for life and I don't think that in the future I would be tempted to pick up one of my selected books for pleasure reading.

Although some students claimed to have developed a liking for books in the course of studying them, the reverse process also took place. Some texts were clearly not substantial enough for the detailed consideration they were given. Several students said that they had enjoyed their first reading of a novel (*To Kill a Mockingbird* was sometimes mentioned) but that extended study had destroyed that pleasure:

- *To Kill a Mockingbird* is an enjoyable book to read but after you have read it over and over again and have practically written it out in your own words it becomes exceedingly *boring*.
- I would have enjoyed the novel more if I hadn't had to study it so much.

Indeed, some specifically distinguished between books which gained from close study and those which did not: 'I began to enjoy the poems and *Romeo and Juliet* more after studying them, but after studying *To Kill a Mockingbird* I was put off it'.

The idea that three disconnected texts (typically a Shakespeare play, a poetry anthology and a novel) can somehow 'represent' literature has always been dangerous, and particularly in schools where the study of those texts has been spread over more than one year. The range is too restricted (much narrower in most schools than the reading diet in any other year), the emphasis is too heavily on low-level knowledge of detail, and there is an inbuilt temptation to treat all texts, whether poetry, prose or drama in the same way (which may account for the frequency with which students in examinations refer to a play as 'this novel' or 'this story').

In the survey, nearly half of the students were indifferent to what they were reading, and over a quarter were definitely dissatisfied. A number of them complained about the narrowness of their courses, which seemed to be exclusively devoted to the set texts. They said that, 'I don't think we were given enough books to read ... we need to compare books more' or that there ought to be at least 'an extra play and another novel'. Several wished to break away from the pattern of a course in which everyone studied the same books. One boy proposed that 'novels and plays could be chosen by the individual ... in order to adapt to people's own likes and dislikes', and a girl suggested that there should be options in which pupils could choose from a selection of texts offered by different teachers.

Courses are already changing markedly with the coming of the GCSE. Perhaps the most important difference is that in place of the sharp division between Language and Literature, English at 16+ is now seen as a unitary subject including both. The National Criteria make it clear that this subject should 'develop the ability of students to enjoy and appreciate the reading of literature' and to 'understand and respond imaginatively to it'.[52] English Literature will be an *additional* subject for some students and here again there is to be a break from the conventional O-level syllabus. The regulations say that even books for detailed study 'need not be prescribed in a set texts syllabus of a traditional kind', the canon is to be enlarged, 'wide personal choice' is to be encouraged, and 'undue emphasis ... on mere recall' is deprecated.[53] The effect of these changes on students and ultimately on A-level courses cannot yet be estimated. They have been greeted with widely differing reactions, from those which see the innovations as 'a major step forward' to those which see them as a symbol of our 'neglect of the literary heritage'.

At A-level, as previously at 16+, courses are almost wholly determined by what happens to be currently on offer by an Examination Board. The Inspectorate have pointed out that many schools had no syllabuses apart from those provided by the Board and that 'the list of set books ... was taken as sufficient as a framework for A-level study in itself'.[54] Little attention seems to be given to articulating 'common or agreed aims' or to serious discussion of different ways of structuring and sequencing the course. The minimum number of texts to be studied is usually seven or eight, though in particular cases it could be as few as five or as many as eleven, according to the choice of options. It is important, then, to be aware of the different implications which the variant forms of A-level syllabuses have for students' views of literature, and of 'appropriate' connections between books. (It is clear from discussions and responses to the questionnaire that texts were frequently seen in isolation, sometimes presented by different teachers, with little attempt to relate them to one another). Three particular forms of syllabus have been common.

- 1 A number of boards still offer - as was common in the 1920s - a study of particular authors combined with a wider study of a particular period. Shakespeare is almost universal; Chaucer is frequently offered with 'other major authors' or 'one other'. Cambridge offers a choice of periods: Renaissance, 1760-1832, the Victorian age and English Literature since 1900. Oxford proposes 1550-1680, 1660-1790, 1790-1832, 1832-1896, 1896-present.
- 2 An alternative course structure prescribes topics, with a list of books in each from which a choice has to be made. London currently offers as themes: satirical comedy, history into literature, peace and war, or African and Caribbean literature. The JMB's even wider titles are: English worldwide, post 1945 or men and women.

- 3 There is also the do-it-yourself curriculum, in which a Board proposes a list of texts (typically about 16 for JMB) and invites teachers to make their own selection, which may emphasise a period or a theme or simply pick a group of winners. In some cases (Oxford and Cambridge) the choice has to include at least one from each of the major forms: fiction, drama and poetry.

The transitional role of the A-level course is nowhere clearer than in this choice of curriculum. The first of these three modes takes its structure directly from the way in which most universities chop up the literary curriculum; the third is simply a more advanced version of what happens at 16+.

What of the student reactions to the courses they were following? Rather more than half of the sample (56%) said that they had criticisms, and the proportion was the same for both sexes. Some of the complaints balanced each other: 'I would prefer more books to be studied' and 'too many books'; 'course is too exam-oriented' and 'we are not well enough prepared for the exam'. As at 16+, however, the most common complaints (voiced by over a third of the students) were about the constraints of the syllabus, or the poor selection of texts (especially the fact that 'students don't have enough choice'). A few were more general: 'I do not like hardly any of the books we are studying', 'I resent having to study authors I despise', 'the books are very old-fashioned', or rather pathetically, 'I would have liked different books'. Other comments suggested weaknesses in the school organisation or selection rather than in the nature of the syllabus itself. Complaining that the books studied were virtually all from the nineteenth century, one girl proposed that 'it would be better to do a book from each period'. Another lamented the fact that 'we seem to take so long on one particular book - we've spent more than four months on *Mansfield Park*'. A third criticised what seemed undue concentration on the direct demands of the syllabus: 'There is too much time spent on studying the set books. You should be able to enjoy and appreciate other books and also be able to adapt your own creativeness'. A number of others mentioned directly or indirectly the way in which detailed knowledge of a limited number of texts swallowed up their time, and led to the exclusion of wider reading, language studies or imaginative writing. Indeed, the second most frequently mentioned complaint (by about 16%) was about the lack of time and the pressure of work. This was proportionately a much more common worry for girls than for boys.

A number of university lecturers were similarly conscious of the potentially cramping effect of over-close adherence to a minimum A-level syllabus, even while acknowledging the responsibility of their own entry targets for some of the problems. In one particularly interesting discussion a lecturer said:

> The thing I would ideally want to change myself/in sixth form programmes/would be the size and the range of texts that people look at/and the kinds of texts they look at/there should be a considerable variety/including a variety of seriousness/they ought to look at minor literature/and try out critical approaches on those too/it ought not to be a miniature great books course/but an introduction to discriminating reading/that some universities seem to think comes out of the air/rather than something you have to train people for.

Later, discussing course structure, he remarked:

> Good schools try/in the lower sixth/to cover a wider range/and in the upper sixth we do the set books/but its the wrong way round/you ought to be giving kids the confidence to deal closely with basic critical matters first/and in the second year you ought to broaden out a bit/prepare for reading two or three texts a week at university.

Those students who were following one of the 'alternative' syllabuses were rather less likely to have complaints about the course than those taking 'standard' A-levels (48% as opposed to 60%), and this may have some significance for the future. Although the changes in methods of assessment promoted in 'alternative syllabuses' are separately discussed in chapter 6 it is worth noting here that such syllabuses have also influenced the *content* of courses. It has become possible, for example, to consider for A-level:

- a single novelist in depth, examining three or four novels.
- a particular movement in poetry or drama.
- a comparative study of two linked writers.
- an aspect of the relationship between literature and other art forms.
- three linked Shakespeare plays.

- the examination and application of writing skills in a particular genre.

Such developments have made it possible to explore the linking of texts in ways other than the purely chronological. Even within the 'mainstream' syllabuses offered by the examination boards there is now available a considerable variety (four choices for London and three for the AEB and the JMB). Courses in Language or Language Studies, involving literary materials, but also other varieties of English, are available from two boards, and a combined Language and Literature syllabus from two. Several boards offer a curriculum of school choice for part of the assessment. Oxford, the one board that has not introduced significant change, announces in its latest (1989) syllabus that, because of the introduction of GCSE and the coming of AS levels, it is 'currently undertaking a thorough review of its Advanced level English syllabus'.

At university level, the problems of presenting an almost unlimited field in terms of discrete courses become extreme. Various structures are outlined in the booklets intended for prospective undergraduates, but rarely with any accompanying rationale. Oxford says broadly that the emphasis is 'on exploring the whole range of English writing from the beginning to the present', but gives few details about how that might be achieved in practice.

Universities differ in what they perceive as an appropriate learning sequence, and particularly in what they offer to new students in their first terms. At Sheffield the pattern is basically chronological: students encounter literature of the Renaissance first and work through towards the twentieth century in part two. At Oxford work begins with literature from 1832 to the present (alongside studies in Old English) and earlier works are considered later. At Lancaster concentration is first on post-1955 literature. At Durham the history of literature is approached first from both ends: the common core involves Renaissance literature and modern drama. At Cambridge, part 1 of the tripos is devoted to the range of English literature from 1300 onwards and part 2 offers more wide-ranging courses in tragedy, practical criticism and options involving classical or other literatures, the English moralists, the novel and so on. Some universities, but by no means all, offer introductory courses in practical criticism, critical theory, or the techniques of different genres; others expect new students to engage in language studies, history of the language, or linguistics;

at others again English Language offers a quite separate curriculum from English Literature (in at least one case offered in a separate department).

In virtually all cases the available choices widen as students move from year to year, frequently allowing them to select from broad, 'basic' or 'survey' options and narrower, more concentrated studies in depth. They may include, for example, Afro-Caribbean, Canadian, or Australian literature (Hull and Kent), bibliography, research methods (Leicester), Scottish literature or the Edwardian novel (Lancaster), or inter-disciplinary courses involving works of art and criticism (Exeter). What is on offer changes from year to year according to the availability and interests of members of staff. In some cases students are allowed to prepare their own topics for detailed study, usually presenting a dissertation or long essay. It is consequently more difficult to offer a coherent picture of undergraduates' reactions to their courses, since they were having very different experiences of very different fields and topics for study.

However, virtually three-quarters of them said that they had criticisms, and although these were more diverse than those of the younger students, nearly 30% were similarly concerned with the selection of authors, texts and periods and 17% with the excessive work load. University students were more likely than those at school to complain about particular courses or the emphasis of certain lecturers, about the lack of personal guidance or about the balance between different elements in their studies. Their general comments on courses were often vigorous ('inadequate choice', 'not relevant', 'tedious, stagnant, restrictive, too pampered'). Two remarked on the results of current pressures on the system:

- Large numbers of students mean that tutors with special areas of interest are often forced to take courses they have no particular liking for - and you can see this.

- In the first year we do nothing but Renaissance (which very few people take to anyway) then for the second year have to choose options that we've never tried.

Particular courses were described by those who did not favour them as 'over-emphasised', 'not useful', 'too difficult', 'very uninteresting', 'should be abolished'. Occasionally the emphasis was on what was omitted:

- The whole approach is far too historical; there is no concentration on creative writing or on the future direction of literature which should be done through study of present-day literature.
- No formal creative writing course.
- No real teaching of critical techniques.

Comments on the pressures of the course sometimes consisted simply of 'not enough time' or 'too much to cover'. Students complained:

- Amount of work required ... not stated clearly enough at the outset.
- Reading lists and workload are too heavy giving little time for looking at literature generally and working on one's weaknesses.
- Pressures of continually moving on means that it's dangerous to dwell on anything too long.
- Being expected to read too much and therefore having no time to give it any thought.
- Expected to cover topics in short space of time.

Asked to pick out those courses or topics which they had found 'particularly helpful or interesting' students did not echo the personal preference for fiction revealed in their answers about favourite reading. Among A-level and undergraduate groups, work on novels was mentioned less frequently than poetry or drama (though the difference was more marked in the A-level group). Both were more likely to find topics in drama the most 'interesting or helpful' (mentioned by nearly 32% of the A-level students and 16% of the undergraduates), followed by poetry (22% A-level; 12% university) and fiction (12% A-level; 10% university). There may be a difference here between those kinds of writing which are enjoyable to read in themselves and those which gain in study, or are associated with enjoyable methods. It may also suggest, of course, that staff are better at *teaching* poetry and drama than the more extended novel form. For example, one 17-year-old girl wrote, explaining her preference for drama:

I love acting plays and reading them aloud in class. We learn to cope with showing our true feelings and capabilities (better in small groups) and in front of people who are in fact going through the same experiences as yourself.

A 19-year-old undergraduate similarly pointed to drama courses as providing 'great opportunities for fun, and for personal character analysis and development'.

For both groups, the most valued topics were not to be identified with particular literary genres. A-level students mentioned critical activities and practice more often than any other single topic (36%) and undergraduates understandably referred most often to period or thematic studies (51%) followed by work in language (26.5%). Typical comments from universities included these:

- The combination of poetry, drama and perspectives on the background did give me a helpful insight into the Renaissance period as a whole, therefore historically it was interesting.
- The courses I'm doing at the moment provide not only knowledge of the literature but also of the history, politics and social climate of the period.
- Linguistics has given me a greater understanding of e.g. language acquisition, propaganda, the strength of the written word, language and solidarity.
- Critical theory opens up a whole new approach to literature - made me realise how narrow my view had been before.

Some indication of teachers' priorities in course elements can be gained from their responses to a question asking them to indicate the degree of importance they attached to various activities. Almost all A-level teachers attributed some importance to practical criticism of unattributed texts, to the social and historical background of texts and to knowledge of critical terminology. Activities perceived as less important were approaches to published criticism, instruction in literary theory, and language study or linguistics (which only one teacher thought very important). This raises some interesting questions. If a knowledge of critical terms is so important, why do a quarter of the teachers think knowledge of literary theory is of 'no importance'? If practical criticism, rated the most highly of all, is such an important activity, then why do only three teachers think it very important for students to acquire approaches to published criticism, from which they would presumably come to understand what criticism is?

Questions are also raised by the lecturers' responses to an

overlapping but wider set of activities. Like the teachers they ranked linguistics as the least important (and well below the historical study of the language). Was this simply a case of supporting the courses currently offered, or a perception of linguistics as a separate discipline? Practical criticism was rated considerably lower than by the teachers. Most importance of all was attached to the social and historical background to texts: the only item which all lecturers believed to be of some importance, and the one which most described as very important. What does this suggest about the nature of English studies? Are critical theory and practice no longer to be seen as the central core of the discipline?

The perceived influence of English courses

Asked 'Do you feel that your present course has had any significant influence on your attitudes or your way of life?' 55% of the A-level group and 64% of the undergraduates answered affirmatively. Those who said yes were asked to suggest briefly what they thought the effects had been, and most responded. Their replies can be related to those discussed in the section of chapter 1, 'What is to be gained from English?'

A few of the A-level students pointed to more than one way in which they had been influenced by their courses, but overall 5.6% suggested negative effects (like the diminishing of confidence or enjoyment), about 35% mentioned specifically literary benefits and 80% referred to positive personal benefits. A few were difficult to classify ('My attitude towards scientists has worsened'; 'It has improved my use of language but confused me on certain moral and political issues'; 'I can now answer questions on *Mastermind* and *University Challenge*', 'James Joyce really freaked me out'), but most fell into clearly marked groups. Those few who thought the influence had been bad made such comments as:

- I think I have become more cynical in outlook ... I live on borrowed ideas.
- My social life has been made almost extinct.
- It is more stressful, making my life harder.
- It has made me extremely cynical towards the 'classics'.

The most frequently advanced personal benefit (mentioned by nearly a third of the respondents) was perceived in terms of greater maturity and self-understanding, a 'broadening of the mind', 'increased awareness':

- It has helped me mature and given me a certain amount of self-knowledge.
- I am a lot more open-minded about things.
- It has made me critical of myself and my actions ... it has made me try to listen to myself realistically.
- It has shown me the importance of developing my own ideas, and increased awareness.

The next most mentioned effect was on awareness of others, sometimes expressed as a capacity to empathise or tolerance of other views: 'more mature understanding of people', 'helped me to understand friends and family'.

- It has made me realise that people are not always what they seem to be.
- A greater insight into people's motives.
- The added perception to understand people around.
- Wider experience of understanding people and their behaviour.
- It makes me stop and think why people say the things they do and do the things they do.
- Appreciate other people's opinions more than I used to; more aware of different attitudes to life.
- Made me more receptive to ideas and opinions that differ from my own.

Increased confidence (especially in conversation) or willingness to express personal convictions was mentioned by about one in seven:

- It has made me a little more confident to voice my opinions.
- I can put forward my own thoughts and ideas, often clashing with other people's opinions.
- The course has helped me gain much more confidence in myself.
- I can have belief in my own feelings.
- Made me more prepared to voice my own opinions.

A similar number pointed to a greater interest in ideas, more concern for issues and a deeper understanding.

- I have become more critical of the commercial and material world, and more perceptive.
- The course has made me more responsive to everyday issues and the ability to assess them and the way I view situations.
- It has made me listen to news more and to read newspapers and to have a point of view.
- Studying modern literature ... often raises contemporary issues or a new perspective on them, and encourages us to think and question.

The most frequently mentioned literary benefit was framed in terms of increased enjoyment or appreciation, more reading or theatre-going.

- My 'turn-off' attitudes to writers has been removed.
- I now visit theatre for pleasure and can enjoy and criticise plays.
- I appreciate literature much more now than I did and my interest has broadened ... I go out more to see theatre and screen adaptations of novels and plays.
- It has opened up new areas of literature to me.
- I appreciate good books more.

A significant number also referred to becoming more discriminating, reading more critically, as a result of the course. (Sometimes ironically, as in 'I no longer dare read Enid Blyton and Beano'.)

- I am more particular in my choice of reading and visit the theatre more.
- I am now extremely critical of authors, films, TV etc.
- Become more critical (on newspaper articles, etc.)
- Appreciation and discrimination (no more *Dallas*).

There was very little difference between undergraduates and A-level students either in the ways they described the influence of their courses or in the proportions responding in particular ways. The university students mentioned negative effects rather more (mentioned by one in ten) but some 75% pointed to personal benefits (80% of the A-level sample) and 31% literary benefits (35% at A-level). There was obviously more temptation for older students to be ironic ('I feel miles more aesthetic', 'My belief in the unified self has been destroyed', 'Are you joking?'), but most attempted to define what some of them saw as a complex series of interrelated changes:

- You tend to think more about everything. Makes you *accept* less for granted. Gives you self-confidence. Makes me unconsciously analyse the verses in Christmas cards, instructions on bean tins ...
- I am less bothered by the desire to conform to the social conventions which determine behaviour, especially marriage and materialistic values.
- Greater confidence. A different perspective on life. Events and attitudes which were important in the past have become trivial. I think for myself a lot more. General experience in practical issues (e.g. renting a house).

It will be clear that many of the most valuable lessons learned have not been consciously taught. As was seen in chapter one, English students are particularly impressed by the indirect benefits they gain. The next chapter therefore goes on to consider the more direct links between teaching and learning.

5

Teaching and Learning

Unanswered questions

The question 'How should literature be taught in the examination years?' has become urgent. For years it seemed unproblematic. As Ball has suggested, English simply took over 'the established methods and approaches of the classics'. In school,

> Literature teaching relied on working through annotated editions of English classics, modelled on classical commentaries, which directed attention to linguistic, archaeological, historical or geographical points.[1]

Indeed, such approaches continue. Students in one A-level group referred to spending all their English periods for more than a term in working line-by-line through a single Shakespeare play. At university, English departments simply took over the conventional pattern of private reading and essay writing guided by mass lectures and possibly smaller group work. It is significant, though, that a 'radical' post-war reshaping of English in a major university (then a university college) could be defined in terms of an innovative 'departmental tutorial system under which students ... are divided into small groups ... a member of staff acts as tutor to each group'.[2]

The failure to ask questions about methodology has been indicated by the fact that until recently there have been very few published accounts or case-studies of successful practice at examination level and that books offering systematic guidance on the topic for student-teachers in training have not been available. In the first of a series of articles on English in the university, F.W. Bateson remarked that 'too little thinking has been done about the teaching of English literature', and one more recent study has concluded that it is 'very difficult to gauge at all how the teaching of literature has taken place within the United Kingdom over the past 40 years'.[3] It was frequently assumed that although English graduates might require guidance about teaching younger children, their degree courses provided both the knowledge and the approaches required for examination work. Equally, few questions were raised about the fact that what English lecturers were trained to do - normally manifested in successful research - bore little relation to much of the teaching that they did.

Early in the seventies discontent about standards of teaching began to surface *within* the universities. One article claimed that the result of too much university teaching was 'murder by steady discouragement, so that people lose enthusiasm for the study':

> There's nothing wrong with the university study of literature, critical appreciation of the works at its centre, *except* the university teachers of the subject - in their 'teaching' and in the mountainous and ever-growing dust-heaps of their publications.[4]

Another article sought for reasons that 'literature teaching is in so much better heart in the schools' than in the universities.[5] The authors suggested that although the schools were doing their task on the whole 'strikingly well' and making English 'interesting and rewarding', they received 'small thanks' from dons who complained of students going stale when actually the universities denied them 'genuinely fresh intellectual stimuli'.[6]

It has to be said that the relationship between teaching and learning in English is a particularly complex one. Teachers learn from their students as well as the other way round and learners teach themselves. The teacher is less concerned with passing on information (still less with passing on judgments) than with establishing situations in which learning can go on. Students and teachers simultaneously pick up and transmit signals about what their respective roles should be. Students enter the examination years with reading and study habits already formed to encounter teachers whose teaching habits are equally ingrained and to begin the process of mutual modification. Every shared discussion of text is unique; it cannot be neatly pre-planned; teacher and students both come to a new understanding of what they are reading. In one influential article on literature teaching in the university, Barbara Hardy remarked that

> the university teacher of literature will *as a teacher* be interested not chiefly in his own relation to his subject but in his pupils' relation to the subject. There are three sets of human particulars in a teaching situation: the particularity of the work and the author, the particularity of the teacher, and the particularity of the student.[7]

Generalisation is particularly dangerous in dealing with the learning relationship of such a set of 'particulars'. Students are individuals who choose to study in the ways that they do. Graham Gibbs has pointed out how unhelpful is generalised advice about study skills, and how shakily based are our ideas of the merits of note-taking, revision, essay-planning and so on.[8]

There are, of course, inevitable broad distinctions between the kinds of pedagogy generally seen as appropriate in schools and in higher education and summed up in the implied difference between a 'teacher' and a 'lecturer'. In school a teacher will usually manage or orchestrate the reading or performance of a text; in universities lecturers will mostly assume (sometimes incorrectly) that students have already experienced and are familiar with the text to be discussed. School readings of works are developmental: the shifting responses of individuals at different stages are part of what is discussed. University discussion of texts is retrospective: it considers the work as a whole, with the implication that students will already have formed a summative judgment. In their writing, school students may be encouraged to keep reading journals, to record shifting views of texts or to respond to them imaginatively. At university the stress is likely to be on the end-product, the 'finished' critical essay, in which more tentative, personal working towards ideas is likely to be seen as inappropriate. Teachers in school, endeavouring to encourage pupils in the formulation of their own responses, will be chary of trying too soon to pass on ready-made their own judgments of texts and their specialised knowledge. A lecture in a university, by contrast, is the occasion for an expert to transmit such knowledge and to defend a particular critical position.

However, it would be unwise to over-emphasise such differences, which are based essentially on no more than differences in the range and pace of work. The first year undergraduate is only a few months older than the A-level student. This book argues throughout that to make too much of that change in institution is unhelpful; that more attention needs to be paid to *continuity* of experience than to differences. Whatever their ages, students will be engaged in the same broad kinds of learning experience.

First, as part of the general developmental process, students will be extending their experience, shuttling between the direct experiences of their immediate world and the represented experiences of books to make sense of both. Studies of the ways in which children describe their reading of stories show both how universal is this process and how increasingly sophisticated it becomes.[9] Second, students will progressively become more able to articulate fluently and precisely their responses to what they read. Again, studies of the stories which children tell *about* stories have begun to indicate some of the ways in which this ability is manifested and developed.[10] As Norman Holland has written, 'one cannot teach literature itself: one can only teach students to make statements about literature'.[11] Third, students will become more used to hearing, reading and evaluating views and ideas *about* literature. In the earlier years this is likely to be mediated by their teachers and achieved through group discussion. Eventually it will involve an acquaintance with literary criticism in the sense defined by James Gribble: 'That form of discourse which undertakes the analysis of works of literature so as to do justice to their "embodiment" of meaning'.[12] Throughout their studies students will be learning to balance different perceptions of texts. Thus, fourth, students will themselves be learning to practise criticism and to see it as an activity rather than as a body of information to be acquired. Reading grows on reading, and the greater their experience of books, the more easily they should be able to approach new texts, to appraise them and to discriminate between them. In the last resort, the ability to read and the ability to criticise are not separate skills but simply different ways of describing the same process, heads and tails of the same coin: 'Understanding involves criticism'; 'The critic must begin by being a reader ... the reader must be a critic'.[13]

The crucial issue, then, concerns the kinds of *teaching* most likely to advance those kinds of *learning*. In the continuing debate about methodology, it is striking how far 'new' approaches have been breaking down the barriers between conventional views of what is 'appropriate' at school or university level. Books like

Experiments in English Teaching: New Work in Higher and Further Education[14] chronicle many methods drawn directly from common practice in schools. Equally *Teaching Literature for Examinations*,[15] with its case studies of skilful A-level teachers at work, proposes some approaches that are familiar in higher education and others that have conventionally been seen as belonging to the pre-examination years. Perhaps continuity in English studies will eventually come about because greater agreement is reached about what 'teaching' English means. There has been little dispassionate observation and commentary on methods at this level, but some guidance has been offered by Her Majesty's Inspectors as a result of two recent surveys.[16] Drawing illustrations from different A-level lessons, and stressing that the achievement of objectives 'requires a willingness and an ability to devise teaching approaches appropriate to them', they distinguish certain features 'associated with work of quality', marking it off from less successful lessons. It is not the purpose of this chapter to advance a case for particular methods of teaching, but the broad principles detected by HMI can be summarised:

- 1 'A balanced range of activities ... which developed various skills.' Successful sessions typically involved practical activities, using recorded source material, pair or small group preparation and presentation, discussion and note-making as well as 'input from teachers'.
- 2 Exposure 'to work of scholarship and excellence'. As well as the stimulation of the teacher's own knowledge, groups were encouraged to hear 'recorded discussions by literary scholars' and to discuss critical opinions at an appropriate level.
- 3 'Extension of work beyond the immediate confines of the examination syllabus and often beyond the classrooms' confines.' The encouragement of wider reading, provision of appropriate books, organising of theatre visits, help from Regional Arts Associations, visits to local colleges and universities, poetry readings and field trips were all mentioned.
- 4 'A high level of student participation and involvement.' In the best work, students led seminar discussions, presented papers, improvised, experimented with varied interpretations of drama texts, carried out investigations, and freely debated opinions. 'In brief, through a variety of activities, the students

were encouraged to develop the skills of independent study and to take responsibility for their own learning.'

By contrast, in some schools students were 'passive' listeners much of the time, there was 'dreary reading round the class', line-by-line 'translation', a 'narrow' range of writing, the use of 'ill-conceived' worksheets and too restricted a range of reading. Overall, however, the judgment was that 'the balance of the work observed in classrooms was more encouraging than otherwise'.

Perceptions of teachers and learners

What are perceived as the most helpful ways of learning and teaching? Responses to several questions and contributions to discussion provide information about this, but the details should be prefaced by a word of warning. The difficulties of interpreting student reactions to teachers and teaching have been illustrated by a mass of research, particularly in the United States.[17] However, the main features of the responses can be briefly demonstrated. There was a marked difference between the responses of O-level and A-level candidates in the pilot study when they were asked the open question, 'What do you think are the most effective methods used in your school for learning about the books on the examination syllabus?' At both ages just over a quarter of the students mentioned seeing productions, films or video-tapes of the books being studied, but if their other responses are grouped under the main headings of reading, writing and talking, the results can be compared:

| | *Percentage of students mentioning at* | |
	O-level	*A-level*
Writing	56	24
Reading	37	40
Talking	33	86

O-level respondents saw making notes as their most important single learning activity of all (27%), but it was mentioned by only 6 out of 96 A-level candidates. Other kinds of writing mentioned included essays, written tests, keeping journals and taking down dictated notes. Of all kinds of reading, directed reading or re-reading in class was seen as most important (23%), and personal, private reading was listed by only 5% at O-level (as compared with over 20% at A-level). Of those who mentioned discussion or listening to the teacher, only 7% referred to talking in small groups (compared with 25% at A-level).

This emphasis on the importance of discussion at A-level has been picked up in other enquiries. One that asked 193 students about the most *enjoyable* (rather than useful) activities found that 130 mentioned discussion, 65 reading aloud, 51 writing silently, and only 32 writing essays.[18] Another concluded that 'the commonest single "strength" cited [by students] was class discussion', and 'enthusiasm for classroom discussion was evidenced by many interviewees'.[19]

The particular significance of discussion in English lessons - as a way of learning from each other as well as from the teacher and with benefits extending beyond the academic - was stressed in one of the later discussions held with an A-level group at the very beginning of their second year:

- In English a lot of it is discussion/you don't get that opportunity in other subjects/it's all taking notes.
- It's the sort of subject in which you can learn an awful lot from other people in your group/there's no other subject like that/you can learn something new and reappraise your own view about it.
- If you can back something up you can still stick to your own idea.
- Nobody feels ashamed to say what they think/it's important in an English group that nobody will turn round and say/that's stupid.
- We all accept each other's ideas.
- And it's not just academic/it helps at a social level as well/you can use the skills learned in discussion in non-academic ways/to get yourself into conversation/to make your views known.

Members of another group picked out the ability to encourage discussion as one of the chief marks of an admired English teacher. They said of her:

- She enthuses you more/she encourages you to say things/she accepts your point of view as well as her own.
- Yes/she takes your opinion/treats all people as equal/everyone's view counts.

- She lets us bring out our own opinions and then discuss them with the whole class/she doesn't discount any interpretation/I prefer that way of teaching.

In the main stage, A-level and university students and their teachers in both cases were asked what relative importance they attached to particular 'methods of study for helping you/them to learn in English'. A-level students and their teachers recorded very similar priorities. Both groups placed whole-class discussion with the teacher first (seen as very important by nearly 80% of the students and by 90% of the teachers) followed by writing essays (very important for 66% of the students and 73% of the teachers). A number felt, however, that the best use was not always made of these essays. One remarked on the fact that although written comments were provided: 'Teachers don't encourage you to go back over essays with them and discuss other points of view. We don't share our essays with one another'. They gave a high rating to small group discussion and to students making their own notes, and more than half of each group thought that seeing plays, films and TV adaptations was very important (the only activity to which no student wished to give less time). Both groups saw dictated notes as markedly the least useful of thirteen listed methods (of no importance at all according to four out of every ten teachers).

These responses seem to be broadly similar to those of the Arts students in the 1967 Schools Council survey (which did not separate results by subject). They were most likely to specify as important 'learning to make your own notes' (mentioned by 69%), 'small tutorial groups of 4 or 5 with a member of staff' (59%), discussions (56%) and 'educational visits' to the theatre or elsewhere (56%). The least important methods were 'having notes dictated to you' (9%) or 'being given duplicated notes' (7%).[20]

Groups were divided about the importance attached to practical approaches to studying drama. Many students thought that acting and improvisation were of little or no importance. Those who had experience of such work, however, generally wished for more of it. One typical complaint, voiced in a group discussion and echoed by other students, was that 'We haven't done enough acting out of plays in class/that's when different interpretations come out'.

It may be significant that the strongest feeling that 'there should be more emphasis on seeing productions of plays' was expressed in a group that had already seen three of their set texts on the stage during the first year of their A-level course. It was particularly helpful to see how well a play with language difficulties, like *The Alchemist*, worked in the theatre. One boy said:

> I think it's important to see different versions of plays/I've seen three or four productions of *The Tempest* /one of them was mostly bad/but they all had their merits/when you come back and read it again/its always helpful to have different versions in your mind that you can relate back to and think/well/is that the right way to do it/how would I do it differently?

A little later in the discussion he added that he had found it valuable in studying another play to discover how it had been performed earlier in its history, to see how ideas of staging had changed over the years.

One group of A-level students was sceptical about the value of film or television adaptations of novels, contrasted with productions of plays, which were 'meant to be performed'. Several of them had found the film of *Tess of the d'Urbervilles* very disappointing because it conflicted with the impressions they had formed from reading. One girl said that it was important to see an adaptation *after* reading the text, because 'you need to realise the book in your mind'. If you saw the film first, it would 'colour your imagination'.

In our separate, related question, in which students were asked whether they would rather spend *less* time on any of the named activities, dictated notes were again revealed as the least popular method (mentioned by a quarter of those who responded to this question), said to be 'boring and doesn't stimulate imagination', 'you tend to switch off and not learn anything'. One girl summed up: 'Your own notes are most important and you should not depend on the ideas of the teacher. Discussion is much more important *and* interesting'. Next in unpopularity came reading texts aloud in class ('pointless - more like drama than English') mentioned by just over one in five. Again this echoes the 1967 survey which found that across the whole range of subjects dictated and duplicated notes were the methods most mentioned as being 'done enough' at school; forms of discussion, tutorials and visits those most described as important and insufficiently employed.[21]

Responding to an overlapping, but not quite identical list of methods, and asked which they thought 'very important', English teachers in 1967 were most likely to say 'Encouraging pupils themselves to consult sources' (85%), discussions (75%), 'having small tutorial groups of 4 or 5' (53%), and 'instructing pupils and leaving them to make their own notes' (51%). Least importance was attached to audio-visual aids (3%), lectures (2%), providing duplicated notes (1%) and dictating notes (0%).[22]

It is interesting that some approaches less tied to close study of texts were seen as more important by the teachers in our survey than by the learners. Over 70% of teachers thought that reading outside the syllabus was very important, but under half the students agreed. Teachers also ranked imaginative writing related to the texts more highly than students (for whom this was the third most frequently mentioned activity on which they would like to spend *less* time) and 30% thought acting and improvising very important (compared with 16% of students). It has to be remembered, however, that the very small teacher sample (48) may not be representative, and that not all students necessarily had first-hand experience of some of the methods. Most of those who wished to spend *less* time on imaginative writing came from the same two or three groups, and need to be balanced against those who in the later discussions expressed a wish for more of such activities. In one group two students said, for example,

- I would like more creative work/critical analysis doesn't stretch your imagination much.
- With Mr --- we were rewriting the story from another character's point of view/making up a missing scene from *The Tempest*/when that happens/I think people work better

There was a similar broad agreement about study methods between undergraduates and their lecturers. Both saw essay writing as the most significant activity (very important for 70% of the students and nearly 80% of the staff). However, essay writing was also the most frequently mentioned activity to which students would like to give *less* time. As one said, essays 'take a disproportionate amount of time in view of their limited learning value'. Tutorials and seminars came next (very important for 70% of both groups), but again these were mentioned by some as activities that could be reduced: 'they depend heavily on the right attitude of tutor and students', they can be 'almost totally unproductive' especially if 'nobody can be bothered to read the text', and 'if the group is not responsive and co-operative and if the atmosphere is inhibiting'. Other ways of working perceived as helpful included making their own notes from books and seminars, the reading of criticism and informal talk with other students. Lectures received a very low rating, seen as very important by only 11% of students and an even smaller proportion of lecturers. This has been a common finding in a number of earlier studies.[23]

Although the school and the university results are not strictly comparable, it is of some interest that methods now becoming more popular in sixth forms are still seen as unimportant in higher education. The Verbal Arts Association will not be cheered to know that although nearly 40% of A-level teachers see imaginative writing related to texts as very important under 5% of English lecturers do so, and a third of them believe it of no importance at all. In a similar way nearly a quarter of the lecturers see no value in performance of plays, films or TV adaptations, whereas over half the teachers see this as very important (compared with under 5% of the lecturers). Those lecturers who have had experience in secondary schools rate these activities more highly than those who have not.

Marked differences between the two sectors also appeared in the other methods which respondents chose to mention as helpful. At A-level, these included the making of diagrams, posters and other visuals, writing pastiches, groups presenting sections of text to the class, working on individual or group projects for sharing with others, writers and other visitors to the group, comparing and criticising the critics and sessions in which the students explained how they wished to tackle a text. At university, suggestions of important study methods included learning poetry by heart, yearly examinations, personal research, very close textual analysis, 'the study of different philosophical thoughts' and one-to-one talks between student and tutor ('very rare' added one, in brackets).

Any survey like this of attitudes towards methods of teaching prompts one overwhelming question: why is so much time spent on approaches that both teachers and learners regard as ineffective? This enquiry, like the wider investigation twenty years earlier, found that of all possible methods copying down the teacher's notes was regarded as distinctly the least helpful. If anything, teachers say that they view it even more critically than students. Nevertheless it is clear that pre-packaged notes are still employed a great deal, indeed that according to another survey it is the commonest practice of all at ages fifteen to sixteen, despite its unpopularity.[24] The same question applies at university level. As fewer than one in ten students and lecturers see lectures as very important (and a number believe them of no value at all), why does lecturing still account in most universities for a considerable proportion of teaching time? One lecturer wrote in frustration: 'Overall I am far more in favour of experiential learning techniques for undergraduates - whereas I see an increasing drift toward lectures and critical theory'.

Proposals for change

Further information can be gained from replies to the question 'Would you wish to see any major changes in the teaching methods practised on your English course? If so, explain what they would be'. In addition, a number of responses to the question, 'Do you have any criticisms of your present course?', chose to deal with teaching rather than with course structure and organisation.

The level of criticism should not be exaggerated. Only a third of A-level students and just under a half of undergraduates said that they wanted 'major changes' in teaching methods. The replies to both questions, however, suggested that undergraduates as a whole are more critical of the teaching they receive than sixth-formers are.

At A-level some of the criticisms were concerned with organisation, rather than with the teaching itself, especially the co-existence of 'different approaches to teaching A-level literature': 'We have three different teachers and none of them knows what the others are doing. We find that we have a constant stream of homework from all three, and have difficulty in keeping up with the work'; 'Our teachers expect us to devote all our time to English. They can't understand that we do have other subjects and commitments'. Others sometimes suggested inadequate literary expertise or preparation ('the teachers don't seem as knowledgeable about the set books as they might').

The most frequent criticism of methodology, apart from the general 'Train English teachers to teach in a more interesting manner', was about authoritarian teaching styles: 'Individual views are suppressed'; 'Only the teacher's views are taken into consideration and the pupils' suggestions and opinions are ignored', 'Less dictation of notes', teachers 'should not talk so much'. This criticism is reinforced by the impressions of the Inspectorate: 'There was still a considerable amount of teacher-monologue in evidence, sometimes reading from inappropriate and old lecture notes'.[25] On the other hand, a few are anxious to be 'instructed' and are resistant to what they see as new

128

'progressive' styles of literary work. One girl wrote, 'I do not like the modern approach, I prefer the traditional methods'. Two others, at another school, remarked:

- I dislike some of the creative writing and imaginative work we do. I find it rather too vague and prefer to do 'solid' work in the form of exam texts etc.
- I don't like the informal lessons because the people with less to say don't get a chance.

Although about a third of the sample (34.2%) expressed a wish for major changes in teaching methods, no single proposal was mentioned by more than about a quarter of these students. In order of frequency, their suggestions were for:

more emphasis on talk or discussion	26.5%
more guidance, individual help	24.1%
'better' teaching (less formal, more enthusiastic, etc)	22.9%
more drama, acting, playgoing	15.7%
more choice, consultation, chance to express views	12.0%

Other suggestions made by small numbers of students were for more imaginative or creative written work, more work on critical theory and practice and more supplementing by outside speakers and visits of different kinds. There was a general feeling that 'simply reading texts aloud in class does not sink in'. Some representative comments will flesh out the analysis given above.

More emphasis on talk and discussion
- I believe we should spend more time in discussion and less in just agreeing with the tutor's notes.
- I would like more discussion lessons and reading for pleasure.
- I wish the teacher would ask me more questions and put me on the spot more often.
- Less discussion by teacher alone - small groups would be better.

More individual help and guidance
- More personal approach.
- Teachers helping more individually.

- I would prefer teachers to spend more time on individuals.
- Giving pupils the opportunity to do more supervised but isolated work.
- More pupil and teacher analysing of mistakes in essays ... on a one to one basis.
- More of our research.
- I would like to see more individual help because everyone has different difficulties.

More drama
- I would like to do some role-playing, a little acting.
- More improvisation and drama to help students understand the plays of Shakespeare more clearly.
- We study Shakespeare plays in the classroom but we do not have a go at acting them out. I think we would benefit greatly if we had time to act out a play.
- Seeing more productions and films of the various books.
- I think we would benefit from visits to our local theatre and from seeing videos of more plays and books that we read.

Other proposals
- Letting the pupils decide which books would be most relevant
- There is not enough creative work.
- More emphasis should be placed on creative writing.
- I would like to see more imaginative essays included.
- More visitors, authors and poets, to discuss work with class.

At undergraduate level, there was a repeated concern that lecturers were not necessarily skilful as teachers. It could be summed up in the suggestion, using capitals for emphasis, 'TRAIN the teachers so they can TEACH'. Students complained, for example:

- Tutors on hobby horses.
- Occasionally the tutors have a rather unhelpful attitude which can be discouraging.
- Some tutorials are vague and time is wasted because the tutor has no fixed plan of what will be discussed.
- Too much emphasis on the tutor/examiner's specific opinion of an author/work rather than being geared to improving analytical capability.
- Suppression of individual response in favour of established views.

130

- A shake-up of the lecturing system wouldn't be bad. All in all the standards of presentation, content and relevance are bad - so bad in fact that lectures can become a waste of a morning.

One student wanted 'more pep, direction and verve'.

With the inevitable risk of over-simplification, it can be said that the overwhelming complaint at both levels is about passivity, about the student being seen as no more than a spectator of the process of reading and understanding, required to conform to 'a preconceived notion of the "correct" answer'.[26] Predictably enough, although students place much of the blame for this on those who teach them, teachers are more likely to blame the examination system, and lecturers to blame the schools for making students dependent.

Whereas in schools questions of pedagogy in relation to curriculum and assessment are being vigorously debated, in universities there seems little contention. It is particularly surprising in view of the range of hotly contested critical positions that wide agreement still exists about the day-to-day practices of instruction: the lecture, the seminar, the tutorial. Accounts of the growth of English as an academic discipline habitually pay little or no attention to the ways in which the subjects have been taught.

The persistence of traditional methods of instruction must surely also in part be due to the continuing belief that lecturers do not require training in how to teach and therefore adapt to what is familiar. In several universities it was suggested that interest in methodology or technique was frowned upon as distracting from the 'proper' concerns of research and scholarship. There was considerable defensiveness about any suggestion of 'appraising' the quality of teaching. Those who become English lecturers are normally those who have done well in the conventional system, and they are therefore unlikely to question it when they themselves come to teach. The methods they use - however well they may practise them - are less appropriate today than once they were. They are simply assumed to be valid, and thus the lecturers ensure their continuance.

We may realize that the forms we teach in continue to mirror an earlier world: the lecture, being an image of the renaissance schoolroom, or the Victorian factory, prolongs that model into our students' future behaviour as managers, teachers, broadcasters. We continue to write and require students to write, in modes which have been superseded by changes in communication: the article, the essay, barely exist outside academe.[27]

It should not be thought that all lecturers are unaware of the weaknesses of traditional methods, or that they are unprepared to experiment with other approaches. In one department visited, they had identified some fifteen different structures for conducting seminars. In another, one lecturer said, 'I've been really dissatisfied with tutorials for a long, long time'. She went on to describe as 'a total disaster' the method she had previously practised: meeting students, talking to them about a text for some time and then asking them vaguely, 'What do *you* think?' Another, who had abandoned lectures and teacher-dominated seminars, said, 'As soon as I shut up, that was the liberating thing'.

What new approaches (such as those developed in DUET - the Development of University English Teaching Project - since 1979) seem to have in common is a shift from concern with the teacher teaching to concentration on how students can best learn. Bruner wrote thirty years ago that the principal concern of instruction was to 'arrange environments' and 'provide occasions' in which successful learning could go on.[28] Effective teaching depends on a close awareness of the teacher's *own* learning. In a fascinating autobiographical article Professor John Broadbent has described his own experiences of such a shift on moving from Cambridge to East Anglia. He writes:

> I am increasingly concerned to organize students in such a way as to release *their* energies to deal with the problems of method ... It is, I believe, *their* activity that matters; only their activity which can truly make academic work meaningful ...[29]

Learning from 'colleagues in schools', from the local College of Education and from the Open University, he outlines the different methods developed to increase 'participation': improvisation and role-play, enactment, notebook keeping, group projects, arts practicals and text editing. He discovered, as others have done, the inevitable risks in confronting set expectations, and the irony that introducing radical new methods may initially force a teacher into 'betraying' principles by 'being authoritarian'. Ultimately, however, what was being achieved was a change in the roles of teacher and learners:

The students must experience the teacher himself in various ways that play upon each other: as lecturer (there must be didactic input, but inside its own boundary or it will disable participation elsewhere): as class tutor; individual tutor; author; organizer; actor. The students need to experience themselves in different roles too: lecture audience, member of a small group; alone with the tutor; leader, pupil; and they must experience the role of teacher.[30]

Jon Cook has similarly written, very self-critically, about the attempts he and some of his colleagues made to break away from the 'traditional didactic mode' in which 'the authority of esoteric texts was transmitted by initiated teachers to uninitiated students'.[31]

The experimental work originally carried out in these DUET workshops, mounted by the Development of University English Teaching Project at East Anglia,[32] has more recently been developed elsewhere. This is only one manifestation of an increasing grass-roots concern to discuss methodology and to participate in staff seminars to share ideas. Predictably it is in general the younger lecturers and those who have worked outside the university sector that are most willing to experiment. Nearly a quarter of our small sample had taught in schools, though this had occupied less than two years for most of them, and only one had worked in a comprehensive school. The two following examples, described in a staff seminar, are presented not as 'models' of good practice but as indications of lecturers questioning their own practice and experimenting with more effective ways of helping students.

One tutor responsible for a third-year option on Commonwealth literature abandoned the conventional one-hour lecture, one-hour seminar, format for a weekly two-hour seminar, with freedom of movement and constant coffee. Each session began with consideration of a worksheet distributed the previous week ('what I might have said had I been giving a lecture'). The group then broke down into smaller groups to discuss three questions about the author or text being considered. Each group chose a scribe and a reporter. In the final stages, each of the four reporters presented their groups' thinking ('they usually came at the same topic from very different angles') and this was followed by more general discussion. The lecturer felt that this approach was 'far more productive than if I'd talked for an hour'. It was, of course, also an approach that would have been familiar to many of the students from their sixth forms, which may have contributed to the fact that all the students became involved so quickly. Their written course evaluations were enthusiastic about the workshop style of learning, described variously as 'exciting', 'brilliant', 'stimulating', 'productive' and 'refreshing'. Students commented on the way in which 'ideas bounce back and forth', on the overcoming of nervousness, and on surprise at 'the maturity of thought within us'. Two of them summed up their judgments: '*Please* suggest this method to other tutors' and 'I hate the idea of going back to the old lecture/tutorial format'.

Another tutor described a number of ways in which, by detailed preliminary planning, she had 'attempted to introduce a greater degree of structure into the seminars'. Her first attempt was to give the five students a worksheet on *Wuthering Heights*, suggesting a number of tasks on particular aspects of the novel (structure, imagery, dreams and voices). Each student was to choose one of these and report back to the rest of the group. Although all of the students described carrying out the specific tasks as 'enjoyable' or 'invaluable', there was some reluctance to report back, and the approach was not a success as a way of initiating discussion. 'With hindsight I see that I attempted far too much,' commented the lecturer. Individualising the tasks was not in itself a good way of overcoming the timidity and inhibition about speaking displayed by some students.

In her next attempt, the lecturer wrote to all students before the course explaining what was going to happen, and suggesting a pooling of ideas by relating specific tasks for individuals to those undertaken by the whole group. The students felt that this provided them with a 'bank of data' and by the end 'restraint was giving way, talk bursting forth ... they wanted to talk more than they normally had opportunity to do'. In a further development, as tutorial preparation she asked students to select one of a number of books to read, to undertake certain tasks (marking key phrases, noting authorial comments, analysing the time scheme) and to prepare to discuss certain questions (the same questions for each of the different books).

Such examples of reflective practice illustrate features that have conventionally been associated with school learning: breaking down a large group into smaller ones, giving students responsibility for organising their learning, encouraging students to teach each other, inviting students to evaluate their experiences of learning and teaching. More significantly, however, they serve as a reminder that a subject is defined not only by its content but by the manner in which it is taught and learned. The temperature rises in staff meetings when it is proposed that there should be changes in teaching methods, because this also involves a change in the nature of what is studied.

6

The assessment process

Doubts about examinations

From the very beginnings of English as a subject, there have been the gravest doubts about whether literature *can* be or *should* be assessed. This, indeed, was one of the chief arguments of those who opposed the introduction of literary studies in the older universities. Objectors said that what could be assessed would either be matters of taste and opinion, which would be subjective and unteachable, or mere facts about books and authors, which would lead to undesirable and irrelevant cramming.[1] Even when the subject was instituted, those who were involved remained uneasy about the process of examining it, because 'examinations have a way of thwarting the best-laid schemes of study'.[2]

At school level, a series of official reports pointed to the dangers of examining literature and, in some cases, recommended that such examinations should be abolished. There was a clear sense that, in this subject particularly, the mode of assessment was controlling the curriculum instead of the other way round. For example, the Dyke Acland Report of 1911 said that

English is a particularly difficult subject to teach well and that nearly all its educational value may be ruined by examination papers set on unwise lines.[3]

According to the Spens Report of 1939, inspections from 1902 onwards showed that 'external examinations were having unfavourable reactions on the work of many schools, often leading to cramming and over-pressure' and that the syllabuses and methods 'often impeded improvements in method'. As far as English was concerned,

> The value of wide reading in Literature is now universally admitted. We have, however, grave doubts as to whether books should be used and studied at this stage in the manner that is necessary if English literature is to be an examination subject. We believe that prescribed books do more to injure the growth of a budding sentiment for literature than to encourage it, and therefore recommend *that books should no longer be prescribed in the School Certificate Examination.*[4]

Similarly, the Norwood Report of 1943 summing up the pros and cons of external examinations said that there was 'no room for doubt' that the system had 'a cramping effect upon the minds of teachers and pupils', confined experiment, limited choice, and encouraged wrong values.

> We would assert our belief that premature external examination of pupils at school in English literature is not only beset with every difficulty but is productive of much harm in its influence on the teaching of English literature and eventually upon English as a whole; and for that reason we would advise against any such form of examination.[5]

Possibly the most influential single article, arguing a case that has never been seriously countered, was that of L.C. Knights in *Scrutiny*. His conclusion was that the educational damage being done by external examinations in literature 'is so gross, obvious, pervasive and inescapable, the time has come to press, firmly, for their abolition'.[6]

Many other authoritative voices have been raised to sing similar tunes. Stephen Potter's lively account of English studies chronicled with many examples the way in which early examinations in literature emphasised such qualities as memorising, categorising and explicating, and ignored any possibility of discussion of personal response to or evaluation of texts.[7] In the 1940s, F.R. Leavis agreed that the system emphasised the most trivial and superficial skills and added that it also undermined real learning by encouraging teacher and student to combine in outwitting the examiner.[8] From the 1960s onwards, working party reports for the

National Association for the Teaching of English and articles in *The Use of English* and *English in Education*, have regularly described English examinations in such terms as 'trivial', 'reactionary', 'stifling', 'inflexible', 'harmful' and 'injurious'.[9] Peter Marris advanced as a truism the assertion that 'Examinations unquestionably do great harm, at all levels of education'.[10] In a particularly important set of articles on the future of English studies, published in 1978, scepticism or hostility towards the examining of literature was a recurrent note.[11] Echoing L.C. Knights, the critic W.W. Robson said that the evidence should 'convert the most cautious to abolition'. Significantly, however, the accompanying editorial, while agreeing that in English examinations were even 'more absurd than in other subjects', added cynically that 'it is not likely that English faculties will be the first to abolish' them.[12]

Such cynicism is easy to justify. The establishment and growth of English as a subject have been linked throughout with the development of external examinations. The Newbolt Report (1921) expressed the view that examining literature at first and second Certificate levels had exerted a beneficial influence in establishing the subject and that without such examining the study of literature in schools would be neglected.[13] The trebling of student numbers passing O-level and A-level English Literature since 1950 has been associated with a shift in the power structure within schools.

> English has been perceived as relatively more 'important' because it provides so many examination candidates; there are more groups to be taught; more English specialists are required; heads of department can argue for a larger slice of the resources cake. Ironically, the examinations that so many English teachers deplore have been a major factor in strengthening their position and giving them chances of promotion.[14]

University English departments have similarly benefited from the massive increase - significantly greater than for almost all other subjects - in the numbers of those qualified to study English in higher education.

Nevertheless, there are good reasons to be perturbed about the influence of the public examination system on English teaching. One of the worst features - and one that seems to ensure its survival - is its use from the very beginning as a series of filters for selection, leading up to professional occupations. Although established to measure present performance, 16+ exams largely decide who will continue in academic study, A-level grades are used to determine who shall enter higher education, and degree classes sift out those who might be permitted to engage in research. Because of their importance as predictors, examinations exert a major pressure on the curriculum and styles of teaching.

Public examinations are not carried out (as *school* assessment may be) for the benefit of the student and the teacher, diagnosing progress and weakness, but for the 'users' of the system: universities, employers and other groups. In other words, the examinations are valued less by those who teach *towards* them than by those who later receive the products. At A-level there are two particularly unfortunate results. First, as indicated in chapter 4, dealing with attitudes to courses, an examination 'qualifying' for university entrance is now imposed on the considerable majority who have other destinations in mind. The injustice of this was not unnoticed by some of the lecturers who discussed the situation. One said firmly that an A-level course 'ought to include kinds of literature and kinds of activity that do not necessarily bear directly on what will happen in universities'. Unfortunately, however, this is made more difficult by the second result of the system. Because of the intense pressure on places in university English departments, and because admissions officers rely on grades as a discriminator, students and teachers are encouraged to work in ways that they believe will gain not just a pass but the requisite high grades for the minority aiming at graduate courses. Schools are forced to waste time 'to prepare those tricks that the universities are thought to require', wrote an English professor in the 1960s, instead of encouraging a 'living and therefore indefinite response to the work'.[15] The process is made even more dubious by the evidence, already illustrated (in the last section of chapter 2), that particularly in English A-level grades have little value as predictors of future degree class. In the spoken and written responses of lecturers, however, there was a resigned acceptance of this state of affairs. A-level English 'is what we're stuck with'; 'the examination is so hard to alter'; 'it's the best indicator we've got'. Although many were 'aware of the danger of A-level production lines' and conscious of the damaging effects of 'the grind for good grades', few would be happy to abandon the setting of targets, even though in English almost all universities require identical grades. It was said to me that the standard offers are 'a spiral it's hard to get out of'; higher grades are 'part of a macho image'; 'we've all been forced to bid ourselves up' because of the view that has been cultivated of a 'pecking order' between departments and universities.

The comments of teachers make it plain that they see the most worrying feature of this process as the amount of time which students spend not on reading and responding to texts but on learning the rules of examinations. A Schools Council paper contrasted this 'artificial' situation with the 'normal operations of the mind'. As a result, 'the pupil acquires a technical facility for dealing with examination papers; he learns to be an examinee'. Students learn 'to welcome notes as the most convenient and economical way of memorising the facts (or ready-made answers)', to 'spot' likely questions, and to engage in 'feverish last-minute memorising of the facts which achieves delusive status under the name of revision'.[16]

Questionnaires and discussions with school students indicate which are the most common practices that they associate with working for examinations in literature. Some of these clearly contribute to their literary education: widening the range of reading, studying certain works in close detail, discussing texts with other students, learning to express responses in writing, comparing and evaluating books, seeing individual works in the context of other books, of other arts or of a historical period, and becoming acquainted with critics and critical theory. Other practices may have a value as desirable study skills, even if they are not likely to contribute specifically to literary education. These include learning methods of note-making (marking or high-lighting texts, summarising and selecting information, organising material in numbered points) and revision techniques (working in pairs, recording information on audio-tape for replay, restructuring notes around key issues, and so on).

Some practices, however, seem directed almost wholly at examination passing and have little to do with developing the abilities mentioned in the previous two categories. Unfortunately these are also the practices that are mentioned most frequently by students. They include learning by heart agreed lists of 'illustrative' quotations, preparing ready-made answers on likely questions (or even learning duplicated model answers provided by the teacher), and exhaustive practice at forty-minute essays set from previous papers. One guide, written by an examiner of 36 years standing, never seems to enquire whether there is any real purpose in the proposed activities beyond getting a good grade. Less able candidates in particular, we are told,

> need to be taken through question after question from old papers and to be instructed in the technique of answering them. They need explanations of exactly what these questions involve, how they are to be tackled, how much illustration is to be expected and so on.[17]

It must surely be seen as a weakness of the examination system if it results in students giving a great deal of time to practices that will be of no ultimate benefit to them. The recent survey by Her Majesty's Inspectors, carried out in 1985, gives a depressing picture of the effects of 'traditional examining methods and their associated classroom pressures' in many schools. Comments like the following indicate how concern for the examinations can restrict both the programme of reading and the types of work undertaken.

> Some of the teaching took place in the constant shadow of the examination with a narrow concentration on essay and context question to the exclusion of other activities, which had the effect of shrouding the vitality of literature in an air of gloomy retribution.

> In nearly every school writing tended to be seen only as a finished item, the short literary-critical essay, not as part of a process by which a dialogue might be sustained with the teacher, leading to further reading and reappraisal... Teachers and students alike were usually too conscious of what were perceived to be the requirements of successful writing for examination purposes.

> Few English departments provided a sustained breadth of reading during the two year course... Most students of English literature at A-level seem to read little beyond the set texts and short critical essays.[18]

I have suggested elsewhere that some teachers (wrongly, in my view) assert that mechanical 'cramming' and narrow text-based approaches are forced upon them by an examination system which is actually more enlightened than their methodology.[19] Douglas and Dorothy Barnes have similarly written that 'some teachers seem to have forged their own manacles'.[20] Nevertheless it was clear from the answers to a question about 'the chief constraints that hamper the kind of work you would wish to do at A-level that the *major* constraint was perceived as the examination and its syllabus. This and the lack of adequate time were the only two points put forward by the great majority of teachers (44% and 42% respectively). Patricia Broadfoot's study has similarly concluded that 'in England teachers already identify assessment procedures - particularly public examinations - as the main control over their practice'.

> This emphasis on 'product evaluation' through examination results is a source of control which secondary teachers in the main seem both to recognize and accept despite its many undesirable effects including the inhibition of curriculum development and an excessive emphasis on exam preparation.[21]

The fact that only three of the 42 university lecturers mentioned the system of assessment as a major constraint illustrates the difference in their situation. For them, examinations are under their own direct control, the results of undergraduates are seen as judgments on the students' capability rather than on those who taught them, and apart from moderation by other lecturers there is no external monitoring of those results. By comparison, recent discussions with teachers in schools suggest that they feel that there is currently a decline in teacher autonomy in curriculum and assessment. Attacks on their professional judgment from government and pressure groups have been accompanied by demands for the external definition of 'appropriate' knowledge and assessment of standards.

What is to be assessed?

It is all too easy to see assessment systems as neutral, somehow 'given', inevitable. As will be seen in the following section, although most students are dissatisfied with the methods used, the changes they look for are mainly quite minor adjustments. Nobody called in question the principle of assessment itself or the notion that all texts *can* be reliably examined. The successive stages of 16+, A-level, first year and finals examinations form a sequence: success at each level predicts an ability to adapt appropriately to the increasing demands of assessment. Students are led to accept the authority of an examination system which only perfunctorily makes explicit the assumptions governing the structure, the approach and the content of the papers.

The dubious validity of these assumptions can be demonstrated by recalling the kinds of assessment common in the early days of literary studies. Degree level students were then asked to name the authors of lists of works, to give the main dates in the lives of writers, to outline plots, or to list the major Shakespeare editors and commentators. At the beginning of this century nine answers might be expected in three hours. Candidates could be asked to:

- Prove that *The Tempest* is one of the latest of Shakespeare's plays.
- Estimate the influence of Italy on the English literature of the sixteenth century.
- Characterize the historical methods of Gibbon, Macaulay and Carlyle respectively.[22]

Presumably at the time the assumption that assessment should be concerned with a broad sampling of whatever factual information had been memorised went largely unchallenged.

Although our views of what should be assessed are likely to be very different today, they also rest upon assumptions that are infrequently debated. For example, we rarely discuss the fact that examinations in English *literature* are largely tests of candidates' ability to *write*. What is being assessed may - at different times - be knowledge about books, critical ability or the sensitivity of response. In all these cases, though, the assessment is based on the degree to which that knowledge, interpretation or response can be articulated. In addition, the assumption is made that of different kinds of writing the literary-critical is the dominant or exclusive mode to be assessed. Despite the evidence that students' question choice can affect their grades, examination papers assume that quite different kinds of question (passages for comment, critical essays, factual recapitulation, personal responses) are somehow 'equal' and carry the same marks. The more specific assumptions that underlie the formulation of questions and the approach of markers are discussed in later sections of this chapter.

One rare attempt to bring assumptions and criteria into the open was made by John Dixon and John Brown in their two-volume study *Responses to Literature - What is being Assessed?*[23] This centred on the commentaries made by a panel of 'expert' readers on some 400 examination and coursework essays written for A-level. The running argument was accompanied by the publishing of an 'exemplar' collection of specimen essays together with the panel's commentaries. The report thus offers not only tentative suggestions for approaching work in literature at A-level but also samples of how the appraisal might be carried out in practice. The disturbing conclusion reached by Dixon was that 'half the students taking A-level Literature may be getting little or nothing from their course, so far as written appreciation is concerned', and specifically that of those given grade B by A-level examiners half seemed to the panel 'as "rather thin", or "very weak", or even as "negative" evidence of literary appreciation'.[24] The implications of this work, and of Dixon's continuing work with Leslie Stratta on responses at 16+, do not yet seem to have been digested.

Students' views of assessment

A majority of students at all stages expressed some dissatisfaction with the way in which their courses were assessed. The proportion decreased with age, which may indicate that assessment methods were more satisfactory for older students, or that these had progressively become conditioned to accept them. In brief, only one in ten of the O-level candidates said that they had no complaints and almost all the others indicated ways in which the assessment could be improved. Asked if they would be in favour of changes, about 61% of the A-level candidates and 57% of the undergraduates said that they would. (Even more strikingly, 71% of the A-level *teachers* wanted change). The university lecturers formed the only group where there was a majority against change (48% against 43%, with a number not replying).

The 16+ sample, consulted shortly before the introduction of the GCSE, were quite clear about what seemed to them the shortcomings of O-level. Over a third of them (36%) expressed a wish that course work should be the partial or whole basis for their assessment. Smaller numbers wished for plain texts to be available in the examination or for an oral test. Another third complained about particular features of the examination: the lack of adequate time, the stress on memory and the discounting of personal response, the narrowness of the syllabus and the lack of choice.

The proposals for GCSE would almost seem to have been framed to meet these objections. Coursework, internally marked and externally moderated, is to become a requirement, and possibly the sole basis of assessment. An emphasis on 'mere recall' and 'learned responses' is decried; instead, candidates are to be tested on their ability to 'communicate a sensitive and informed personal response to what is read'. In addition to detailed knowledge of texts, students must show evidence of 'wider reading'. In the examination mode, 'provision of lengthy extracts or complete plain texts' is encouraged. It will be interesting in due course to see what the effects are of these major changes, first on the work of students continuing with English at A-level, and second on the pattern of A-level examining, where there are already a considerable number of experimental syllabuses and schemes in operation.

There was a significant difference in attitudes towards A-level examinations between those who were taking formal examinations only and those who were also being assessed by coursework or projects of different kinds. The all-examination candidates (178 of them) were much more likely to say that they would like changes in their examination board's methods. Whereas they were more than two to one in favour of change (70% to 30%), more than half of those being assessed by other means expressed no such desire (58% against and 42% in favour of changes). It is also interesting that those taking all-examination courses were proportionately more likely to be numbered in the small group of those who said that they now regretted taking English at A-level, though the difference is not major (24% as opposed to 16% of those also being assessed by other means).

There was widespread agreement about the sort of change which the dissatisfied had in mind and their ideas were very close to those of the O-level group. A number of suggestions were put forward by a few students: an oral element, open book examinations or a long project. Overwhelmingly, however, there was pressure for coursework to be assessed. This point was made by eight out of ten of those who wanted change (82.8%). Dissatisfaction with the standard examination format was widespread. Students wrote, for example:

- To write four essays in three hours is not only an inadequate way of assessing someone's knowledge and appreciation; it is insulting to the authors who wrote the literature we study.

- I think continuous assessment should be carried out because examinations are not 'natural' conditions - you are under much more pressure.

- Get rid of the present examination system and the teaching methods that go with it. English should be enjoyed and appreciated. Continuous assessment of essays done throughout the year is a better way because it singles out the people that work at the last minute. You have to work all the year round.

This disquiet with the A-level examination came out in the discussions held with student groups. They said that the situation was 'false', that there was 'too much stress on memory', that it was 'scary' to have two years work so briefly assessed, that the examinations come 'at a time when there's the most pressure on you', that best work is not produced 'when you're not relaxed', that if you have a bad day 'there's nothing to show for two years work'.

It was suggested that the three hour examination militated against any genuine response. One student said 'you can't discover what you really think because there's too much to do in a short period of time' and another added 'you need to have the whole essay jam-packed in your head before you begin to write'. According to a third, 'it takes four hours to write a decent essay/and so there's not enough time in an exam/to give a sensible answer'. Their feelings were summed up by one who said 'exam technique is a skill that you do learn/but it may not be a valuable one'.

Suggestions for modifying the system were mostly moderate: increasing the time limit, giving advance notice of some questions so that answers could be prepared beforehand, the use of plain texts, shorter tests 'in stages throughout the course', the inclusion of teacher judgments ('not of what you remember but of what you can do with it'). Some felt that despite the practical difficulties 'it would be good to have an oral element in the exam ... an examiner you discuss your ideas with, to test how you react in developing ideas, to see if you can argue your case'. Others wanted an assessment of wider reading beyond the set texts and more questions which required comparison of different authors and works rather than questions simply 'on' one.

The commonest suggestion was for coursework to be included: 'there should be a chance to assess some of your best work done during the course'. As one boy said, to apparent approval, 'the best would be a compromise between examination and continuous assessment/there will always be some people who prefer one or the other'.

Tests of practical criticism were not very popular. Two repeated remarks in group discussions were that guided questions were over-analytic (parodied by one boy who complained of being asked 'What use has the author made of the word *and* in line 7?') and that more open forms of appreciation encouraged insincerity. One student felt that teacher guidance in technique was actually disguised pressure to respond in particular ways, thought to be acceptable to examiners. He wanted freedom to record 'what it actually does for you rather than what it *should* be doing for you'.

The feelings of undergraduates were even more clearly distinguished according to the kind of assessment being practised than those of the A-level groups. The traditional 'big bang' of three-hour papers still operates in some universities, but changes are becoming more widespread. At Oxford two out of eight finals papers can take the form of 'library papers' written over three or four weeks earlier in the year, and a thesis can be offered for assessment on any subject in the field. At Cambridge one dissertation is compulsory, and another can be presented as an option. At the University of East Anglia, coursework counts for half of the total assessment. At Newcastle there is a mix of conventional papers, submitted work and 'take-away' papers, with the choice of a dissertation. Many universities permit the submission of a file of creative work. At York, six methods of assessment are practised: three hour papers (with the possible use of texts), papers to be taken away and answered over several days, submission of tutorial essays, long essay, oral assessment of seminar contributions and viva-voce.

In this survey those who were being judged by a mixture of examinations and other methods (course-work essays, long projects and so on) were almost two to one against change (and many of those wanting change were simply in favour of less weight being given to the examination). In the group whose assessment depended entirely or virtually wholly on examinations, those wishing the system to be changed outnumbered the others by nearly four to one. Their comments made substantially the same points as those of the younger students. There was considerable resistance to formal examinations, which 'rest on luck' and chiefly test 'the dubious ability to pass examinations'. They suggested:

- Continuous assessment rather than exams as a much fairer and more accurate method - and more interesting for lecturers as it promotes real discussion and progress.
- I would prefer to see some continuous assessment concerning essay marks - a lot of time is given to essays and good essays should be rewarded - also it would ease exam pressure a little.
- Continuous assessment to be given equal, or best of all, greater importance than exams. Formal exams for three hours or so at the end of three years give no idea at all of your grasp of the subject or critical ability. Merely test memory and ability to function under pressure.
- Why not more essay assessment done under conditions conducive to sensitive study, rather than three hours of panic and memory tests?

Staff views of assessment

Teachers who responded to the questionnaire were even more dissatisfied with the conventional three-paper A-level examination than their students, and this impression has been reinforced in meetings with groups of teachers. Among some written comments one young teacher said 'I'd like to see a completely different system ... I am very dissatisfied with the A-level syllabus and exam as it stands', and another, who had taught three different A-level syllabuses, remarked that even in the best of these 'I am still preparing students for exams in which they have no access to the texts they are required to write about: this seems ridiculous'. Conventional examinations resulted in 'generations of students who can quote Dryden but haven't heard of Pope, who know "Hamlet" by heart but couldn't say who wrote "The Tempest"'. There were repeated complaints about 'undue pressure', 'lack of range' - all attributed to the fact that 'A-level English is hampered by the structure of the final examinations'.

Teachers were quite clear about how the situation might be improved. The seven out of ten who expressed a wish for change were virtually unanimous in defining what that change should be: 'partial or total continuous assessment', 'assessment work done over longer periods of time', 'coursework element', 'assessment of essays written during the course', 'a large element of continuous assessment'. Most of those teachers in the sample who expressed no wish for change were working in schools that already operated the 'Sheffield' syllabus (now JMB syllabus C) or that belonged to another consortium that included the assessment of course work. A few of these wished for further change: '*more* coursework', or the total disappearance of examinations as 'coursework should be the sole basis for assessment'. One or two teachers recorded that they were actively considering changing to one of the 'experimental' schemes: 'we are looking into this at the moment', 'we are currently changing to a scheme which includes course work to be assessed'. An experienced teacher who had made such a change to the Sheffield syllabus described it as 'a vast improvement', and another described the effects in these terms:

> The emphasis is on coursework (4 essays) and originality, one of the examination papers being an open book examination. We have freedom of choice and freedom from rote learning. At first this course makes greater demands on the students who *want* to be given notes and to be *told* what to do, but eventually in the Upper VI year they begin to think for themselves and are able to cope successfully with paper III and the Shakespeare paper, more successfully than under the traditional system. We prepare them for the course by doing NEA syllabus B 16+ at fifth form level, based on continuous assessment.

The one example of a teacher who was resisting such a move, despite the urging of a local adviser, made it clear that this was not because of any regard for the traditional system: 'I want to teach them about life/people seen through authors' eyes but for the sake of the students' grades I must teach them to jump through examination question hoops'. The 'only reasons for not changing to the Sheffield syllabus' were understandable fears about the extra burden of marking on members of the department and the fact that the course 'still has the unseen Literary Criticism to worry pupils'.

Three other proposals for change were made by a significant number of teachers, in most cases combined with a wish for continuous assessment. About one in seven wanted plain texts to be available in any examination, about one in ten favoured a long essay or other major project, and a similar number wished for creative responses as well as critical ones to be assessed. One highly qualified teacher accompanied a wish for 'a large element of continuous assessment' with the need for 'more possibilities of giving credit for extended writing about texts and less "orthodox" forms of writing'. Another, complaining that examination essays 'do nothing to test a student's response to literature', urged 'the submission of a portfolio of work: creative writing, critical essays, responses to texts'. A third felt that there was 'room for a lengthy project/dissertation on texts of the student's choice', which might give more emphasis to 'American and third world literature'. He went on to suggest the introduction of 'a wider range of disciplines: linguistics, Computer AI, cross-cultural uses of English, philosophy as expressed in literature, psychology and literature - perhaps a modular approach'. Another teacher felt that some of the damaging effects of an examination might be reduced if there was 'a paper that is open i.e. 9 a.m. - 3.30 p.m., as they do at university'.

These clear-cut opinions of the teachers contrast strikingly with those of the university lecturers who responded to the questionnaire. As a group they were much more divided, both about the merits and demerits of A-level examinations and about the assessment system being practised in their own universities. Several did not reply to these two questions, but of those who had a clear opinion a small majority believed that the influence of the A-level was 'helpful for undergraduate work in English' (60%) and did not favour any changes in the way that their degree courses were assessed (52.6%).

A difference was to be expected, of course, between those who are actually engaged in preparing students for the examination and those who basically use the results to decide which students shall be admitted to degree courses. However, it seemed surprising that so many lecturers were uneasy about expressing an opinion, either about the examination itself or about possible changes in the system. It was particularly surprising since almost all of them (95%) believed that their students were badly prepared for university work after their A-level. It might have been expected then that lecturers would wish to consider whether the pressure of the examination was responsible for some of these student weaknesses.

A number of them felt that the question was too wide ('In 25 words or less?'), that the issues were too complex ('impossible to answer', 'yes and no', 'neither and both') or that the situation was somehow irremediable: 'A-level is an unavoidable *rite de passage*, therefore cannot be improved', 'unanswerable as A-level is it is what we are stuck with for the time being'. If, like some, one felt that 'it depends almost totally on the quality of the A-level teacher', then perhaps the somewhat tongue-in-cheek proposal for change of one senior academic should be followed: 'Doubling of teachers' salaries, and the destruction of all TV sets'.

Cautious responses can be applauded as being academically scrupulous. On the other hand, if the implication is that university lecturers do not *need* to think about the A-level situation and how it might be improved, then the picture is more worrying. When being asked about what changes might produce an improvement, it seems dismissive to retort 'Impossible to say, without consideration of alternatives'. Alternatives were, after all, being solicited. The existence of A-level does not make the question 'unanswerable', since changes and experiments *are*, in fact, constantly taking place, although very few of the lecturers revealed much, if any, awareness of this.

No particular pattern of response seemed discernible, except that those who had experience as A-level examiners were more likely to see the influence of the examination as helpful and those who felt it *un*helpful were more likely to be younger lecturers (though the age-difference was on average only just over four years). It is, perhaps, more interesting to consider the views of those who suggested changes in the A-level systems. Three-quarters of them, like many of the school-teachers, felt that A-level encouraged too much stress on memorisation of 'right' answers rather than an appreciation and personal response:

- Help them to see there are no simple answers to questions about literature.
- Students still want to write 'character studies', to ask for a list of themes, etc. I think this is an attitude encouraged at A-level...
- Shifting emphasis away from narrowly academic questions.
- It seems to cultivate a play-it-safe, syllabus-based attitude to literature.

However, their remedies nearly all seemed to take the examination format itself for granted. They dealt with extending the syllabus, changing the approach or altering the ways in which questions are framed. Typical comments included these:

- Questions are too narrowly based.
- Get them to read *far* more, specialise less.
- A more flexible, wider based and more culturally adventurous preparation would be better.

- I would like to see a course more concerned with wider reading (a bit like the International Baccalaureat) and less with minute dissection of individual (or even bits of) text.
- They should study texts in meaningful groups.
- More texts studied somewhat less intensively might be an improvement.
- A greater degree of contextualising of text - literary works do not exist in a vacuum.

Only two made points which resembled the teacher's often-repeated desire to break away from exclusively critical writing being assessed solely in examinations:

- More flexibility in exam format; more attention and priority given to students' choice of texts; a coursework component; emphasis on language and variety; less of a 'set texts' approach.
- Probably more practical work in writing both creatively and critically.

It is interesting then, that although they do not seem to support teachers' suggestions for modifying A-level, lecturers advance precisely the same suggestions for changing *university* assessment. Although, as has been stated, rather under half of the sample wished to make such changes, the actual modifications that were proposed by this group were identical with those that the school-teachers wanted. Continuous assessment of coursework was mentioned by 40%, a long essay, project or dissertation by 28%, and greater variety of assessment methods (including creative and practical work), possibly offering students a choice, by 40%.

- *More* dissertations and long essays; *less* emphasis on examinations.
- I would opt for less and less formal examination.
- More stress on prepared essays and comparatively less on timed essay exams.
- A greater flexibility in examining methods, making available a wider number of options to the formal examination.
- More emphasis on coursework. Exploration of alternative methods of assessment from 3-hour papers.
- *Everyone* should do a 6000 word thesis on a topic of his own choice.

- The opportunity for students to *choose* methods of assessment.

These comments give the general flavour. One or two other points were put forward by individuals. For example, one very experienced lecturer proposed more frequent and briefer examinations (with better 'communication between the assessor, the assessed, and the teacher'), while another was critical of a particular course that was orally assessed because 'the results seem often unpredictable and unfair'.

However, it is the discrepancies between teachers' and lecturers' views of A-level, and between lecturers' views of desirable changes in the system at A-level and in degree courses that are intriguing. One lecturer, who had also had experience of teaching in school and in a college of education, began his views on desirable change with the words: 'A consideration of our aims followed by an examination of how we are to achieve them'. There may be some reason to believe that not much serious discussion of aims and principles of assessment goes on at present. Interviews suggest that while individuals or small groups in English departments think this important, they doubt whether most of their colleagues would share their interest. Whereas in the teacher sample, staff from any school tended to answer in similar ways about assessment - suggesting that there was an agreed policy - this was not true of the university departments, all of which seemed to contain colleagues with very different attitudes.

Examiners' views of assessment

The opening of this chapter and the last two sections briefly recapitulated some of the mass of material alleging that the effect of examinations in literature has been to narrow the range of work studied, to substitute 'safe' views for genuine feelings and to acquire a special written mode for critical discussion. It is ironical, then, that examiners and examination boards *deny* that 'approved' answers, in-depth knowledge of a minimum number of texts and formal critical writing are what they want. Their reports are equally critical of 'prepared answers', 'lifeless English', 'restricted reading' and 'conformity'. In 1983 the GCE Boards agreed on a 'common core' statement which said that the aim was:

> To encourage an enjoyment and appreciation of English Literature based on an informed personal response and to extend this appreciation where it has already been acquired.

The centrality of *enjoyment* and *personal response* in this statement seems clear, although it has to be said that it is not fully supported in the accompanying list of *skills tested*. That list in itself - knowledge, understanding, analysis, judgment, sense of the past and tradition, and expression - may be unexceptionable, but the glosses suggest something more restricted than might be gathered from the aim. 'Knowledge of the content of the books' and 'factual comprehension' seem to have squeezed out the imaginative ability to 'construct' meaning and significance from the text. *Analysis* is seen as an inert cataloguing process: 'the ability to recognise and describe literary effects'. *Expression* is defined solely as 'the ability to write organised and cogent essays on literary subjects', with no reference to other modes of writing. There has to be some doubt, then, whether the development of these *skills* (always a dangerous word) will result in achieving the *aim*.

The tension that seems to exist in the 'common core' statement between a desire to encourage active personal response and a wish for evidence of specific literary skills runs through many of the examiners' reports and other publications of examining bodies. Generalised assurances, such as the JMB's objective of testing the candidate's 'response to literature, jointly affective and evaluative' and the Oxford criteria, 'Above all we seek evidence of a candidate's personal enjoyment with his reading, and of his active response', are reinforced by more specific examiners' comments.

There are frequent statements that examiners genuinely want the personal, 'imaginative and critical' views of students, and that there are no pre-ordained 'right' answers. Twenty years ago one A-level report said that 'Examiners are generous in rewarding independence of thought and freshness of response, even when they do not agree with the views expressed'.[25] More recently, others have criticised candidates for a 'lack of confidence' revealed in 'a reluctance to give frank expression to personal opinion when invited to do so' and assuring them that examiners do not have a 'party line'; 'examiners do not decide in advance on one right answer or one right approach'.[26] They have praised the original 'perception of unexpected qualities' in those good scripts which 'show a freshness of personal response',[27] have remarked that 'it is always encouraging and exciting for examiners to come across scripts which do reveal personal, informed response',[28] and even gone so far as to suggest that 'in general the candidates who showed at least the beginning of a personal response were marked up, even if that response was, in some cases, misconceived'.[29]

Despite these assurances, it is clear that the need to see examination scripts as 'evidence' of understanding, critical ability and coherent expression cannot always be reconciled with the encouragement of free individual response. The boards may say that there are no 'right' answers, but an examiner from Cambridge University can go on record complaining that students of Hardy have read the 'wrong' books and acquired 'out-of-date concepts' or 'distorted attitudes'. Her view was quite clear: candidates must hold appropriate views of texts (i.e. must share those of the examiner) and 'should not be permitted to reproduce inaccurate and discredited concepts'.[30] A standard guide to the practice of A-level assessment pays lip-service to the principle that very different perspectives and interpretations are acceptable, but adds that 'at this level too exclusive a treatment often becomes unacceptably limited in practice'.[31] The suggestions offered by examiners to help candidates make clear that there are principles which take precedence over any individual response to text or question. For example, the duplicated notes provided by one board repeatedly refer to texts as the source of illustrations for already existing ideas:

> An essay short of illustration is unlikely to receive high marks ...
> Most of the best scripts provide many short and apposite textual references. Frequent but brief illustrative quotation woven deftly into the sentence structure is characteristic of the really good candidate, working with argument and text clear in his head.

The reports of most boards understandably stress the importance of answering the questions set: 'however well-informed an answer may be, it has little value unless it keeps to the point of the question',[32] 'pursuit of an arbitrary angle remote from the question will not do'.[33] Nevertheless, the common assertion that candidates should 'let the angle of the question and its topic and key terms determine the structure and content of the answer'[34] seems to give little scope for the free play of personal response.

This issue is seen at its clearest in the different messages currently being offered about whether the examination room is a site for delicate retuning of pre-prepared material or for a new articulation of response and thinking through of ideas. The paper already quoted assumed that a good candidate would work 'with argument and text clear in his head', and the assessment guide says that 'honest adaptation of preparatory work is rewarded'.[35] Examiners who share this view make repeated complaints about 'candidates who tried to work out their argument in the very process of writing' or who 'started to write too soon, that is, before (s)he knew what (s)he was going to say'.[36] The assumption is that a good candidate is one who has the structure of an argument, complete with supporting quotations, ready-made to adapt to the particular question set before beginning to write. However, such an assumption no longer goes unchallenged. One board complains of candidates who 'instead of thinking freshly in the examination room in response to unfamiliar questions ... take refuge in reproducing previously prepared work'.[37] Particularly in reporting on alternative syllabuses there is a recent trend to value what one report called 'this sense of exploration, of continuing to think in the examination room'.[38] Tentativeness and uncertainty, particularly but not only in the practical criticism of unseen texts, can be seen as meritorious: 'candidates were not frightened to say what they still did not understand ... and were still bold enough to attempt an explanation'.[39] By contrast with the view of examination writing as final product, the report last quoted claimed that the scripts in question were 'fascinating to mark' specifically because of their 'emphasis on reading as process and the ability to convey the stages involved in the process'.

Indeed, there are wider and marked differences between the tone and the content of examiners' reports on 'traditional' and 'alternative' syllabuses. A comparison within a single board, AEB, shows that in recent years reports on the 'traditional' syllabus 652 have wearily repeated the same complaints, frequently giving over half of the report to a listing of errors in organisation, punctuation ('by now a lost cause'), spelling and vocabulary ('ugly coinages' and 'modish terminology').[40] The strongest criticism is of failure to answer the questions as set: 'a common fault was irrelevance arising from a faulty examination technique'. There was evidence that whole groups had prepared the same answers and illustrations: 'a bank of questions is often used in common by all the candidates from quite large centres'; 'Although there was some excellent work, many candidates displayed little critical ability and a number showed a lack of understanding of the texts'. What such reports strikingly do *not* do is to question whether any of the weaknesses may be a direct result of the mode of assessment.

The reports on alternative syllabus 660 make a striking contrast. A typical overall judgment is that 'the general standard of work offered for this syllabus continues to be very high, showing signs of detailed study, skills in organisation and learning and a high degree of commitment and response'. (Response is hardly mentioned in the reports on syllabus 652.) It is less the enthusiasm ('examiners were struck ... by the number and quality of really outstanding scripts') than the grounds for the enthusiasm that are interesting. There is praise for candidates who have 'been able to develop a personal and individual "voice" during the two year course', for the 'wide range of approaches to textual interpretation and response', for the extension of 'modes of written response' and for candidates' willingness 'to reveal themselves and their own interests'. It is hard not to believe that this team of examiners, operating open-book examinations and the moderation of course-work assessment, is seeking qualities (if not criteria) that are different in a number of ways from those valued on syllabus 652.

Examinations at 16

Because until now the format of examinations at 16 has remained largely constant, some critics of the system have assumed rather too easily that what is being required of students has remained equally unchanging. In fact the dominant modes of questions have shifted significantly over the years, they reflect (after an appropriate time-lag) university-based developments in critical thinking and literary theory, and they imply different views of what teaching and learning involve in the field of literature. An analysis of questions set by the major boards over half a century shows that the majority fall into a small number of categories, that the popularity of different question-modes changes over time, and that each implies particular views about how a student will read a given text, how a teacher will work with a class and how an examiner will judge the candidates. Some typical examples with accompanying commentary will demonstrate this argument.

(i) 'What have you learnt about?'

Particularly in the years following the 1939-45 war some questions continued to treat literature as a quarry for information:

What have you learnt from the novel about food, pastimes and communities at the end of the 17th century? (London 1947).

What have you learnt about London from the several essays in which the *Spectator* describes Sir Roger's visits? (Cambridge 1948).

What impressions of eighteenth century social life have you gained from the poem? (London 1951).

The implication is of non-literary reading: that books are to be treated as transactional discourse, as if they existed to provide information. Other questions demanded knowledge of T.E. Lawrence as a reporter of Arab food, Chaucer as a source of facts about war and fighting, or Milton as providing us with 'ideas of Hell'. The role required of the teacher is simply to instil detailed knowledge by repeated readings and note-making. Little attention need be paid to style or literary effects and still less to any response. Assessment can only be based on the amount of memorised detail that can be recapitulated in a given time.

(ii) 'What does the author say?'

Questions of this kind assume, in Quiller-Couch's terms, an author in direct contact with the reader, and take for granted that in the act of reading students can tell what was in the writer's mind:

What does Wordsworth say he has owed to memories of his previous visit to the Wye Valley? (London 1947).

What impression have you gained from this play of how Shakespeare thought a country should be governed? (London 1948).

What lesson does the poet wish us to learn from this poem? (JMB 1948).

It is assumed that there can be no question of what an author's intentions and reasons are. Typical openings include:

State Wordsworth's reasons for saying ... (London 1946).

Say what you think was Tennyson's intention ... (London 1946).

Show with what purpose Shakespeare ... (London 1948).

Why do you think Shakespeare ... (Cambridge 1953).

What are the effects the author wishes to produce ... (JMB 1965).

At its most extreme, this can lead to a confusion of the writer as person and the writer as producer of text:

> Which two writers in this volume would you most like to meet and know? Show from details in their writings why you choose them. (AEB 1955).

Another question asks candidates to arrange a number of pilgrims from the *Prologue* 'in what you think would have been Chaucer's order of preference' (Cambridge 1956). The reader is manoeuvred into seeing texts not, perhaps, as a source for factual information, but as a guide to writers' experiences and views. You have to be ready to 'illustrate' (another recurrent word) John Masefield's feelings for the sailors in *Dauber* (London 1949), Wordsworth's belief in the power of Nature (Oxford 1952), or Jane Austen's views of a happy marriage (JMB 1965). Questions in this form are commoner about poetry (and some plays) than they are about fiction. For the teacher, the pressure is to speak *for* the author, to explain 'What Shakespeare is really saying here', to paraphrase and to explain the author's 'intention'. The assumption that reasons and intentions are overt means that examiners are likely to impose their own 'privileged' views of what the author says in judging what candidates have written.

(iii) 'Give an account of'

The two previous categories largely disappeared in the fifties, and 'Give an account of ...' was for many years the dominant mode of O-level (particularly in dealing with novels or plays):

> Give an account of *one* of the practical jokes played in *Twelfth Night*, and show how far it advances the plot. (Oxford 1959).

> Give a detailed account of the scene in the church. Write your account in such a way as to reveal the characters of Leonato, Beatrice and Benedick. (JMB 1962).

With close reference to book IX, summarize the arguments by which the serpent persuades Eve at the tree to taste the forbidden fruit. (London 1963).

The implication of such questions is that readers will see the novel or play predominantly as equivalent to its story-line, which can be recapitulated adequately in the reader's own words. Those variants of the question that ask about characters suggest that they will be viewed as though they are real people with fixed, undebatable personalities. There is no suggestion that different readers might have very different reactions to Sergius, say, or to Bluntschli. For example:

Sketch the characters of Gripplestraw and of Mrs. Garland. How far does Hardy succeed in making them real people? (London 1951).

In what respects is Bluntschli a more attractive character than Sergius? (AEB 1955).

Sketch the character of *either* Gilbert Glossin *or* Dominie Sampson, illustrating your points by reference to events in the novel. (Cambridge 1956).

The popularity of questions of this kind helps to explain the sales of Coles notes and other 'guides'. Faced by such an examination, a teacher is likely to emphasise the making of plot summaries and of character studies, collecting 'useful' quotations drawn from what characters say and from what is said about them. The implication for plays is that the concentration is on the text ('Give a clear account of the scene ... referring closely to the text') rather than on a performance. The assessment will be based on the degree of success with which candidates can undertake a quite sophisticated written task: taking a literary narrative text, reducing it selectively to a factual framework and adding an analytic critical commentary. 'Write an account' is almost always followed by some such phrase as:

showing how the author ...
pointing out the features ...
indicating the ways ...

This, as will be suggested in the next section, implies the 'Cambridge' mode of demonstrating elements of technique, of literary effects, manifestly there on the page, except that in this formulation certain specified features and not others are to be demonstrated.

(iv) 'Show how'

This, the other prevalent mode for many years, brings to the fore what is sometimes the second part of 'Give an account of ...' questions.

> We are evidently intended to feel from the play that life in the Forest of Arden is finer and nobler than life at the court. Show, with some brief quotation, how Shakespeare conveys this feeling. (Cambridge 1953).

> Show how Shakespeare creates an atmosphere of beauty and romance in his scene in Capulet's orchard (the balcony scene) when Romeo declares his love to Juliet. (Cambridge 1962).

> Show clearly by what means we are led to feel sympathy with Macbeth in spite of his murderous actions and intentions. (Cambridge 1965).

> By what means does Cowper make his poem 'John Gilpin' entertaining? Give examples from the poem to support the points you make. (AEB 1985).

Questions framed in this way assume that readers will all agree with the imposed judgment. There is no possibility of arguing that life at court is finer than life in the forest, or that we do not feel sympathy with Macbeth. Any view of the effects created by the balcony scene has to be reduced to a discussion of 'beauty and romance', and 'John Gilpin' has to be taken as 'entertaining'. There is also the buried implication of what the reader's 'proper' motive for reading the books should be: that we turn to Gray's 'Elegy' because 'its sentiments find an echo in every heart' (London 1947), that we read Tennyson either because of his 'moral lessons' (JMB 1965) or for his 'sensitive and musical qualities' (London 1965). At its worst, readers may be asked to 'Explain the humour' in the opening of *Northanger Abbey* (JMB 1962). The teacher's approach to an examination including such questions will have to be one demonstrating particular qualities by close attention to selected key sections of the books. Importance is attached to the spotting of likely questions and to teaching how a generalisation can be applied to discussion of the text. 'What qualities make *Rogue Male* a gripping novel?' or 'Point out the main characteristics of Robert Frost's poetry' (AEB and JMB 1985) encourage detached rather than responsive approaches to books. From the examiners' point of view, these questions are perhaps nearest to the formulation in university examinations, and therefore might be congenial to university markers. They seem to reward a capacity for flexible critical gymnastics: a willingness to argue any case that is 'given', rather than having strong genuine conviction about a text.

(v) 'Say what you think'

Although it occurred occasionally in earlier years, significant use of the pronoun *you* has only become common in the eighties. It seems to be a marker of the increasing influence of reader-response criticism in schools.

> Give an account of *one* occasion in *Richard II* when you find yourself feeling sympathy with or liking for the king; and also of an occasion when you have little or no sympathy with him. Make clear the reasons for your feelings towards him on each occasion. (Cambridge 1957).

> In your reading you may have found a poem which describes an experience very familiar to you. Write an account of such a poem, making clear the qualities to which you have responded. (AEB 1984).

> Many people find it easier to sympathise with Juliet than to sympathise with Romeo in the play. How do *you* feel? Why do you feel this way? (Cambridge 1985).

> At which point in *A Midsummer Night's Dream* do you feel embarrassed or annoyed because of the way the characters are behaving? Explain carefully why you have these feelings. (Cambridge 1985).

Questions formulated in this way see reading as the creation of meaning and significance in the mind of the individual reader. The focus is on reading experiences, about the feelings and ideas of candidates, rather than on any view of the text as object. From the teacher's standpoint this involves a shift in role from reconstituting some agreed view of a text to facilitating the expression and discussion of a range of personal responses. The questions often deliberately suggest that a variety of views is legitimate. For the examiner there are inevitable difficulties in assessing responses to '*How* do you feel and *why*?' Seeking evidence of genuine response to texts is a different assessment process from ticking the points in some impersonal presentation of 'facts' or 'evidence'. It is noticeable that 'Say what you think' questions have been particularly associated with plain-text examinations, where candidates can be directed to a particular passage about which their reactions are sought: recreating and interpreting the experience, reflecting on what is significant and evaluating it.

(vi) 'Imagine'

Like the last category, this formulation was not unknown in earlier years but has only recently become prominent. It marks some erosion of the traditional division in literary studies between the critical and the creative.

> Write an imaginative dialogue in which Brutus and Cassius discuss the reasons for the failure of the conspiracy against Caesar. (AEB 1957).

> Imagine you are Helen Burns on the afternoon when Mr. Brocklehurst and his family visit Lowood Institution. Give your own account of that visit, and your attitude to Mr. Brocklehurst and his school. (Cambridge 1983).

> Imagine that you are able to overhear Mrs. Kingshaw and Mr. Hooper discussing, after the discovery of Charles's body, what can possibly have happened to him. They will, no doubt, recall what they know of his recent activities and behaviour. Write what you hear. You may if you wish write in the form of a play. (Cambridge 1985).

Questions of this kind stress the importance of 'active' reading, realising the text, filling the 'gaps'. They offer the teacher an opportunity to unify work in 'language' and in 'literature' and emphasise the kinds of activity that are now more common in the earlier secondary years: supplying missing scenes, reframing events from the viewpoint of another character, adapting one genre for another. Questions on plays invite candidates to imagine 'If you were producing *Macbeth*' or 'How you would play the part in a school production'. In such ways they try to overcome the criticism that plays have too often been treated as texts for reading rather than as scripts for performance. The first sets of specimen questions for the GCSE suggest that this mode is likely to be important in the near future. The NEA, for example, includes a question on *An Inspector Calls* inviting candidates to imagine a fourth act to the play in which they have to invent what two of the characters might say to the real police inspector ('You may set out your two accounts as if they were sections of the play'). Such tasks have been common in coursework assessment, but including them in the examination mode involves a further change in the examiner's role. The most obvious problem concerns the relative importance to be given to creative flair (the ability to write an effective pastiche of an author's style, maintaining a sense of genre and convention) balanced against direct perceptions of the set text.[41]

In one example of interesting inter-penetration between examinations at different levels, a lecturer in higher education has recorded how his degree level practice has been affected by his work as an O-level examiner. He said how impressed he had been by the 'vitality' of answers in which candidates wrote letters (one from Jaques and one from Audrey) about happenings in Arden, or Bianca's diary entry on the night of her wedding (*The Taming of the Shrew*), or a scene from 'Bottom's Dream', following the success of 'Pyramus and Thisbe'. As a result, he designed a new, creative 'workshop' approach to *As You Like It*, in which his students wrote letters from characters looking back on Arden and developed these into poems (some of which he quoted). All the students 'remarked on how the assignment had made them read and re-read the play - a form of preparation apparently not always forced upon them by my seminars or their formal essays!'[42]

It seems likely that the coming of GCSE will not only encourage different modes of assessment and different kinds of examination question but also require different attitudes from examiners. The NEA report on the 1986 joint 16+ examination in English expresses 'enthusiasm' for the 'freedom' which course work 'naturally encourages', and opens with these significant comments:

With the development of GCSE very much in mind, examiners were this year asked to concentrate on the positive qualities of scripts, rather than dwell on their inadequacies. In other words, they were required to mark what the candidates had done, not what they had failed to do. From this viewpoint it is salutary to note that it was a tiny minority who could communicate virtually nothing of value, while the skill of the very best was often astonishing.

Set against such real achievement, the near hysterical concern for spelling and punctuation expressed in some quarters appears disproportionate.

In addition, of course, virtually all teachers of 16+ groups are now also becoming examiners: a task for which some do not necessarily feel adequately prepared. The wider sharing of the role of assessment, with the accompanying need to agree standards between classes and between schools, will itself be productive of change. English teachers as a profession will have to be more directly concerned with debating the principles, modes and applications of assessment.

Examinations at 18 and beyond

Compared with the changing form of 16+ questions, which give increasing importance to readers' responses and to imaginative reactions to the text, A-level questions appear relatively constant. Experimentation seems to have been channelled into the 'alternative' syllabuses. For a variety of reasons the topics set at 18 bear a close resemblance to those offered in universities, more or less adapted for younger students. It would be possible to point to the traditional role of the universities in defining the sixth-form curriculum, to the considerable number of lecturers who work as A-level examiners, to the fact that most sixth-form teachers are themselves products of the English degree system, or to the use of the examination as an element in university selection. The result has been to devise a form of assessment that will initiate students of seventeen and eighteen into ways of thinking about literature seen as appropriate at university, and that will prepare them for the ultimate test of Finals.

A comparison of A-level and English Finals papers over the last decade confirms how similar the chief modes of questioning are. The university examinations are frequently more conceptually demanding and often require knowledge of more than one work to be shown in a question, but the level is not always apparent from the formulation given. Could we unhesitatingly say which of the following ten questions were set for A-level and which for Finals?

- Write an essay on the variety of styles in Milton's *Minor Poems*.
- Analyse the distinctive features of Pope's imagery.
- 'Donne is a scholar, not a poet'. Discuss.
- 'A Victorian romantic'. How accurate is this description of Tennyson as a poet?
- The faults and weaknesses of Antony and Cleopatra are revealed in the action of the play, their magnetic power and nobility in its poetry'. Discuss.
- 'Excellent falsehood'. How far does this phrase sum up the behaviour of the protagonists in *Antony and Cleopatra*?
- 'Keats is much concerned with the relationship between Art and life'. Discuss.
- Write on the title of *Wuthering Heights*.[43]

What kind of knowledge is suggested as important by the commonest modes of questioning? At A-level, easily the most popular form - frequently accounting for more than half of the questions in any paper - is the one requiring candidates to discuss some quoted (but frequently unattributed) critical judgment of the text. Not only does this restrict a student to that particular aspect, it also involves reacting to another's view, validating or questioning it, rather than to one's own direct experience of the text:

- 'Archdeacon Grantly is Trollope's greatest creation in *Barchester Towers'*. Discuss (London 1980).
- 'To insist too much upon Jane Austen as a *comic* writer is to distract attention from the emotional depth and moral scope of her work'. Consider the validity of this statement with reference to *Sense and Sensibility*. (Cambridge 1981).
- 'The description of physical conditions in *Great Expectations* heighten, sometimes almost create, the emotional moods of episodes in the novel'. Do you agree? (Cambridge 1984).

It must be doubted whether such formulations are helpful to a young student working under examination conditions. Is 'creation' only to be applied to the *characters* of Trollope? Is the implied balancing of *comic* against *moral* in Jane Austen a fruitful topic for discussion? Can the reader really *dis*agree with the judgment on *Great Expectations*, and - if so - how? This form of question is possibly even more dominant at university level:

- 'Webster's tragedies would be hopelessly melodramatic without the saving grace of black humour'. Discuss.
- 'Clare's poems abound too much in mere description: they are deficient in feeling and human interest'. Discuss.
- 'Elitist and defeatist'. Would you agree with this view of T.S. Eliot's poetry?
- 'For all his bracing, manly style, Browning was a sentimentalist at heart'. Discuss.

In order to stimulate response, a striking remark is offered for discussion, but whether such over-simplification provides an agenda for a critical essay under examination conditions is more doubtful.

Sometimes the quotation seems to be employed to force A-level students towards an unreal choice between views which are not strictly alternatives to each other.

- 'The strength of *The Mayor of Casterbridge* lies in the clarity of the episodes, rather than in the individuality of the characters'. Do you agree? (London 1980).
- 'Less a satire than a romance'. Discuss this view of *Brideshead Revisited* with detailed illustrations from the novel. (JMB 1981).

Separating out narrative from character in this way, or demanding the defining and balancing of terms like *satire* and *romance*, seems more likely to inhibit than to encourage genuine critical response. Undergraduates will perhaps have had sufficient practice not to be flustered by similar questions.

- *Gulliver's Travels* has been labelled 'a comic satire' and 'an eighteenth century tragedy'. Does either or neither description satisfy you?
- Does *King Lear* represent the triumph or the defeat of humanity?

- 'Shelley's strength, which is also a measure of his weakness as an artist, lies more in the qualities of vision and insight than in the quality of his poetic language'. Discuss.

The other most popular A-level form - frequently overlapping with the first - is the one which isolates a particular theme from the set work, and which tests candidates by their ability to abstract that from all other features for their attention.

- How important is the religious theme and background to our response to *The Power and the Glory*? (JMB 1981).

- In the preface James refers to 'the most modern of our current passions'. Discuss the importance of this theme of collecting antiques in *The Spoils of Poynton*. (Cambridge 1981).

- 'Loneliness is the real subject of all T.S. Eliot's poetry'. Discuss. (Oxford and Cambridge 1984).

Theoretically candidates could argue that the selected theme is not particularly 'important' or 'essential' or the 'real' subject. In practice, however, the bland assumption is made (implied by phrases like 'important ... to *our* response') that candidates and examiners will think alike. Questions on Finals papers are often even more directive:

- Consider the themes of imprisonment and release in Coleridge's poetry.

- 'Temptation is Milton's most dramatic theme'. Discuss.

- The dominant motif in *Othello* is alienation, separation.

In the last example, the absence of the usual word 'discuss' seems to reinforce the notion of an impersonal 'truth' which is to be extracted and illustrated. Some themes can reappear conveniently attached to other authors. In consecutive years, students could be invited to 'Discuss Conrad's treatment of the theme of betrayal' and to 'Discuss Hardy's treatment of betrayal...'

Even when the formulation includes such a saving phrase as 'how far' or 'to what extent' ('How far is Thackeray's *Vanity Fair* simply variations on a theme of contrasting value?') a student who dismissed the theme as unimportant and went on to discuss the greater significance of a quite different one would be held to have failed to answer the question set. Indeed, at A-level thematic questions are sometimes framed to exclude any discussion of what the text is 'about'. The candidate is not permitted to question the judgment; it has to be accepted in order to answer the question at all:

- *The Spire* has been called 'a conflict between Faith and Reason'. Discuss the book in these terms. (London 1980).
- Consider *Jane Eyre* as a moral pilgrimage. (London 1981).
- Consider the view that *Mansfield Park* is mainly about personal integrity. (London 1984).

A further variant of this type of question is the one which appears to suggest that a book is written (or read) to demonstrate a particular proposition. Despite the use of phrases like 'how far' or 'to what extent', it is difficult to reject the implication that books are essentially concerned to offer illustrations of general truths.

- 'A nation torn between cultures'. To what extent does *A Passage to India* illustrate this theme? (JMB 1981).
- 'A great exercise to demonstrate the thesis that the universe is totally indifferent to men and women'. How far is this an adequate description of *The Return of the Native*? (AEB 1982).

As these examples suggest, A-level questions seem largely concerned that students should neutrally evaluate the evaluations of others in relation to certain aspects of texts, rather than writing about their own encounters with books. The implication is that the reader of 16-18 should be learning to understand and describe the qualities and effects of certain texts that must be 'known' and to draw appropriate conclusions. The reader's role in 'realising' the text is largely irrelevant. Consider this example: 'What is Waugh's view of his central character as it is expressed in either or both of the set novels?' (London 1980). Can we know Waugh's view from the novel in which it is supposed to be 'expressed'? Are we to assume that the implied narrator's voice is identical with that of the author? Can we be sure that what is 'expressed' is what all readers will receive? By framing the question in this way, rather than asking for the *reader's* views of the central character, a particular concept of learning and teaching in A-level courses is being conveyed. Similarly, when we read ' "In *Vanity Fair* Thackeray makes us delight in Becky despite our moral disapproval of her". Discuss' (Oxford 1984), the stress is laid on the author's creation of response ('makes us') and on the universality of that response (makes *us*, *our* disapproval). The text is to be seen as the source of authorial techniques, which candidates are to discuss, rather than as the source of readers' reactions, which have to be grounded in what they perceive as significant factors. It is in the questions on *alternative* syllabuses that questions are posed which seem to value a reader's encounter with the text, rather than the organising of ready-made material to reach some pat conclusion. One such paper, for example, providing a list of quotations, asks:

> There are frequent references and appeals to God in this play. What do you think 'God' means to any three characters in *The Crucible*? Go on to suggest what you think Miller achieves by setting his play in a specifically Christian context. Some of the statements you might like to consider when thinking about your answer are shown below. (AEB 1984).

Even such a brief discussion as this illustrates the point made in a previous section: that there is a tension between examiners' stated desire that candidates should write honestly about their personal responses and the format of the questions they set for those candidates. Their problem has been well documented by Helen Butler in a study of all the Boards' examination papers in English and the ensuing examiners' reports for a single year.[44] The overall picture is one of students being conditioned in the sixth form to practise the kinds of writing perceived as appropriate in degree-level studies. Ironically, as new modes of assessment and question-setting become common for GCSE, so the gulf will widen between that stage in literary education and the next.

Throughout the system, it has been argued, students are picking up messages from the pattern of their examination questions about how they should read and study, about the kinds of knowledge that are seen as valuable for students of English, about the sorts of performance that are rewarded, and about the nature of 'progress' associated with literary studies.

The similar kinds of message that were being picked up a decade ago in the United States were vividly described by Professor Ohmann. He showed how disconcerting or even subversive literature was subtly changed by the kind of study that ended in assessment. In such an approach to the work, 'self is abstracted into *character*': 'feeling is transformed into *attitude*', and the same process 'turns ideas into *themes*'. As presented in an examination, a text

> contains themes, and it may even contain issues, but there is no suggestion that it may actually contain an idea or press a claim. It is intellectually bloodless.[45]

Conclusion

The preceding chapters have considered the current state of 'English' studies during the examination years, and particularly the perceptions of such studies formed by students and those who teach them. The concern has been with what *is*, rather than what *ought* to be. There are inevitable dangers in trying to sum up the range of opinions expressed by so many different voices without gross over-simplification. Nevertheless, some attempt must be made to consider the broad implications of this study particularly for those who teach, examine and frame policy.

Although there are few surprises in the points which emerge most strongly it may be helpful to have some evidence to support gut-feelings and anecdotes. The survey suggests that there is good reason to believe:

- That those taking English courses at A-level and at university are generally happy to be doing so, chose the subject chiefly because they enjoyed it, and are satisfied with the result.
- That the majority believe that they gain personally as well as academically from their English courses (but that there is some conflict between their perceptions and those of their teachers).
- That English is not perceived as important in career terms as providing a qualification for particular occupations.
- That at all stages students feel that their previous work has failed to prepare them adequately for what they are doing (and this view is shared by those who teach them).
- That in curricular terms there is insufficient continuity in content, methods and approaches between 16+, A-level and degree courses.
- That students value active modes of learning in which they feel personally involved (particularly discussions in small groups), and believe that learning would be improved (especially at university level) by less impersonal modes of teaching.
- That although on the whole students feel that teachers encourage them to make their own responses to what they read, the system itself (essay grades, tutor reactions,

examinations) frequently prevents them from revealing their true views.
- That there is a widespread dissatisfaction with the examination system, and a strong desire for more assessment of work done during the course.

More important, perhaps, are the issues that are raised by some of the differences of opinion, and particularly those where there is a mis-match between the views of students and their teachers, or between those in school and those in university. Some questions that emerge most urgently in the previous chapters can be summarised.

- What practical advantages and disadvantages result from the fact that those involved in the subject have very different perceptions of what English is and what its aims are? Does it matter that teachers of English, even in the same department, frequently hold quite different or even irreconcilable paradigms of English teaching? Should those within the profession be more concerned with the views of those outside it (and particularly the combination of a high value attached to the subject but a critical view of teaching and its results)? How far can it be assumed today that 'it is in society's interests to train and pay enough teachers, scholars and critics to ensure that literature exercises its civilising influence'?[1]
- What effects on public perceptions of English are created by the make-up of its students in terms of gender, social background and academic results? Can anything - and should anything - be done to increase the proportion of men studying English after 16? Why are boys more likely to take English in independent schools than in comprehensives? What are the effects on student perceptions and relationships of gender differences in staffing? (Although women considerably outnumber men in secondary school English departments, men seem to do at least as much A-level teaching as women. Most university English lecturers - and almost all professors - are men, although their undergraduates are three-quarters women.)
- Does there need to be more wide-ranging discussion of the extent to which the syllabuses and courses offered shape students' views of literature and of literary studies? Is it

adequate for each university department to plan its courses in isolation, and for schools to select from what examination boards have on offer? Should there be more agreement, for example, about the place of critical theory in schools and universities, the range of kinds of writing to be studied and practised, or the extent to which other media should be included?

- In view of the clear evidence from students and teachers that the literary curriculum is seen as disjointed, and that students feel unprepared for work at successive stages, can anything be done to make the process more coherent? Does the continuing work on models of developing response offer a basis for such a programme? In particular, how can the transition from school English to Higher Education be eased?

- What effects are likely to be caused by the increasing range of post-16 'English' courses and examinations, and by their co-existence in some institutions? In particular, what is likely to result from the teaching of AS English candidates together with those taking A-level? What kinds of 'knock-on' pressure on A-level courses and assessment are likely to be exerted by the new approaches of GCSE?

- What steps can be taken to ensure that those involved in English teaching can be kept up to date in a period of swift change? The HMI report that 'relatively few' A-level teachers 'had experience of recent professional training which was directly relevant to their present teaching duties'.[2] In particular, how can those on either side of the 18+ transition become more conscious of what is happening across the divide? Should those in universities discover more about new styles of teaching, learning and assessment being practised with A-level groups? Could they offer more support to schools in the discussions over such matters as the amount of English being taught by non-specialists, in the heavy demands of course-work assessment, or the pruning of funds for the purchase of texts and library books? Should teachers be better informed about the constriction being suffered by English departments in universities, the lack of mobility and the difficulties of promotion?

- Is it appropriate that university English teachers should still not be required to undergo any formal training in how to teach? How can those groups and units that attempt to give such guidance be strengthened? Could the lack of examples of successful teaching and learning, particularly at university, be partly overcome by the commissioning of more written case-studies with examples of student work, video-tapes of sessions and more sharing (of experiences and sometimes of classes) within departments?

- What are the chief aims of assessment in English thought to be, and by what methods can they best be achieved? Does everything done *have* to be assessed? Is there a place for self-assessment in sixth forms and universities? Should university students have any choice in modes of assessment? How can the assessment of coursework be adequately monitored? How can legitimate expectations be defined at any stage about what students should be expected to have read, what kinds of critical ability they should display, and what language skills they should have mastered? (Because many lecturers are A-level examiners they influence the situation in schools, but there is no reciprocal influence on the universities.) Is the considerable increase in coursework assessment for GCSE English likely to produce pressure for similar changes at A-level and beyond (as students appear to wish)? What effects will the increased involvement of English teachers in the assessment process at 16 and 18 have on their attitudes towards the ways in which universities select candidates for entry?

- How can selection for university break away from the image of a buyers' and sellers' market? Can schools make clearer to lecturers what they hope to achieve in an A-level course, and can universities define the criteria by which they make their selection? Could there be a unified movement to end the over-reliance on A-level grades? If so, what might replace this?

It will be clear that finding answers to most of these questions would depend on the willingness of those who teach English in different kinds of institutions to talk to one another. Unfortunately, in times of heavy and often philistine pressure on teachers, there is a strong temptation to restrict attention to the immediate task and to avoid the consideration of wider issues beyond the particular school or department. This enquiry suggested that many teachers and lecturers were very concerned about such matters, but felt powerless to do much more than to express that concern. The achievement of continuity between school and university, thought so desirable in 1950 (see the beginning of chapter 3), seems no nearer. Peter Hollindale wrote recently that 'the lack of professional unity between school and university teachers has not noticeably changed in the last twenty years', indeed, since the mid-sixties attempt to achieve this.[3]

Between 1962 and 1967 the Critical Quarterly Society sought, through its publications and through conferences, to bring together those concerned with literary education in schools and in universities. In particular its journal *The Critical Survey* printed two series of accounts of principles and practice: one by Professors of English describing the situation in their departments, the other by English teachers mostly concentrating on work in sixth forms. Why did this admirable initiative seem to produce so little actual result? In part it may have been affected by the change from a period of heady expansion to one of contraction. (*The Critical Survey* ceased publication in 1973.) However, re-reading those journals suggests other underlying reasons.

First, as Emrys Evans noted in his 'Survey of the surveys', although the notion of *continuity* in literary education was a recurrent one, it occurred virtually exclusively in the accounts of the school-teachers.[4] They wrote of the lack of any 'sense of continuity between the various stages of English teaching', and of the need for a 'continuing syllabus and examination system'.[5] Describing the damaging effects of the examination system, one Hull teacher went on:

> If there is a remedy, it would seem to lie in establishing a principle of continuity in English teaching, ranging from the primary school to the university, by virtue of which the process becomes more important than the examination and the teacher becomes fully conscious of the part played in the over-all pattern by the stage for which he is personally responsible.[6]

Such ideas were absent from the accounts coming from the universities.

Second, and related to the first point, whereas the teachers referred frequently to the universities for which their students were bound, their requirements and the courses they offered, the professors said almost nothing about the schools from which they drew their students. Almost all the teachers described how far their courses and methods were constrained by the demands of A-level and university entry. By contrast, university accounts simply outlined courses and organisation in particular institutions with little acknowledgement of the context in which they existed.

Third, from 1969 onwards *The Critical Survey* became the vehicle for the *Black Papers* on education. Many teachers were repelled by the naked hostility and the suggestions of failure presented by academics who had previously shown little desire to be informed about schools. Peter Hollindale has written of the Black Papers:

> These documents asserted the prerogative of English academics to act as *cultural* critics, and hence to pontificate authoritatively about education, social behaviour and popular taste in general. The broadly cultural critique becomes almost inevitably political in nature, and the right-wing political alignment of the Black Papers was barely disguised. The convictions underpinning the Black Papers were voices in a tone of authoritative ill-temper which is characteristic of literature-based cultural criticism; also characteristic was a cavalier acceptance of aggressive and slipshod arguments which the contributors in their *literary* critical role would scarcely have tolerated.[7]

Teachers saw the criticisms of curriculum and methodology as those of unqualified amateurs. Even today it is difficult to persuade groups of English teachers that anything good can be said about those professors chiefly associated with the Black Papers.

In the mid seventies there was a similar clash when a public letter from 26 senior academics expressed their 'alarm' at the 'prospect of O-level examinations in English being more and more assessed internally by schools and of A-level in due course following the same pattern'. In a tell-tale phrase, the professors expressed their preference for the work of examination boards 'over which the universities have some control'.[8] Teachers who responded to the letter were doubtful whether the universities *should* have such control, disliked the suggestion that the needs of 90% should be over-ridden by the most able 10%, and thought it ironic that universities assessing the students *they* taught should seek to deny the same right to schools. In particular, however, there was resentment at the hierarchical impression: that dons saw themselves as 'consumers' of the products provided by schools rather than as members of a wider English-teaching community engaged in the joint process of literary education.

There are, of course, much more encouraging signs of mutual understanding. Recently teachers have given the warmest praise to courses for staff and students provided by university lecturers and lecturers have commended what one called 'the dedicated and imaginative teaching in difficult circumstances' carried out by secondary staff.

Those who have frequent contacts with both teachers and lecturers will be familiar with the mixture of admiration, concern, suspicion and occasional irritation with which each group still regards the other. The final survey question put to each of these sets of respondents asked them whether they would personally be in favour of 'closer liaison' between university lecturers in English and A-level teachers of the subject. In their replies eight out of ten in the former group and nine out of ten in the latter said that they would. With such a high measure of agreement we may wonder why it does not come about.

However, the suggestions they made for 'particularly helpful' kinds of liaison reveal a marked difference between the two groups. Those in school generally had clear ideas about what they would favour; the university responses were more undecided and ambivalent ('I have not thought about this', 'I cannot imagine', 'Who knows what practicality might devise?'). Not all lecturers who rejected closer liaison did so because they were unsympathetic to teachers. One or two in this category wanted the schools to be more independent of universities. They did not want 'another bureaucratic structure' and felt that 'the school syllabus cannot afford to be too exclusively geared towards the universities'. Another, who *did* favour closer liaison, still said that 'basically I feel schools are not sufficiently independent of universities'. The need for better understanding was expressed by one lecturer in these terms:

> I think there is a big gap in communication between 'A' level teachers and university lecturers - a lack of understanding of each others' aims and criteria of judgment. Teachers think that we are looking for some mysterious quality of 'flair', 'potential', 'literary intelligence'; we think we're looking for simple realistic qualities (e.g. wide reading) which might actually not be realistic in the context of 'A' level work.

However, when one lecturer said in discussion that he favoured liaison because it is necessary 'to meet and talk and devise intelligently a set of procedures and expectations different from the ones we've got at the moment', a colleague remarked that he was doubtful whether such a desirable process could succeed. 'You're asking most university lecturers to start to think in terms of the whole educational programme, which they're very loath to do from sheer habit'. He felt that most preferred to concentrate on their own particular studies, and on the processes with which they were familiar: 'Changing the focus of interest is going to require a great deal of effort'.

Practical proposals for achieving better liaison demonstrated the sense of hierarchy in the educational system. Lecturers were five times more likely to mention kinds of help and guidance which they could offer to schools than to suggest ways in which they might learn something from teachers. Those in schools seemed even less likely to propose ways in which universities might learn from them rather than the other way round.

The most common kinds of assistance offered (and sought) were in literary updating and in the process of entry to higher education. Examples of the first category included this one from a young lecturer, the tone of which some teachers might find rather patronising:

> I suspect that good graduates who go into teaching rapidly sink to the level of the standard syllabus - they shy away from poetry and most literature pre-1850. In order to help them, there should be regular in-service training, in which they return to university for seminar work on texts they find intimidating and approaches they have forgotten.

Others proposed courses 'purely on literature' (since teaching methods for A-level should be the preserve of school-teachers), study days on set texts, information on 'current thinking in English departments', lectures and conferences on 'new approaches to texts'. Several gave details of such courses and conferences in which their own universities were already engaged. One felt that this might be a way of bringing about changes in school practice. She saw it specifically as 'an opportunity to influence the way in which the earlier parts of the syllabus - Chaucer to the Metaphysicals - are taught and examined'. Teachers similarly mentioned - frequently from experience - the potential value of university courses and 'day schools', though with the proviso that 'their value depends very much on the quality of the lecturers'.

Several specifically referred to their need for periodical updating: 'the opportunity to learn about critical theory and new approaches to established authors from lecturers whose main job it is to work with literature at a higher level'; 'I feel particularly cut off from developments in critical theory and approaches to the study of literature'.

There was some difference between the two groups in the way that they viewed the transition between school and university. In brief, lecturers saw the process in terms of their own institutions: their expectations and the degree to which those from school fitted their courses. Teachers were more concerned with the problems of preparing their students for a variety of different institutions, with varied courses and entry procedures. Several lecturers commented about ways in which the transition between school and university might be eased. One proposed 'periods of discussion about the overall process from A-level to degree studies' and another talked of guiding teachers about 'what we shall be expecting from students - that the study of literature doesn't stop at A-level and that students are going to have to read more quickly, more self-reliantly and more adventurously than A-level requires from them'. Teachers were more narrowly concerned with obtaining information about the emphases of different university courses and the criteria by which undergraduates are selected. They said, for example,

- It would help to know more about English degree courses and the qualities which universities looked for in prospective students.
- Clearer explanation of what universities are trying to do and clearer agreement on what English is.
- I'd like to know what sort of background an English lecturer expected from a student - what she feels would be useful preparation for a course.
- We need updating on university/college course requirements.
- To discover from lecturers what they are looking for in selecting students for English courses.
- I should like to know *what* is going on in English departments in various institutions, so that I could feel greater confidence in encouraging my students as to the usefulness of their making applications.
- If lecturers told us in clearer terms what they require, and put pressure on exam boards to alter syllabuses to meet those

requirements, then perhaps there would be less cause for dissatisfaction.

It was suggested earlier that relatively few lecturers mentioned any need for themselves to find out much about schools, or to go into them, though one experienced lecturer who had also spent some years in school-teaching remarked that 'more university teachers ought to understand what happens in schools'. It is, perhaps, possible therefore to sympathise with one very well qualified sixth-form teacher who exclaimed:

Liaison! When do we ever see them in schools? What interest do *they* take in schools, or specifically A-level teaching?

As has been suggested, the A-level teachers were very willing to learn, but a number (particularly the more experienced) felt that lecturers also needed to discover more about what was actually happening in schools, rather than depending on anecdotes and media coverage. They said: 'I think lecturers have a lot to learn', and mentioned more specifically:

- Universities should be more aware of the limitations of school and more involved in the teaching.
- In many cases lecturers seem to have minimal understanding of, or interest in, the range of reading, study skills or ability in the very mixed groups now taking A-level English.
- I'd like to see lecturers visiting schools and involving themselves in teaching and discussion where possible.

One fuller response outlined a wish for

English lecturers coming down to earth and (a) actually being aware of which are the set texts at A-level for a major board, (b) being aware of the constraints on school teachers - lack of technician support, cost of duplication facilities etc, (c) I am appalled to find that many lecturers are still as hooked on 'lit crit' as all my sixth form teachers were over 20 years ago - to the *great* detriment of my personal responses and genuine understanding of literature.

Reactions like these indicated a side-effect of the teachers' general acceptance of a hierarchy in which the lecturers were somehow 'above' them as 'experts'. They resented the impression that the staff in universities controlled the work in schools (through the examination system and by competitive entry criteria) but had unreal expectations because they knew little or nothing about the conditions in which teachers had to work. The significant terminology of one teacher was used to suggest that lecturers should be invited to meet 'ordinary mortals' so that they would not be seen as 'intellectuals inhabiting ivory towers deriding the efforts of mediocre talents in schools, but concerned about the quality of teaching and seen to be doing something to improve this'.

Perhaps as a result of such feelings the teachers as a group were very much more likely than the lecturers to put forward kinds of liaison which involved genuinely joint activities or exchanges. About 65% of the small school sample made such suggestions, compared with 29% of the lecturers. References to working in each other's institutions were mostly brief and lacking detail: 'teacher-lecturer exchange on a termly basis', 'interaction between staff on exchange visits', 'exchange of roles for limited periods', 'secondment for a term or so in both directions'. One more detailed suggestion proposed 'some kind of exchange between willing teachers/lecturers to discover what kinds of learning experiences students are having in the two different kinds of institutions from observation - and perhaps to exchange briefly as teachers'. Two lecturers did make similar proposals - one for limited exchange of classes, the other for a more radical transfer which 'perhaps should be made *compulsory* after, say, 6-7 years in any one institution'.

Although one or two lecturers did mention possible reciprocal arrangements ('liaison work both ways, i.e. including teachers helping lecturers' or 'university lecturers should hear papers by teachers on what they've found in their close teaching of texts'), teachers were much more likely to see joint activities ('a common approach', 'closer working links between both') as desirable. Some of their suggestions included:

- Seminars, informal and formal, that would lead to an increased understanding of each other's teaching aims and methods, and of the viability of their application to each of our needs.
- More workshops rather than lectures ... participation is important.
- Opportunities for meeting and discussion on choice of texts, questions, criteria for assessment.

Conclusion

- *Joint* refresher courses of short duration for both.
- Perhaps a group of teachers in each LEA should liaise with schools, [examination] boards and universities, part of whose brief was to invite lecturers to teachers' centres and assess teacher response to what is offered at A-level.

Some of those who wished for more joint activities suggested that the actual function of these was less important than establishing human contact and greater mutual understanding. One lecturer suggested

> Any kind of forum - lecturers visiting schools, day/residential courses for teachers and universities, joint conferences - in which teachers and lecturers can meet to discuss common problems, exchange ideas, and actually get to *know* each other's attitudes and needs.

The tone of this is very like that of the teacher in school who said that

> Any kind of communication between people in the same field cannot be other than helpful - exchange of ideas on certain topics, and advice to pupils about what to expect out of school.

It appears, then, that although both groups *say* that they would welcome closer liaison, it is mainly the teachers who feel that they have something to gain from this. Most lecturers see liaison as a process in which they would be giving rather than receiving. Only in a few cases does there seem to be a real sense that both groups are essentially engaged on the same work, and that this might be viewed as a partnership. Perhaps this fact in itself suggests how urgent it is to achieve a greater sense of professional unity.

By compartmentalising the developmental processes involved in English studies, ignoring what comes before and after each stage, we have avoided having to grapple with the basic, underlying questions posed in the introduction to this study. Jack Thomson speaks for many of us in a recent book when recording that it was only at the age of 27, after teaching for seven years in secondary schools and embarking on a Masters' degree in English literature, that he was at last 'beginning to learn how to read'. He had moved with apparent success through the different student stages but without ever really comprehending what his English studies were intended to achieve. Those who taught him in school or university, he writes, all proceeded on a series of unspoken and untested assumptions.

> Between what we claim to be teaching in literature and what most of our students are actually experiencing and learning there lies a gigantic chasm.[9]

This book has tried to map some features of that chasm, and to suggest that bridging it will demand the united efforts of all those who work with students of English.

Notes

Introduction

1. D.G. James, 'The teaching of English in universities', *Universities Quarterly*, vol. 5, no. 3, May 1951, p.235. James seems to be echoing T.S. Eliot's 'difficult' question, whether 'the teaching of English literature can rightly be included in any academic curriculum' (*The Use of Poetry and the Use of Criticism*, Faber, 1933, p.36).

2. George Steiner, 'To civilize our gentlemen', *The Listener*, 28 October 1965.

3. These last three questions were raised in R. Ohmann, *English in America*, Oxford UP, New York, 1976, p.257.

4. E.g. Stephen Potter, *The Muse in Chains*, Cape, 1937; E.M.W. Tillyard, *The Muse Unchained*, Bowes & Bowes, Cambridge, 1958; D.J. Palmer, *The Rise of English Studies*, Hull University, 1965; Jo McMurtry, *English Language, English Literature*, Archon, USA, 1985; Gerald Graff, *Professing Literature: an Institutional History*, Chicago UP, 1987.

5. John M. Bowen, 'The subject of "English": psychology and pedagogy from Bain to Richards', Ph.D. thesis, Birmingham University, 1985, p.9.

6. A helpful summary of information about this stage is given in Alan Gordon and Gareth Williams, *Attitudes of Fifth and Sixth Formers to School, Work and Higher Education*, Lancaster University, 1977, pp.12 ff.

7. Bob Redpath and Barbara Harvey, *Young People's Intentions to Enter Higher Education*, HMSO, 1987, p.1.

8. E.g. Peter Marris, *The Experience of Higher Education*, Routledge & Kegan Paul, 1964; W.A. Reid, *The Universities and the Sixth Form Curriculum*, Macmillan, 1972; NFER School to University Research Unit, *The Prediction of Academic Success*, NFER, Slough, 1973; Scottish Education Department, *Transition from School to University*, HMSO, Edinburgh, 1973; University of Western Australia, *Problems of Transition from School to University*, 1973.

9. Scottish Education Department, *Transition from School to University*, HMSO, Edinburgh, 1973, pars. 1.1 and 1.3.

10. Robert Protherough, *Teaching Literature for Examinations*, Open University Press, Milton Keynes, 1986, chapters 1-3.

11. Roma Morton-Williams, *et al.*, *Sixth Form Pupils and Teachers*, Schools Council, 1970, and Bob Redpath and Barbara Harvey, *Young People's Intentions to Enter Higher Education, HMSO, 1987*.

Chapter 1 English as a Subject

1. D. Duckworth and N.J. Entwistle, 'Attitudes to school subjects: a repertory grid technique', *British Journal of Educational Psychology*, vol. 44, 1974, pp.76-88.

2. E.g. *Educational Studies in Mathematics*, vol. 13, no. 4, 1982; *Teaching History*, vol. 33, June 1982; *British Journal of Language Teaching*, vol. 21, no. 1, 1982 and vol. 21, no. 3, 1983.

3. E.g. Lynda Measor, 'Gender and the sciences', in M. Hammersley and P. Woods, *Life in School*, Open University Press, Milton Keynes, 1984, pp.89-105; R. Deem, *Schooling for Women's Work*, Routledge, 1980.

4. P. Woods, 'The myth of subject choice', in Hammersley and Woods, *Life in School*, pp.45-60.

5. Duckworth and Entwistle, 'Attitudes to school subjects' p.79.

6. DES, *Young School Leavers*, Schools Council Enquiry 1, HMSO, 1968, pp.61-2, 67, 70. Compare Lynda Measor, 'Pupil perceptions of subject status' in I.F. Goodson and S.J. Ball, *Defining the Curriculum: Histories and Ethnographies*, Falmer Press, Lewes, 1984, pp.201 ff: 'Everyone agreed that maths and English were the most important subjects'.

7. Robert Witkin, *The Intelligence of Feeling*, Heinemann, 1974.

8. M. Stubbs and S. Delamont, *Explorations in Classroom Observation*, Wiley, 1976, p.57.

9. Paul Bench, 'Pupil responses to reading and literature at O-level in secondary schools', M.Ed. dissertation, Birmingham University, 1985.

10. *British Social Attitudes*, SCPR, Gower, 1986.

11. *Sunday Times*, 17 March 1963.

12. *Guardian*, 6 April 1987.

13. Ken Fogelman, *Britain's Sixteen-year-olds*, National Children's Bureau, 1976, p.46.

14. Ibid, p.45.

15. Brian Goacher, *Selection Post-16: the Role of Examination Results*, Methuen, 1984, pp.47-8.

16. NFER School to University Research Unit, *The Prediction of Academic Success*, NFER, Slough, 1973, p.21.

17. Ibid, p.26.

18. See J.T. Hodgson, 'Changes in English teaching: institutionalization, transmission and ideology', Ph.D. thesis, London University, 1975; Gerald Grace, *Teachers, Ideology and Control*, Routledge and Kegan Paul, 1978; Douglas and Dorothy Barnes with Stephen Clarke, *Versions of English*, Heinemann, 1984; S.J. Ball, 'Competition and conflict in the teaching of English: a socio-historical analysis', *Journal of Curriculum Studies*, vol. 14, no. 1, 1982; S.J. Ball and C. Lacy 'Subject disciplines as the opportunity for group action', in Peter Woods, *Teacher Strategies*, Croom Helm, 1980.

19. Harold Rosen, *Neither Bleak House nor Liberty Hall*, University of London Institute of Education, 1981, p.5.

20. For a fuller treatment of this topic see Robert Protherough's chapter on 'English' in M. Rayner and P. Wiegand, *Curriculum Progress*, Croom Helm (in press).

21. R. Morton-Williams *et al*, *Sixth Form Pupils and Teachers*, Schools Council, 1970, p.366.

22. Caroline St John Brooks in Goodson and Ball, *Defining the Curriculum*, pp.39-40.

23. Considering the annual primary and secondary language surveys of the APU, Peter Silvester HMI writes, 'It is pleasing to report that there has been an evident improvement over the five years in reading as well as a small improvement in writing' (APU *Newsletter*, no. 9, Spring 1987).

24. E.g. T. Christie and G.M. Forrest, *Standards at GCE A-level 1963 and 1973* (a pilot examination of examination standards in three subjects), Macmillan, Basingstoke, 1980.

25. Stephen J. Ball, 'A subject of privilege: English and the school curriculum 1906-35', in Goodson and Ball, *Defining the Curriculum*, pp.34-7.

26. C. Burt, 'The mental differences between children', *Black Paper Two*, 1969, pp.23-4.

27. Dr J. Marenbon, *English, Our English*, Centre for Policy Studies, 1987, pp.33-5.

28. Ibid, p.38.

29. Ibid, p.39.

30. Philip J. Hartog, *The Writing of English*, Clarendon Press, Oxford, 1907, and J.H. Fowler, address of February 1908.

31. E.A. Peers, *Journal of English Studies*, vol. 3, no. 1, June 1914, p.15 and S.P.B. Mais, *Journal of English Studies*, vol. 2, no. 3, Jan-May 1914, pp.187-8.

32. Cambridge UP, 1987.

33. Ian Michael, 'The historical study of English as a subject: a preliminary enquiry into some questions of method', *History of Education*, vol. 8, no. 3, 1979, p.201.

34. Robert Protherough, 'The figure of the teacher in English literature 1740-1918', Ph.D. thesis, Hull University, 1981.

35. Ivor F. Goodson, *School Subjects and Curriculum Change*, Croom Helm, 1983.

36. See Thomas S. Popkewitz, *The Formation of the School Subjects*, Falmer Press, Lewes, 1987.

37. See Gerald Graff, *Professing Literature: an Institutional History*, Chicago UP, 1987.

38. Brian A. Doyle, 'English and Englishness: a cultural history of English studies in British higher education 1850-1980', Ph.D. thesis, CNAA, Thames Polytechnic, 1986, p.91.

39. S.J. Ball, 'English for the English since 1906', in Ivor F. Goodson, *Social Histories of the Secondary Curriculum: Subjects for Study*, Falmer Press, Lewes, 1985, p.53.

40. A.N. Applebee, *Tradition and Reform in the Teaching of English: a History*, NCTE, Urbana, Illinois, 1974, p.1.

41. See Louis Wright, *Middle-Class Culture in Elizabethan England*, North Carolina UP, Chapel Hill, 1935, and Frank Davies, *Teaching Reading in Early England*, Pitman, 1973.

42. Richard Mulcaster, *The Educational Writings*, James Maclehose, Glasgow, 1903, pp.183, 186.

43. Ibid.

44. James Cleland, *The institution of a young noble man*, J. Barnes, Oxford, 1607 (Scholars facsimiles and reprints, New York 1948).

45. Charles Hoole, *A New Discovery of the old Art of Teaching Schoole*, J.T. for Andrew Cook, 1660, (facsimile Scolar Press, Menston, 1969).

46. John Brinsley, *Ludus Literarius: or the Grammar Schoole*, Thomas Man, 1612 (facsimile Scolar Press, 1968).

47. Edmund Coote, *The English Schoole-maister*, Jackson and Dexter, 1596 (facsimile Scolar Press, 1968).

48. Mulcaster, *The Educational Writings*, James Maclehose, Glasgow, 1903.

49. J. Lawson and H. Silver, *A Social History of Education in England*, Methuen, 1973, p.113.

50. Margaret Mathieson, *The Preachers of Culture*, George Allen and Unwin, 1975, p.17.

51. See David Shayer, *The Teaching of English in Schools 1900-1970*, Routledge and Kegan Paul, 1972, chapter 1.

52. Michael Paffard, *Thinking about English*, Ward Lock, 1978, p.14.

53. Alice Zimmern, 'Literature as a central subject', *The Journal of Education*, September 1900, pp.588-9.

54. See Edward C. Mack, *Public Schools and British Opinion 1780-1860*, Methuen, 1938.

55. S.J. Ball, 'A subject of privilege: English and the school curriculum 1906-35' in Goodson and Ball, *Defining the Curriculum*, p.83.

56. Lawson and Silver, *A Social History of Education in England*, p.345.

57. Mathieson, *The Preachers of Culture*, p.43.

58. Lawson and Silver, *A Social History of Education in England*, pp.304-5.

59. Ball, 'A subject of privilege', p.35.

60. Graff, *Professing Literature*, p.99.

61. Ibid, p.79.

62. Board of Education, *The Teaching of English in Secondary Schools*, HMSO, 1910, para. 1.

63. Commissioner Bruce's internal memo to Morant, 8 December 1910, cited Ball, 'A subject of privilege', p.69.

64. *The Teaching of English in Secondary Schools*, para. 7.

65. Shayer, *The Teaching of English in Schools, 1900-1970*, p.67.

66. DES, *A Language for Life*, HMSO, 1975 and HMI, *Aspects of Secondary Education in England*, HMSO, 1979.

67. S.P.B. Mais, 'Some results of English teaching at public schools', *Journal of English Studies*, vol. 2, no. 3, Jan-May 1914, pp.187-8.

68. *The Cambridge Magazine*, 31 January 1914.

69. Introduction to W.H. Mason, *For Teachers of English*, Blackwell, Oxford, 1964.

70. *The Teaching of English in England*, HMSO, 1921, para. 237.

71. Ibid, para. 11.

72. Ibid, para. 2.

73. Margaret Mathieson, 'Persistence and change in the claims for English in schools', *Educational Studies*, vol. 2, no. 3, 1976, p.217.

74. *The Teaching of English in England*, para. 259.

75. Doyle, 'English and Englishness', p.178.

76. *The Teaching of English in England*, para. 6.

77. Board of Education, *Report of the Consultative Committee on Secondary Education*, HMSO, 1939, pp.173, 218.

78. Board of Education, *Curriculum and Examinations in Secondary Schools*, HMSO, 1943, p.91.

79. Terry Eagleton, *Literary Theory: an introduction*, Blackwell, Oxford, 1983, pp.31-2.

80. Anne Beezer *et al*, in David Punter, *Introduction to Contemporary Cultural Studies*, Longman, 1986, p.95.

81. Board of Education, *The Teaching of English in Secondary Schools*, para. 2.

82. See Alan Bacon, 'Attempts to introduce a school of English literature at Oxford: the national debate of 1886 and 1887', *History of Education*, vol. 9, no. 4, December 1980, and Jo McMurtry, *English Language and English Literature*, Archon, USA, 1985.

83. E.M.W. Tillyard, *The Muse Unchained*, Bowes and Bowes, Cambridge, 1958.

84. Marjorie Daunt, *Universities Quarterly*, vol. 5, no. 3, May 1951, pp.239 ff.

85. P. Doughty, J. Pearce and G. Thornton, *Language in Use*, Arnold, 1971.

86. S.J. Burke and C.J. Brumfit, in *English in Education*, vol. 8, no. 2, Summer 1974.

87. *Universities Quarterly*, vol. 5, no. 3, May 1951, p.237.

88. E.D. Hirsch, Jr., *Times Literary Supplement*, 10 December 1982.

89. Graff, *Professing Literature*, p.67.

90. Winifred Bryan Horner, *Composition and Literature*, Chicago UP, 1983, p.5.

91. See Robert Protherough, *Teaching Literature for Examinations*, Open University Press, Milton Keynes, 1986, pp.46-51.

92. J. Hillis Miller, in Horner, *Composition and Literature*, pp.41-2.

93. G.D. Atkins and M.L. Johnson, *Writing and Reading Differently*, Kansas UP, 1985, p.3.

94. David Kaufer and Gary Walker, ibid, p.71.

95. Nancy R. Comley, ibid, pp.130-1.

96. Peter Marris, *The Experience of Higher Education*, Routledge and Kegan Paul, 1964, pp.28-30.

97. Derek Bosworth and Janet Ford, 'Perceptions of higher education by university entrants: an exploratory study', *Studies in Higher Education*, 1967, p.10.

98. Donald Hutchings, *The Science Undergraduate*, Oxford University Department of Education, 1967, p.10.

99. Linda Garratt, 'Factors affecting subject choice at A-level', *Educational Studies*, vol. 11, no. 2, 1985, pp.127-32.

100. P. Woods, 'The myth of subject choice' in Hammersley and Woods, *Life in School*, pp.45-60.

101. Bob Redpath and Barbara Harvey, *Young People's Intentions to Enter Higher Education*, HMSO, 1987, p.25.

102. Malcolm Yorke, *English in Education*, vol. 8, no. 2, Summer 1974, and vol. 13, no. 1, Spring 1979, and *Use of English*, vol. 29, no. 3, Summer 1978.

103. Roma Morton-Williams *et al*, *Sixth Form Pupils and Teachers*, point out the continuing popularity of this combination, especially for girls.

104. Ball, 'A subject of privilege', p.75.

105. Schools Council, *The Examination Courses of First Year Sixth Formers*, Macmillan, 1973.

106. Redpath and Harvey, *Young People's Intentions to Enter Higher Education*, p.32.

107. NFER School to University Research Unit, *The Prediction of Academic Success*, p.23.

Chapter 2 The Students of English

1. Douglas and Dorothy Barnes with Stephen Clarke, *Versions of English*, Heinemann, 1974.

2. John Dixon, *Education 16-19*, Macmillan, 1979, p.20.

3. See the Further Education Unit, *Language for All*, 1986, pp.17-19.

4. Bob Redpath and Barbara Harvey, *Young People's Intentions to Enter Higher Education*, HMSO, 1987, p.7.

5. *Duet 8* working papers, University of East Anglia, 1987, p.4.

6. Brian Austin-Ward, 'English, English teaching and English teachers: the perceptions of 16-year-olds', *Educational Research*, vol. 28, no. 1, February 1986, p.37.

7. Ibid, p.39.

8. Ibid, p.37.

9. Ibid, p.38.

10. Nicola Burston, 'English and communications at 16+: a study of courses, literature and student and staff responses', M.Ed. dissertation, Birmingham University, 1987.

11. Ibid, pp.50-1, 76.

12. Ibid, pp.52-67.

13. M.E. Williams, 'Communications and general studies in further education - some students', staff and employers' views', B.Phil. (Ed.) dissertation, Birmingham University, 1977, pp.47-51.

14. Ibid, pp.39-40.

15. Dixon, *Education 16-19*, p.43.

16. Board of Education, Consultative committee on the differentiation of the curriculum for boys and girls respectively in secondary schools, HMSO, 1923.

17. These and the following figures are drawn from the DES annual *Statistics of Education*.

18. Roma Morton-Williams *et al.*, *Sixth Form Pupils and Teachers*, Schools Council, 1970, p.26.

19. DES statistics and Redpath and Harvey, *Young People's Intentions*.

20. DES *Statistics of Education*.

21. HMI, *A survey of the teaching of 'A' level English literature in 20 mixed sixth forms in comprehensive schools*, DES, 1986, para. 2.2.

22. Paul Lodge and Tessa Blackstone, *Educational Policy and*

Educational Inequality, Martin Robertson, Oxford, 1982, p.207.

23. Peter Marris, *The Experience of Higher Education*, Routledge and Kegan Paul, 1964, p.30.

24. Redpath and Harvey, *Young People's Intentions*, p.32.

25. Figures supplied by the Graduate Teacher Training Registry.

26. Ibid.

27. DES *Statistics of Education.*

28. Redpath and Harvey, *Young People's Intentions*, p.72.

29. Alan Gordon and Gareth Williams, *Attitudes of fifth and sixth formers to school, work and higher education*, Lancaster University for the DES, 1977, p.188.

30. Gordon and Williams provide a convenient summary of much of this work on pp.15-17, 128-30, 188ff.

31. Redpath and Harvey, *Young People's Intentions*, p.63.

32. Ibid.

33. This suggests that there has been little change since the 1970 Schools Council Survey, which classified 52% of sixth formers' parents in the upper two social groups and only 8% in the lower two.

34. E. Rudd, 'Students and social class', *Studies in Higher Education*, vol. 12, no. 1, 1987, pp.99-106.

35. *Committee on Higher Education*, HMSO, 1963, Appendix 1, p.46.

36. Lodge and Blackstone, *Educational Policy and Educational Inequality*, p.210.

37. Redpath and Harvey, *Young People's Intentions*, p.26.

38. Ibid, p.27.

39. UCCA reports.

40. HMI, *A Survey of the Teaching of 'A' Level English*, para. 2.2.

41. Ibid, para. 2.2.

42. Ibid, para. 2.3.

43. W.A. Reid, *The Universities and the Sixth Form Curriculum*, Schools Council, Macmillan, 1972, p.58.

44. Ibid, p.43.

45. Brian Heap, *Degree Course Offers 1986*, Careers consultants, 1987.

46. Reid, *The Universities and the Sixth Form Curriculum*, p.75.

47. Ian Robinson, 'UCCA to what?', *Use of English*, vol. 34, no. 3, Summer 1983, pp.23-33.

48. NFER School to University Research Unit, *The Prediction of Academic Success*, NFER, Slough, 1972, pp.35 and 63; Kevin Sear, 'The correlation between 'A' level grades and degree results in England and Wales', *Higher Education*, vol. 12, 1983, pp.609-19; Tom Bourner, *Entry Qualifications and Degree Performance*, CNAA, 1987.

49. A.H. Iliffe, *The Foundation Year in the University of Keele: a Report*, Keele University, 1969.

50. Arnold Kettle and Gordon Martin in D. Craig and M. Heinemann, *Experiments in English Teaching*, Arnold, 1976, p.20.

51. Reid, *The Universities and Sixth Form Curriculum*, pp.75-6.

52. Ibid, pp.40-1.

53. See Robert Protherough, *Teaching Literature for Examinations*, Open University Press, Milton Keynes, 1986, pp.6-7.

54. Marris, *The Experience of Higher Education*, p.177.

Chapter 3 Development and Continuity

1. *Universities Quarterly*, vol. 5, no. 1, November 1950.
2. Ibid, p.22.
3. Ibid, p.16.
4. Ibid, pp.22-3.
5. Ibid, p.17.
6. *Universities Quarterly*, vol. 5, no. 3, May 1951, p.217.
7. Robert Protherough, *Developing Response to Fiction*, Open University Press, Milton Keynes, 1983, pp.9-12.
8. APU, *Language Performance in School*, Secondary Survey report 1, HMSO, 1982, pp.49-50.
9. I am grateful to Judith Atkinson for these recent student comments on GCSE English.
10. Roma Morton-Williams *et al.*, *Sixth Form Pupils and Teachers*, Schools Council, 1970, pp.75-93.
11. E.g. A.N. Applebee, James Britton, John Dixon, David Holbrook, D.W. Harding, Barbara Hardy, Margaret Spencer, Michael Tucker, Frank Whitehead.
12. E.g. Protherough, *Developing Response to Fiction*, chapters 1-3; Judith Atkinson, 'How children read poems at different ages', *English in Education*, vol. 19, no. 1, Spring 1985; and Jack Thomson, *Understanding Teenagers' Reading*, Methuen, Australia, 1987.
13. Frank Whitehead *et al.*, *Children and Their Books*, Macmillan, Basingstoke, 1977 (see especially pp.113, 125-9, 151-3).

Chapter 4 Courses of Study

1. HMI, *English From 5 to 16: the Responses to Curriculum Matters 1*, DES, 1986.
2. Peter Medway, 'What counts as English?' Ph.D. thesis, Leeds University, 1986.
3. Raymond Williams, 'Literature *in* society' in Hilda Schiff, *Contemporary Approaches to English Studies*, Heinemann, 1970, p.30.
4. DUET no. 8 papers, University of East Anglia, 1987.
5. Richard Lanham, 'One, two, three' in W.B. Horner, *Composition and Literature: Bridging the Gap*, Chicago UP, 1983, pp.15-16.
6. Roma Morton-Williams *et al.*, *Sixth Form Pupils and Teachers*, Schools Council, 1970, pp.166-7.
7. Horner, *Composition and Literature*, p.4.
8. Raymond Williams, *Keywords*, Fontana, 1976.
9. Rene Wellek, *The Attack on Literature and Other Essays*, Harvester Press, Brighton, 1982, p.15.
10. *Critical Quarterly*, vol. 28, nos 1 and 2, Spring/Summer 1986, p.4.
11. Sir Arthur Quiller-Couch, *On the Art of Reading*, Cambridge UP, 1921, p.95.
12. This point is more fully treated in Robert Protherough, *Developing Response to Fiction*, Open University Press, Milton Keynes, 1983, pp.26-9.

13. Terry Eagleton, *Literary Theory: an Introduction*, Blackwell, Oxford, 1983, p.208.

14. F.R. Leavis, *Education and the University*, Chatto and Windus, 1943.

15. *Times Educational Supplement*, 10 December 1982, symposium 'Professing literature'.

16. Ibid.

17. Robert Protherough, *Teaching Literature for Examinations*, Open University Press, Milton Keynes, 1986, pp.70-1, 96-7, 123-4.

18. B.W. Caws, 'A consideration of the effect upon candidates' performance in Advanced level of (1) textual choice and (2) question choice', M.Phil. thesis, Southampton University, 1977.

19. See Gill Parsons, 'English literature: teachers, relevance and the "great tradition" ' *Education for Development*, vol. 6, no. 3, April 1981, pp.31-41.

20. Dr John Marenbon, *English, Our English*, Centre for Policy Studies, 1987, p.26.

21. George Steiner, 'Why English?' in Schiff, *Contemporary Approaches to English Studies*, pp.9, 11, 19.

22. Colin MacCabe, 'Broken English', *Critical Quarterly*, vol. 18, nos 1 and 2, Spring/Summer 1986, p.4.

23. Schiff, *Contemporary Approaches to English Studies*, p.25.

24. Tony Bennett, *Formalism and Marxism*, Methuen, 1979, p.8.

25. Gerald Graff, *Professing Literature*, Chicago UP, 1987, p.7.

26. Ibid, p.8.

27. Quiller-Couch, *On the Art of Reading*, p.vi.

28. Ibid, pp.67-9.

29. Ibid, pp.91-2.

30. Ibid, p.70.

31. Ibid, p.35.

32. Ibid, p.71.

33. Ibid, p.75.

34. Ibid, p.93.

35. Ibid, p.8.

36. F.R. Leavis, *How to Teach Reading: a Primer for Ezra Pound*, Minority Press, Cambridge, 1932, p.26.

37. Ibid, p.26.

38. Ibid, pp.34 and 40-1, my italics.

39. Ibid, p.26.

40. Ibid, pp.40-1.

41. Ibid, pp.40-2.

42. I.A. Richards, *Practical Criticism*, Kegan Paul, Trench, Trubner & Co., 1929.

43. E.L. Black, 'The difficulty of training college students in understanding what they read', *British Journal of Educational Psychology*, vol. 24, 1954, pp.17-31.

44. I.A. Richards, 'What is involved in the interpretation of meaning', in William S. Gray, *Reading and Pupil Development*, supplementary educational monographs 51, October 1940, University of Chicago, p.49.

45. Louise Rosenblatt, *The Reader, the Text, the Poem*, South Illinois UP, 1978, p.ix.

46. Ibid, p.11.

47. Ibid, p.137.

48. Ibid, pp.142-3.

49. Jonathan Culler, *On Deconstruction*, Routledge & Kegan Paul, 1983, p.37.

50. Morton-Williams *et al.*, *Sixth Form Pupils and Teachers*, pp.369-71.

51. W.W. Robson, *The Definition of Literature and Other Essays*, Cambridge UP, 1982, pp.1-19.

52. General Certificate of Secondary Education, *The National Criteria: English*, HMSO, 1985.

53. Ibid.

54. HMI, *Aspects of Secondary Education in England and Wales*, HMSO, 1979.

Chapter 5 Teaching and Learning

1. Stephen J. Ball, 'A subject of privilege: English and the school curriculum 1906-35', in I.F. Goodson and S.J. Ball, *Defining the Curriculum: Histories and Ethnographies*, Falmer Press, Lewes, 1984, p.65.

2. V de S. Pinto, 'Notes on the School of English Studies in the University of Nottingham', *Universities Quarterly*, vol. 5, no. 3, May 1951, p.230.

3. F.W. Bateson, *Essays in Criticism*, vol. 9, no. 3, July 1959, p.265, and John Michael Bowen, 'The subject of "English": psychology and pedagogy from Bain to Richards', Ph.D. thesis, Birmingham University, 1985, pp.359-60.

4. J.M. Newton, 'Literary criticism, universities, murder', *The Cambridge Quarterly*, vol. 5, no. 14, pp.335-54.

5. K. Brown and C. Campos, 'Lit. Studies and Eng. Lit. - the logic of success', *Universities Quarterly*, vol. 26, no. 1, Winter 1971, p.53.

6. Ibid, p.48.

7. *English in Education*, vol. 7, no. 1, Spring 1973, p.27.

8. Graham Gibbs, *Teaching Students to Learn*, Open University Press, Milton Keynes, 1981, chapter 4.

9. Robert Protherough, *The Development of Readers*, Hull University, 1983, pp.55-71.

10. Robert Protherough, 'The stories that readers tell', in E. Evans and W. Corcoran, *Readers, Texts, Teachers*, Open University Press, Milton Keynes, 1987, pp.75-92.

11. Norman N. Holland, *Poems in Persons*, Norton, New York, 1973, p.130.

12. James Gribble, *Literary Education: A Revaluation*, Cambridge UP, 1983, p.32.

13. R. Bolt and R. Gard, *Teaching Fiction in Schools*, Hutchinson,

1970, p.15; Louise M. Rosenblatt, *The Reader, the Text, the Poem*, S. Illinois UP, 1978, p.137.

14. D. Craig and M. Heinemann, *Experiments in English Teaching*, Arnold, 1976.

15. Robert Protherough, *Teaching Literature for Examinations*, Open University Press, Milton Keynes, 1986.

16. In what follows the main headings are taken from *Experiencing A-level - Aspects of Quality*, DES, 1987, pars. 2.4 - 2.7, with supporting details from *A Survey of the Teaching of 'A' level English*, DES, 1985.

17. Conveniently summarised in Herbert W. Marsh, 'Students evaluations of university teaching: research findings, methodological issues, and directions for future research', *International Journal of Educational Research*, vol. 11, no. 3, 1987.

18. Audrey Third, 'Talking books', *Times Educational Supplement*, 2 October 1982.

19. Martin Reed, 'A study of literature teaching in two colleges', Birmingham M.Ed. dissertation, 1985, pp.48-50.

20. Roma Morton Williams, *et al.*, *Sixth Form Pupils and Teachers*, Schools Council, 1970, p.198.

21. Ibid, pp.200-1.

22. Ibid, p.368.

23. E.g. John McLeish, 'Lecture, tutorial, seminar: the students' view', *Education for Teaching*, Spring 1968, pp.21-7.

24. David Raffe, *Fourteen to Eighteen*, Aberdeen UP, 1984, pp.62-4.

25. HMI, *A Survey of the Teaching of 'A' level English*, para. 3.3.

26. Ibid.

27. John Broadbent in David Punter, *Introduction to Contemporary Cultural Studies*, Longman, 1986, p.318.

28. J.S. Bruner, *Towards a Theory of Instruction*, Oxford UP, 1960.

29. Craig and Heinemann, *Experiments in English Teaching*, p.37.

30. Ibid, p.38.

31. Punter, *Introduction to Contemporary Cultural Studies*, p.121.

32. Ibid, pp.314-28.

Chapter 6 The Assessment Process

1. Alan Bacon, *History of Education*, vol. 9, no. 4, December 1980, pp.303-13.

2. D.J. Palmer, *The Rise of English Studies*, Hull University, 1965, p.165.

3. Board of Education, *Report of the Consultative Committee on Examinations in Secondary Schools*, HMSO, 1911, p.76.

4. Board of Education, *Report of the Consultative Committee on Secondary Education*, HMSO, 1939, pp.78-9, 175.

5. Board of Education, *Curriculum and Examinations in Secondary Schools*, HMSO, 1943, p.76.

6. L.C. Knights, 'Scrutiny of examinations', *Scrutiny*, vol. 2, no. 2, September 1933, p.158.

7. Stephen Potter, *The Muse in Chains*, Cape, 1937.

8. F.R. Leavis, *Education and the University*, Chatto and Windus, 1943.

9. Similar criticisms from individual teachers had, of course, been common in the 1920s and 1930s (see David Shayer, *The Teaching of English in Schools 1900-1970*, Routledge & Kegan Paul, 1972, p.115).

10. Peter Marris, *The Experience of Higher Education*, Routledge & Kegan Paul, 1964, p.180.

11. 'The future of English Studies', *Times Educational Supplement*, 25 July 1968.

12. Ibid, pp.773-4.

13. Board of Education, *The Teaching of English in England*, HMSO, 1921.

14. Robert Protherough, *Teaching Literature for Examinations*, Open University Press, Milton Keynes, 1986, p.7.

15. G.K. and S.K. Hunter, 'The transition from sixth form to university', *Aspects of Education*, no. 4, Hull University, 1966, pp.102-9.

16. Schools Council, *Sixth Form Examining Methods*, HMSO, 1968, pp.4-5.

17. Elizabeth Gordon, *Answering English Literature Questions*, Macmillan, 1983, pp.vii-viii.

18. HMI, *A Survey of the Teaching of 'A' Level English Literature in 20 Mixed Sixth Forms in Comprehensive Schools*, DES, 1986, pars. 3.3-3.5.

19. Protherough, *Teaching Literature for Examinations*, pp.20-1.

20. D. and D. Barnes, *Versions of English*, Heinemann, 1984, p.215.

21. Patricia Broadfoot, 'Assessment constraints on curriculum practice: a comparative study', in M. Hammersley and A. Hargreaves, *Curriculum Practice: Some Sociological Case Studies*, Falmer Press, Lewes, 1983, pp.251-69. Also see the essays by Glenn Turner, John Scarth, and Richard Bone and Geoff Whitty in the same volume.

22. See John Butt in *Universities Quarterly*, vol. 5, no. 3, May 1951, pp.219-21; Stephen Potter, *The Muse in Chains*, pp.152-3; Lionel Gossman in *New Literary History*, vol. 13, no. 2, Winter 1982, p.369; John M. Bowen, 'The subject of "English": psychology and pedagogy from Bain to Richards', Ph.D. thesis, Birmingham University, 1985, pp.147-9 and 438-9.

23. John Dixon and John Brown, *Responses to Literature - what is being assessed?* Schools Council, 1985.

24. *The English Magazine*, no. 12, Spring 1984, pp.21-2.

25. London, 1969 (references to examiners' reports on English at A-level here and in the following cases simply give the name of the Board and the date).

26. Oxford, 1984.

27. Oxford and Cambridge, 1984.

28. AEB, 1985.

29. Cambridge, 1984.

30. Ann Turner, 'Wanted: good Hardy teacher', *Use of English*, vol. 32, no. 2, Spring 1981, p.14.

31. P.A. Lapworth, *Marking A-level English Literature*, JMB, Manchester, 1983, p.10.

32. London, 1969.

33. Lapworth, *Marking A-level English Literature*, p.7.

34. JMB, 1984.

35. Lapworth, *Marking A-level English Literature*, p.7.

36. AEB, 1984 and 1986.

37. Oxford, 1984.

38. AEB, 1985 (alternative 660).

39. AEB, 1984 (alternative 753).

40. AEB, 1986.

41. See Jim Sweetman, 'Examining literature through the creative response', *English in Education*, vol. 21, no. 1, Spring 1987, pp.55-62.

42. John Saunders in Richard Adams, *Teaching Shakespeare*, Robert Royce, 1985, pp.98 ff.

43. Questions 1, 3, 5, 7 and 9 are from A-level papers and the others from Finals.

44. Helen M.L. Butler, 'The reader's response and A-level English literature', M.Ed. dissertation, Birmingham University, 1984.

45. R. Ohmann, *English in America*, Oxford UP, New York, 1976, pp.58-60.

Conclusion

1. R. Ohmann, *English in America*, Oxford UP, New York, 1976, p.24.

2. HMI, *Experiencing A-level - Aspects of Quality*, DES, 1987, para.4.20.

3. Peter Hollindale, 'University English and the sixth form', *Use of English*, vol. 37, no. 2, Spring 1986, p.34.

4. Emrys Evans, *The Critical Survey*, vol. 3, no. 3, Winter 1967, pp.184-8.

5. David Self, *The Critical Survey*, vol. 1, no. 3, Autumn 1963, p.176.

6. G.D. Grayson, *The Critical Survey*, vol. 1, no. 4, Summer 1964, p.215.

7. Hollindale, 'University English and the sixth form', p.36.

8. *Times Educational Supplement*, 9 January 1976.

9. Jack Thomson, *Understanding Teenagers' Reading*, Methuen Australia, 1987.

Index

A-level English, 2, 7, 17, 22, 23, 28, 33, 34, 35, 36, 37, 38–39, 40, 41, 46–7, 58–60, 61–6, 83–4, 106–7, 138, 139, 143–4, 145, 148–50, 151–3, 154–7, 165–71, 174, 177
A-level English: alternative syllabuses, 107, 108–9, 145, 148–9, 156–7, 170
A-level English language, 22, 80, 109
A-level English language and literature, 22–3, 80, 109
A-level survey, *see* Her Majesty's Inspectorate
AS-level English, 23, 109, 174
Assessment of Performance Unit, APU, 10, 56
Art of Reading, on the, 87–9
assessment, 1, 2, 4, 7, 77, 92, 136–71, 175; views of students, 140–1, 142–3, 144, 173; views of 16+ students, 75, 144; views of A-level students, 144, 145–7; views of university students, 76–7, 144, 147–8; views of teachers, 50, 141–2, 148–50; views of university lecturers, 50–1, 142, 150–3; *see also*: continuous assessment, examinations

Black Papers, 177
Bullock Report, the (1975), *A language for life,* 17

Certificate of Extended Education, CEE, 37, 40
classics, 10, 13–14, 15–16, 19, 22, 117
Code of Regulations, Board of Education (1904), 16–17, 21
communications (*see* media studies)
continuity, 4, 54–77, 119–20, 121, 172, 174, 175–84; views of 16+ students, 71–2, 105, 122–3; views of A-level students, 57–8, 67–8, 68, 69–70; views of university students, 58–9, 68, 69–71; views of teachers, 51–3, 60–1, 62–3, 127; views of university lecturers, 51–3, 60
continuous assessment, 5, 6, 145–6, 148, 148–9, 152, 175

Critical Quarterly Society, 176–7
criticism, literary, 23, 25, 31, 58, 59, 64, 67, 71, 78, 81, 82, 87–92, 93, 98–100, 111, 112, 113, 118, 119, 120, 128, 140, 157, 174, 175; views of students and teachers, 73, 93, 98–100
curriculum, English in, *see* English in the curriculum
curriculum, literary *see* literary curriculum, the

Dartmouth Conference, the, 66
Department of Education and Science, DES, 17
development of response, 66–77, 120, 174
drama, 21, 34, 82, 124–5, 130
Development of University English teaching project (DUET), 132, 133
Dyke-Acland Report (1911), 136

English Association, the, 17, 18
English as subject, 1, 2, 4, 5–35, 78; views of students, 5–6, 6, 7, 26–8, 31–2; views of 16+ students, 3, 6, 28–9; views of A-level students, 3, 28–32, 49–50, 80, 172; views of university students, 3, 30–1, 50, 172; views of teachers, 3, 7–8, 26–8, 29, 30–1; views of lecturers, 3, 7, 8, 26–8, 30–1;
English, as subject, history of, 2, 11–21, 136–138
English as dual subject, 16–17, 21–26
English courses of study, 4, 78–116; views of students, 78; views of 16+ students, 56, 104–6; views of A-level students, 49, 100–2, 107–8, 108–9, 111–12, 113–15; views of university students, 50, 102–4, 110–12, 113, 115–16; views of teachers, 60–1, 62–3, 112; views of university lecturers, 63–4, 108, 112–13
English from 5 to 16, 9, 78
English in Education, 138
English in Further Education, 37–40, 46
English in the curriculum, 6–7, 9, 11, 12, 16–17, 21, 42, 82

Index

English language, 9–10, 13–15, 23–6, 65–6
English lecturers, 48, 50–1, 52, 53; see also views of lecturers
English leterature, 1, 15–16, 19, 21, 22, 39–40
English, perceptions of, 5–11, 37–40, 78–9, 172; see also views of students; views of A-level students; views of 16+ students; views of university students; views of teachers; views of lectures
English students, balance of sexes; see gender differences
English, students' motives for studying 1, 2, 15–16, 19–20, 26–32, 172; see also influence of English courses
English, students of, 1, 2, 4, 36–53; see also views of English students; views of 16+ students; views of A–level students; views of university students
English, students of, A-level, 41–3, 44–5, 46–7; see also views of A-level students
English, students of, university, 41, 43, 45–6, 46, 47; see also views of university students
English students, their academic record, 41, 46–7, 173
English students, their social background, 41, 44–6, 49, 173
English students, their subject choices, 32–5
English, teachers of, 1, 2, 6, 7, 12, 17–18, 19, 40, 43, 48, 50, 51, 52–3, 65, 73–6, 92–3
English teachers, training of, 43–4, 66, 128, 130, 174, 179–80
English, teaching methods, 1, 4, 87, 87–92, 117–135, 120–135, 139
English teaching, paradigms of, 8, 173
English, university, 1, 2, 3, 19–20, 20, 23–6, 34, 78–9, 81, 84, 85–7, 109–10, 117–18, 119–20, 131–5, 136, 147, 165, 166, 174–5
English, writing in, 1, 9–11, 15, 21–22, 24–26, 79, 80, 81, 111, 126, 129, 149–150, 163–4
examination boards, 22–3, 153–7, 170, 177
examination questions, examples of, 143, 158–63, 166–170

examinations, 2, 7, 136–71; see also A-level English; AS-level English; CEE; GCSE; O-level English; sixteen plus English; university examinations
examiners, attitudes of, 140–1, 153–7, 157–65

GCSE English, 22, 23, 36, 47, 56–7, 80, 105–6, 109, 145, 153–4, 164–5, 174, 175
gender differences, 7, 16, 32, 41–4, 47, 49, 73, 100, 101, 173
grammar, 9–11, 11, 14, 15

Her Majesty's Inspectorate, HMI, 9, 10, 17, 121–2
HMI A-level survey, 42–3, 46, 47, 121–2, 141
Higginson Committee, 48
How to teach Reading, 89–90

influence of English courses, 113–16, 172
International Federation for the Teaching of English, 18

language studies, 21, 22–3, 80, 109
learning in English, 1, 4, 49, 57–8, 73–7, 87–92, 111, 117–135, 139
literacy, 9–11, 13–15, 22, 37–9
literary curriculum, the, 1, 3, 19–20, 21–5, 48, 54–5, 56, 58–60, 60–6, 68–71, 79–116, 173–4
literature; definition of, 83, 93–8
literature, views of students; 16+ students, 6, 68–9, 71–2, A-level students, 68, 69, 69–70, 73–6, 93–8 university students, 68, 70–1, 76–7, 93–8

media and cultural studies, 7, 21, 40, 82

National Association for the Teaching of English (NATE), 18, 137–8
National Council for the Teaching of English (NCTE), 18
National Foundation for Educational Research (NFER) study (1973), 34
Newbolt Report (1922), 17, 18–19, 19–20, 138
Norwood Report (1943), 20, 137

O-level English, 27, 36, 46–7, 55–6, 60–1, 138, 157–65, 177
Office of Population Censuses and Surveys (OPCS) Survey (1987), 4, 27, 34, 44, 45

199

perceptions of English; see English, perceptions of
perceptions of subjects, 5–6
practical criticism, 112–13, 147, 149
public schools, English in, 10–11, 15–16, 17–18, 19, 45–6

(The) Reader, the Text, the Poem, 91
reading, theories of, 25–6, 67, 78–9, 82, 87–92
response, 71–7; *see also* development of response
Robbins Report (1963), 45

Schools Council Survey (1970), 4, 8, 124
Schools Council Survey (1972), 48, 51, 53
Secondary Examinations Committee (SEC), 22, 23, 33
sixteen plus English, 7, 11, 22, 36, 83–4, 157–65
Spens Report, the (1939), 20, 136–7
Students of English Research Project, ix, 3

teaching methods; views of students, 172; views of A-level students, 49, 57–8, 73–6, 111, 117, 122–5, 128–30; views of university students, 76–7, 124, 126–7, 128, 130–1, 134; views of teachers, 124, 125–6, 131; views of university lecturers, 126–8, 131–2; *see also* English, teaching methods
Teaching of English in Secondary Schools, the (1910), 17, 21
texts, selection of, 83–7, 105, 106–7, 109, 148
tertiary colleges, 40
transition; to sixteen plus courses, 55; from sixteen plus to A-level, 55; from school to higher education, 2–3, 55, 174, 180–2; from school to further education, 36–7, 54–5

university English; see English, university
university examinations, 8, 52, 76–7, 137–40, 143, 147–8, 152–3, 165–6, 167, 168, 170–1, 173, 175
university selection, 34, 46, 48–53, 139–40, 165, 175
university selection, criteria for, 50–3, 66, 175
Use of English, the, 20, 138

views of students; on assessment 140–1, 142–3, 144, 173; on continuity and development, 67; on courses, 78; on criticism, 73; on English as subject 5–6, 6, 7, 26–8, 31–2; on learning and teaching, 172; on literature, 71
views of students at 16+; on assessment, 75, 144; on continuity and development, 55–7, 67, 68–9; on courses, 56, 104–6; on English as subject, 3, 6, 28–9; on learning and teaching, 71–2, 105, 122–3; on literature, 6, 68–9, 71–2
views of A-level students; on assessment 144, 145–7; on continuity and development, 57–8, 67–8, 68, 69–70; on courses, 49, 100–2, 107–8, 108–9, 111–12, 113–15; on English as subject, 3, 28–32, 49–50, 80, 172; on learning and teaching, 49, 57–8, 73–6, 111, 117, 122–5, 128–30; on literature, 68, 69–70, 73–6, 93–8
views of lecturers; on assessment, 50–1, 142, 150–3; on continuity and development, 51–3, 60; on courses, 63–4, 108, 112–3; on criticism, 93; on English as a subject, 3, 7, 8, 26–8, 30–1; on learning and teaching, 26–8, 131–2; on liaison with schools, 178–84; on literature, 98
views of teachers; on assessment, 50, 141–2, 148–50; on continuity and development, 51–3, 60–1, 62–3, 127; on courses, 60–1, 62–3, 112; on English as a subject, 3, 7–8, 26–8, 29, 30–1; on learning and teaching, 124, 125–6, 131; on liaison with higher education, 178–84; on literature, 98
views of university students; on assessment, 76–7, 147–8; on continuity and development, 58–9, 68, 69–71; on courses, 50, 102–4, 110–12, 113, 115–16; on criticism, 99–100; on English as subject, 3, 30–1, 50, 172; on learning and teaching, 76–7, 124, 126–7, 128, 130–1, 134; on literature, 68, 70–1, 76–7, 93–8
vocational courses, English in, 37–9

writing, *see* English, writing in